IS THIS A PHASE?

IS THIS A PHASE?

Child Development & Parent Strategies, Birth to 6 Years

Helen F. Neville, B.S., R.N.   ◆   Illustrated by Jenny Williams

PARENTING PRESS
Seattle, Washington

Printed in the United States of America
Cover and text illustration by Jenny Williams
Edited by Carolyn J. Threadgill
Designed by Judy Petry

Library of Congress Cataloging-in-Publication Data

Neville, Helen, 1943-
Is this a phase? : child development & parent strategies,
birth to 6 years / by Helen F. Neville ; illustrated by Jenny Williams.
    p. cm.
Includes bibliographical references and index.
ISBN 1-884734-63-4 (pbk.) -- ISBN 1-884734-64-2 (lib. bdg.)
1. Child development. 2. Child rearing. 3. Parenting.
4. Parent and child. 5. Temperament in children. I. Title.
HQ767.9.N48 2007
649'.122--dc22
                    2007014009

 PARENTING PRESS
P.O. Box 75267
Seattle, Washington 98175

*To see all of our helpful publications and services for parents, caregivers,
and children, go to* www.ParentingPress.com.

◆ Foreword

by Thomas Breese, M.D.
Fellow, American Academy of Pediatrics
Asst. Clinical Professor of Pediatrics
University of California Medical Center, San Francisco

I once received a call from a tearful mother who was distraught because she and her husband had a disagreement surrounding toilet training of their toddler. Dad insisted on an aggressive approach to which his son was very resistant. When Dad departed for work that morning, Mom discovered the child in Dad's closet, deliberately urinating into his father's shoes.

What to do? How to handle this problem? If this family had been in possession of *Is This a Phase?*, I could have referred them to the section on "Toilet Learning," a bountiful resource on the subject, helping them modify their plan appropriately. Indeed, they could have arrived at a disposition before Dad's shoes dried!

Is This a Phase? is an authoritative reference, carefully compiled, accurate, reliable, and just plain good reading. It is easy to use, and covers a broad range of topics in health, behavior, and human needs. Of particular importance, Ms. Neville defines the norms for developmental milestones and childhood behaviors. She gives parents and others concerned with children valuable insights, reassuring them when their child is within the normal *range* and alerting them to seek help when the child is not.

Ms. Neville explains the interplay between development and temperament that affects children's behavior, comforting parents when they wonder why their child behaves in a particular manner and if it's a phase that will pass.

I particularly like the chapter entitled "The Work of Being a Parent" because child rearing is such an exhausting experience for most of us. The information about identifying children's inborn temperaments, understanding how parental roles change as children grow, and realistically viewing time spent in direct child care are immensely helpful. Parents need these supportive and realistic words to encourage them over the long haul.

Ms. Neville is reassuring and practical on topics ranging from art to stress, including choosing the best child care situation when parents work. Information on infant sleep patterns and crying offers solace to parents at 0200 hours on a particularly difficult night. Parents will benefit from her discussion on discipline, always a common source of concern. The "Around the World" notes contrast child rearing in other parts of the world and show the latitude of acceptable parenting techniques, as long as they contain the critical ingredient, *love*.

Ms. Neville and I worked closely together in a large multidisciplinary pediatric clinic for many years. She was in charge of developing and running the Pediatric Advice Center. In this professional capacity, she was much revered by parents and staff alike for her sensible, informative advice and her caring manner. Her book reflects both these attributes. I am overjoyed that she is still serving parents and children on the larger scale allowed by the publication of *Is This a Phase? Child Development & Parent Strategies, Birth to 6 Years.*

◆ Dedication

To my granddaughter, Morgan Catherine Morel, her parents, and all others who lovingly care for young children.

◆ Acknowledgments

I wish to extend many thanks to all who helped along the way:

Elizabeth Crary, Carolyn Threadgill, and Parenting Press for their vision of this book;

Judy Petry for her creative design work and Jenny Williams for her captivating illustrations;

John Neville, M.D., my husband, for his support throughout the writing process and his thoughtful review of the material;

Eric Neville and Sonya Neville-Morel, our adult children, who long ago lit my interest in child development;

Catherine Moore-Fowler, my mother, who always supported my efforts and Pete Fowler, my father, who was dedicated to scientific facts;

Mona Halaby, M.A., Diane Clark Johnson, and Jan Kristal, M.A., who helped build my confidence as a writer;

The staff of Bananas Inc. Child Care Resource and Referral Service: Betty L. Cohen, M.S.W.; Ánh Kim Tran; Madeline Meyer Riley, L.M.F.T.; Carol Wang, Ph.D., and others;

The researchers cited in the bibliography whose probing questions have resulted in valuable information about young children and their families;

Kathy Briccetti, Ph.D.; James Cameron, Ph.D.; Chris Essex, M.A.; Leah Fisher, L.C.S.W.; Herman M. Frankel, M.D.; Frances Grahamjones, M.S., CCC-SLP; Susan Jensen, R.N., M.S.N., C.P.N.P.; Nancy Kaplan, Ph.D.; Ellen Lerner, M.S.; Lynne Miles, Montessori Credentialed; Sheldon Orloff, M.D.; Betty Eastonson, M.Ed.; Peter Levine, M.D.; Michele Forte Ramos, R.N.; Liz Rebensdorf, M.A.; Judith G. Rogers, O.T.R.; David Rudiak, O.D.; Karen Raven, B.A.; Susan V. Scaff, Ph.D.—the many friends and colleagues who helped me collect, verify, and clarify information, as well as to all others who helped in any way.

— *Helen F. Neville*
Oakland, California

◆ Contents

◆ List of Charts and Diagrams

Getting the Most Out of *Is This a Phase?*

How Will This Book Help Me?

Part One, Chapter 1. Here is the overall job description for parents and caregivers. We sometimes get discouraged and wonder, "Will this phase last *forever?*" Chapter 1 shows what is around the corner and how our job description changes over time. What is different about caring for infants? For 2s? For 4s? How much time does it take to care for children of different ages? You'll also meet the children who bring this book to life, and you'll likely find one rather like your own.

Part One, Chapters 2–8. Read the chapter that matches your child's age right now and check out the phase just ahead. "What's Happening" tells what is special about this age and "Ways to Make Life Easier" gives coping strategies. When we understand what's going on, the job is easier. When we know what to do, we feel more competent and have more fun.

Part Two is an alphabetical reference. Over the course of more than 30 years as a pediatric advice nurse and parent educator, I've learned what parents want to know. Concerned caregivers want to know about children's *bodies, minds, and relationships.*

Is This a Phase? is about your *whole child.* Here you will find information on dozens of topics that parents deal with as children grow from birth to 6 years. Development weaves through every aspect of children's lives, including art, discipline, friends, humor, imagination, muscles, music, and more. In Part Two, topic by topic, you will see the striking perspective of six years of development condensed into a few pages. You will clearly see the amazing growth that takes place during these few short years. Like Part One, Part Two includes both development and daily coping strategies.

Important Features of *Is This a Phase?*

Realistic expectations. If we expect too little, we limit our children's growth. If we expect too much, everyone gets frustrated and discouraged. To feel

---

Notice!

All children develop at their own pace. Individual growth, personal abilities, and inborn temperament all affect the pace at which children develop. Throughout most of this book, the ages you see report when *most* children do something. These are only averages, which means that *many* children arrive sooner and *many* later at the same point.

All children develop more quickly in some areas and more slowly in others. However, they go through almost all the phases *in the same order.* The important thing is that they progress through one phase to the next and the next.

Understanding the process of development helps us be more realistic about what is happening now and what is likely to happen next.

If what you read doesn't sound like your child right now, look ahead or back in time to find a better description of where your child is at this point.

successful, we need to be realistic. When *do* most babies sleep through the night, or when *will* toddlers learn to share? When *can* children begin to read, or remember to feed the dog? Chapter 1 clarifies overall expectations for the early years. In Chapters 2–8, read "Family Goals" for what to expect and what *not* to expect during each phase. In Part Two, as you learn more about development, your expectations will automatically become more realistic.

Temperament and culture. Just because children are the same age doesn't mean they act the same way. Inborn temperament also plays a major role in day-to-day behavior. Throughout *Is This a Phase?*, examples show how temperament colors the course of development. In addition, boxes titled "Around the World" are scattered throughout the text. They remind us that there is no single "right" way to raise children.

Ways to talk to young children. During these early years, all life's big topics come up, including friendship, honesty, sex, money, and death. Because children think in pictures and know fewer words than we do, it is often a challenge to answer all their questions. Throughout these pages, you'll find specific examples of ways to talk to young children. Everyone will, of course, adapt such examples to fit their own beliefs and comfort level.

Red flags. Sometimes, if our child acts quite differently from others, we wonder whether something might be wrong. In this case, consult Part Two, "Help—Is My Child Okay?" This section outlines very specific ages by which children should be able to do certain things. If they can't, it is wise to get further information from professionals. Often, such children are developing fine, just "marching to their own drummer." Sometimes, getting special help early is very important. In other parts of the book as well, you will find sections entitled "When to Get Help."

Who Is This Book For?

Whether you are a single-parent family, a two-parent family of mixed or same gender, a grandparent, or a nonrelative raising a young child, an at-home or work-away parent, or child care provider, *Is This a Phase?* answers your questions about child development. Caregivers and others who work with young children will quickly find information to better understand growing children.

Trustworthy information helps all of us feel more appreciative of our children, more patient, and more confident that we are doing our part to build their future. Better understanding makes our job easier and helps us enjoy our children for who they are in any given month or year.

PART ONE

PHASE BY PHASE

What's Happening Now?

CHAPTER 1

All Ages: The Work of Being a Parent

Why does my child act so differently from others her age?

Babies and toddlers take so much time! Will it always be this way?

As my child grows, it seems harder to know what's best for him. Why is that?

Is This a Phase? is about child development and how it affects behavior within the family. To begin our exploration, we will look briefly in this chapter at four important aspects of living with children.

Development. There is a general order to development over the years. One predictable phase tends to follow another. Babies say sounds before words and toddlers walk before they run. With an overview of these fairly predictable phases, we'll be less surprised and more confident as the months go by.

Temperament. Children are different because they each have their own set of inborn temperament traits. If we expect all 2s to act alike, we'll be confused and frustrated. To clarify the range of inborn difference, we will take a quick look at inborn temperament.

Time. Most newborns, toddlers, and 2s take our full, moment-to-moment attention. Will we ever have a life of our own again? Yet there will come a time when most of us will exclaim, "The time went by so fast! How can this be?" Once again, an overview helps us see how much the demands on our time change over the course of the few remarkable years from birth to age 6.

Parents' changing roles. As children develop, *we* need to take on new roles as parents. Changing our behavior to be who our children need during different phases is one of our greatest challenges. Once again an overview, a map, is helpful.

Children's Development

Child development is the natural process of growth and learning in physical, emotional, thinking, and social skills. Between birth and 6 years, healthy children learn many important things, including the following:

1. Babies learn that caregivers can be trusted to provide physical care and emotional support.
2. As babies crawl, they learn that it is safe to explore and discover their world.
3. Toddlers (between 18 months and 3 years) learn they have wishes and feelings that are different from their parents—they are separate individuals.
4. Preschoolers (between 3 and 6 years) gradually learn many new skills, so they feel more capable. With growing ability to think and understand their world, they gradually make more effective decisions about how to get what they want and need.

Each child grows at his or her own pace. Disruptions in a child's health or family life can cause temporary slowdowns or backsliding. Because of individual differences, we can't know for sure, ahead of time, exactly when things will happen.

Nonetheless, development usually leads us on a roller coaster of easier and harder periods. Knowing about the likely waves ahead of time lessens our surprise when our child grows through a typical but challenging phase. This knowledge may help us plan the best times for changes in routines or child care, as well as trips away from home. Chart 1, page 19, is a general overview of life with many typically developing children.

Children's Inborn Temperament

Both season of the year and where we live affect the weather we experience daily. Similarly, both development and inborn temperament affect children's day-to-day behavior. A quick look at temperament will help you see how the two fit together for *your* child.

Before we cradle our babies in our arms, they have already acquired unique qualities—their own set of temperament traits. Their particular traits will dictate *how* they do things. For example, one trait that is obvious during pregnancy is the baby's activity level. Babies who kick more before they are born are usually high in energy and continue to be more active than others after birth.

Dr. Stella Chess and Dr. Alexander Thomas began to study temperament in the 1950s. They observed nine different inborn traits. On each trait,

1. The Ups and Downs of Parenting

Child's Age	Parents' Life	What's Going On
Birth to 3 mo.	Harder	Parents are sleep-deprived; there are new routines: a period of hard work for everyone. Especially difficult with a high need baby.
3 to 8 mo.	Easier	Most babies have settled in by now. Good time for a trip to visit distant relatives and friends.
8 to 15 mo.	A little harder	Babies are more likely to experience separation anxiety.
15 mo. to 2 yr.	Easier	Many of these toddlers are cute and cooperative.
2 yr.	Easier	For all its bad press, this year usually begins easily.
2½ yr.	Harder	The demand for independence makes this period a famous challenge.
3 yr.	Easier	A relatively easy period for most children.
3½ yr.	A little harder	More fussing, whining, and complaining are common.
4 yr.	Easier	Many 4s feel happily confident, capable, and grown up.
4½ yr.	Harder	Feeling so competent, 4½s now wish to run everyone's life and the household, too—often with an attitude. This is a challenging period.
5 yr.	Easier	5s tend to be settled and cooperative.
5½ yr.	A little harder	5½s may become somewhat anxious and worried.

Compiled by Helen F. Neville

a particular child may be at either extreme or anywhere in between. Where that child falls along each scale will have important effects on his or her behavior. Over the years, we learn to modify such behaviors but we still show evidence of our inborn traits.

Temperament traits are not good nor bad, just different. Knowledge of temperament helps us understand children, hold more realistic expectations of them, and meet their needs more effectively. Many inborn traits become clear by 4 months. Think about where your child falls in a range from low to high on each of the nine temperament traits described below.

The Nine Inborn Temperament Traits

Regularity (from regular to irregular body rhythms). Some children get hungry or tired at the same time each day. Others get hungry or tired at unpredictable, or irregular, times.

Regular   Irregular

Activity (from low to high energy). Some children have a great deal of energy and are more physically active. Others have less energy and naturally spend more time sitting.

Low   High

Intensity (from mellow to dramatic emotions). Some children are intense and have strong feelings about almost everything. They laugh, yell, have tantrums and meltdowns more often. Others are mellow. They smile, whine, and frown.

Mellow   Dramatic

Sensitivity (from low to high awareness). Some individuals are much more sensitive than others to temperature, lights, noise, or how clothing feels against their skin. Some always notice small changes, such as when someone gets new glasses. Others are less sensitive to their environment.

Low   High

Curiosity (from curious to cautious in new situations). Some children step right up to meet new people and like to touch and try new things. Others hang back until they have had more time to get comfortable. The cautious child is sometimes referred to as "slow to warm."

Curious   Cautious

Adaptability (from fast to slow adjusting). Some individuals adjust quickly to almost anything. Changes—such as stopping play to go eat—are easier for them. The same is true for shifts in daily routines. Some children adjust more quickly when the space around their bodies changes, as when putting on hats, coats, or seat belts. Other less adaptable children need extra time to flip to a different "channel" in their minds. They plan ahead and expect to see the same blue bowl at breakfast or to have their toast cut the same way. Consequently, for some natural planners, an unexpected red bowl is cause for a meltdown.

Fast   Slow

Reaction to frustration (from manages frustration well to bothered by frustration). Some children naturally try again when something is hard to learn, while others get frustrated and quit. Some feel very frustrated by limits, so they test rules repeatedly. Others easily accept limits.

Manages   Easily
frustration well   frustrated

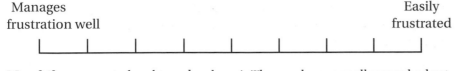

Mood (from easy to hard to calm down). Those who are mellow and adapt-able quickly settle down after being upset. Those who are intense and slow to adapt need more time to calm down. Thus, over time, some children are more lighthearted while others are more serious.

Calms   Hard to
quickly   soothe

Distractibility (from focused to distractible). Focused children naturally pay attention to one thing for a while. Distractible children quickly shift their attention due, in part, to the temperament traits listed above. If highly sen-sitive, they keep noticing their surroundings. Active kids keep moving, cu-rious ones search for whatever is new, and easily frustrated ones quickly move on when the current activity seems hard.

Focused   Distractible

The Children in This Book

All the examples in *Is This a Phase?* are based on real life with real chil-dren. For the sake of privacy and illustration, all these children have been blended into six characters who appear with their parents throughout the book. Three pairs—a boy and girl in each—represent different, *general* tem-perament types.

Easy Evan and Elena are naturally *even* tempered. Because they don't have a lot of energy, they usually prefer to walk rather than run. Most of the time they are *easy* to manage. About 40% of children are rather like Elena and Evan.

Moderate Malik and Melody have mixed temperament traits. Along with overall moderate to easy traits, they may also be either high in energy, or have very sensitive bodies, or trouble with new things, or get easily frustrated. Accordingly, they have their temperamental moments, especially as they pass through more challenging phases of development. About 50% of children are rather like Melody and Malik.

Spirited Spencer and Shauna. *Many high need infants become much easier after about 3 months of age.* Others, about 10% of all babies, continue on as spirited children. They are highly emotional, easily frustrated, and need more time to make changes. They are usually highly sensitive, have lots of energy, and are either very curious or very cautious. Life is never dull and there are many wonderful times. However, Shauna and Spencer's caregivers have to work much harder than others to bring out these children's positive qualities. Mary Sheedy Kurcinka popularized this description in her book, *Raising Your Spirited Child.*

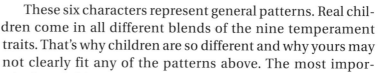

These six characters represent general patterns. Real children come in all different blends of the nine temperament traits. That's why children are so different and why yours may not clearly fit any of the patterns above. The most important message is that children are different. The next message is that in the long run, all temperament traits have advantages and disadvantages. (However, where traits lie and how they combine makes life more challenging with some kids than others.) You can do a more complete evaluation of your child's temperament at www.PreventiveOz.org.

Temperament affects development. For example, a very active baby is likely to learn to crawl sooner than another who prefers to sit and watch. A relaxed, slow-moving preschooler is likely to enjoy sitting and coloring before a very active one does.

When we look at development and inborn traits together, we can see more clearly when our parenting job may be easier or harder. The graph at the top of the next page takes a general look at these three sets of children whose different temperaments influence how they move through developmental phases.

2. Temperament Creates Peaks of Challenging Parenting

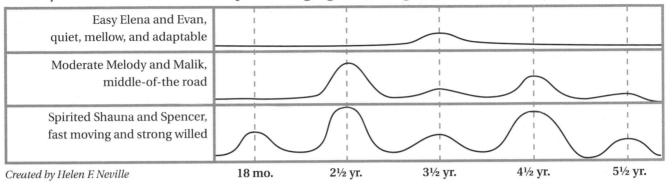

Created by Helen F. Neville

| | 18 mo. | 2½ yr. | 3½ yr. | 4½ yr. | 5½ yr. |

At the top of the graph, life with easy Elena and Evan usually flows along quite smoothly because the differences are less obvious from one developmental phase to another. Their more gentle bid for independence comes later than usual—around 3½ years.

In the middle, Melody and Malik, of moderate temperament, have some notable ups and downs at fairly predictable times.

At the bottom, spirited Shauna and Spencer are fast moving, slow to accept changes, and easily frustrated. Their challenging periods of development last longer and are more dramatic than usual. They begin to declare their independence between 14 and 18 months of age—long before other children do. All along the way, they need a great deal of day-to-day time and support.

How Does Children's Development Affect Parents' Time?

Frustrated parents often complain that young children don't entertain themselves. They are right: young children don't. Humans are social creatures. Most children love to and need to interact with other people most of the time. When families were large and neighborhoods full of children, there was less pressure on adults to spend time with children. *Our lifestyle has changed: children have not.*

During the early months of new life, time often creeps in a slow-motion haze of baby care and lost sleep. Time also crawls as we repeatedly reread the same bedtime story and while we take deep breaths during spells of dawdling. It seems these little ones will never grow up. Then suddenly they are off to kindergarten. It all went by in the blink of an eye. What happened?

How children spend *their* time dramatically affects how we spend ours. Some children need more of our time than others. Those who sleep less need more hours of care while awake. Temperament affects the demand for moment-to-moment parenting. We must watch a curious, fast-moving child (who may fall or break something in a flash) more closely than a cautious, slow-moving one. Individual differences aside, there are still some general patterns of time.

First, we'll look at different kinds of time while children are awake: a) personal care time, b) time with other kids, c) time alone, d) assisted learning time, and e) connection time. In *The Irreducible Needs of Children*, T. Berry Brazelton, M.D., and Stanley I. Greenspan, M.D., recommend, aside from personal care and time with other kids, that the remaining time (c, d, and e) be divided into about even thirds. Here is a closer look.

Personal care is the time when little ones need us to feed, soothe, dress, bathe, and get them to sleep. At 3 years, the amount of personal care time is about half what it was before crawling.

Time with other kids. Babies, of course, spend their time with adults, not other children. Once kids get old enough, they may spend time with others in the neighborhood, in playgroups, home day care, child care centers, or preschools. In large and busy child care settings, it is often hard for children to build close relationships with each other. Thus 3s, 4s, and 5s benefit from some one-on-one time with friends (outside of group care) at least several times a week.

Time alone (⅓ of remaining time). Little ones who are mellow and quiet may *seem* content to spend more time alone. If, however, we leave them to themselves, they miss out on important learning and connection time with us. Some children, especially 2s and older ones who get easily frustrated, cannot manage this much time alone. Some quiet, focused 3s happily play alone in their own rooms for short periods. For the most part, however, it is recommended that kids under 4 are in sight of adults even when they play by themselves. Once they are 4 and 5, most can safely play alone within earshot, if not within sight.

Assisted learning (⅓ of remaining time). This is the time when adults help children learn. For example, we make sounds and faces; talk with them; help them with puzzles; read stories; show them how to put on their shoes, do chores and projects together; and show them how to pick out bananas at the grocery store.

Connection time (⅓ of remaining time). Also called "floor time" or "time-in," this is the time that builds positive, long-term relationships. Connection time works because we *follow* children's actions, interests, and feelings. We follow their lead in what to do, how to do it, and at what pace to do it. When we join children, they feel seen, accepted, and appreciated.

What do we do during connection time? We may give a massage or back rub, dance, or wrestle. With toddlers, we may simply copy them move by move. With preschoolers, we may join their make-believe play. We take the role they assign us, or create a less powerful role. For example, we may pretend we are the baby or a puppy. We don't take over, prod with questions, or give directions or commands (unless someone is in danger). If they ask questions, we keep our answers short.

As responsible parents (and child care providers), it is tempting to concentrate on assisting children's learning. But good relationships require connection. Dr. Brazelton and Dr. Greenspan recommend that ideally babies, toddlers, and preschoolers get *equal amounts* of assisted learning time and connection time from both parents and caregivers.

Toddlers do best with little bits of connection time throughout the day. More difficult preschoolers and quiet, withdrawn ones need responsive, focused connection time for a total of *at least* 20 minutes a day in order to build relationships. Some mellow preschoolers seem to do fine with longer periods several times a week. As children get older, connection time can also include outings of mutual interest as long as we remember to let the child be in the lead about half the time. Some adults easily switch back and forth between assisted learning and connection time. Others have an easier time setting aside specific periods on a regular basis in order to build connection.

Now let's look at time and development together.

Babies need lots of personal care and connection time. This is no surprise to anyone who has lived with one. After 3 months of age, if not before, most babies are content to spend some short periods alone while awake. Before they can crawl, we may put them in swings or surround them with interesting objects and textures that they can explore with mouth, fingers, and eyes.

Crawling through 3 yr. takes even more time! Because 2s are older than babies, we assume they will take less of our time. This is not true. They are awake more than infants. Toddler attention spans are extremely short—just a minute or two. Unlike babies who sit and wait for us, crawlers, toddlers, and 2s come to find us, wherever we are. There is so much they want to show us and tell us, and so much they can learn from loving, interested people. We are their favorite and most important toy. They don't like time alone—except to slip off and get into trouble. They treat playmates as furniture—to push, pull, and climb upon—so they need constant supervision. As one father commented, "The difficulty is not that 2s take half your time, it's that they take five minutes out of every ten!" Welcome to the time-intensive 2s.

3s and 4s need us, but not constantly. Time with adults is important; it is still also important to divide it fairly evenly between assisted learning and connection time. Threes and especially 4s usually enjoy friends a great deal and gradually learn how to get along with each other. By 4 playmates

Around the World

In traditional cultures around the globe, from **Mexico** through **Polynesia** and **Africa,** most parents do not spend much time with 2s. This time-intensive child care is managed nearby by older children—most effectively by those age 7 and up.

become very important. Depending on age, size, and temperament, they need more or less supervision when they play with their friends, brothers, or sisters. Most 3s and 4s actually enjoy and make good use of brief periods alone. Overall, however, they still want and need more time with people than alone.

5s spend more time with other kids and much less with us. They enjoy other children and disappear into the separate world of kindergarten for a number of hours each week. They want time with us, time with their friends, and most can manage some time alone.

The following chart is a general look at how children's development affects adults' time on regular weekdays—not weekends with their family outings. No parent gives 13 hours a day of full attention to one toddler. At home, this time is necessarily mixed with care of household or siblings. Parents often share the personal care and learning and connection time with caring, involved child care providers. The main point is that taking care of children is much more time-intensive during some phases than others.

3. How Child Development Affects Adult Time

	Activity	Newborn	Before Crawling	Crawling to 3 yr.	3 yr.	4 yr.	5 yr.
	Total Hours per Day	24 hr.	24 hr.	24 hr.	24 hr.	24 hr.	24 hr.
Full Caregiver Attention	Personal care	10 hr.	4 hr.	3½ hr.	2 hr.	2 hr.	1½ hr.
	Assisted learning	—	2 hr.	3 hr.	2 hr.	1½ hr.	1 hr.
	Connection time	—	2 hr.	3 hr.	2 hr.	1½ hr.	1 hr.
	Adult-managed play with other kids	—	—	½ hr.	½ hr.	1 hr.	½ hr.
Little Caregiver Attention	Alone, in sight	—	2 hr.	1 hr.	—	—	—
	Alone in earshot (or in sight)	—	—	—	2 hr.	1½ hr.	1 hr.
	Playmates with little supervision	—	—	—	3 hr.	4½ hr.	5 hr.
	Screen time (video, television, computer, etc.)	—	—	—	½ hr.	½ hr.	1 hr.
	Kindergarten	—	—	—	—	—	3 hr.
	Sleep	14 hr.	14 hr.	13 hr.	12 hr.	11½ hr.	11 hr.
	Total Adult Time per Day*	**10 hr.**	**8 hr.**	**10 hr.**	**6½ hr.**	**6 hr.**	**4 hr.**

* Note the change over the years.

Compiled by Helen F. Neville

4. New Roles for Parents as Time Goes By

	4 yr. and Up	**5. Problem-Solving Coach:** "What do you think you could do next?"
Crawling and Up		**4. Life Teacher:** Allows learning from experience, which is sometimes uncomfortable. **3. Bearer of Bad News, Limit Setter:** "You can't always have your way."
Birth and Up		**2. Nurturing Parent:** Feeds, supports, and protects little ones from discomfort. **1. Family Manager and Problem Solver:** Balances needs of all in the family and makes family decisions.

Compiled by Helen F. Neville

Parents' Roles and How They Change

Although we spend less time with children as they get older, our parenting job becomes more complicated. One of the most difficult things about being a parent is that our job description keeps changing. This fact is made more complex because the new roles sometimes conflict with the earlier, ongoing ones. Depending on our own temperament and family background, we'll find some roles easier to assume than others.

1. Family Manager and Problem Solver. Because babies and toddlers are naturally self-centered, they don't consider the needs of others. Even 4s and 5s can't understand the complex needs of adults. Therefore, *we* are necessarily the problem solvers and decision makers who balance everyone's needs—including our own. Even though we invite 2s to make some tiny personal decisions, we need to manage the big picture.

2. Nurturing Parent. We are the guardians of life itself as we feed and protect our infants, a role that's essential for human survival. This role is often very satisfying and sometimes overwhelming. We soothe our babies, and do our best to *prevent discomfort*. Over the years, we continue to offer emotional support to our children. We share their joy. When they are upset, we offer hugs, listen, and try to understand.

3. Bearer of Bad News, Limit Setter. This change in our lives as parents often comes as a shock when babies start to crawl. Life is no longer a straightforward matter of nurturing. Now little ones reach for electric cords, hit friends, refuse baths, and try many other unexpected and uncivilized things. We suddenly have an important but unhappy job of bearing bad news: "You can't have or do everything you want."

The world is far more complicated than a toddler can understand. During the toddler phase, we become gentle animal trainers—not too much explanation, just "this is what we do next." As children become able to understand, we give simple reasons for the necessary limits and rules.

4. Life Teacher. Our teaching role is even more important once babies begin to crawl. The new role of Life Teacher sometimes conflicts directly with the Nurturing Parent. When the going gets hard, Nurturing Parent says, "Come here and I'll hold you," while Life Teacher says, "Keep trying! You can do it." Nurturing Parent, left to her own, overprotects, which can lead to resentment and anger from toddlers and teens alike. Many things are best learned from experience, and experience can be uncomfortable. Nurturing Parent and Life Teacher need to find a balance between support and protection versus letting a child learn from experience.

5. Problem-Solving Coach. This role conflicts with our long-time role as Family Manager and Problem Solver. We have spent years figuring out all the answers. Around 4, however, with their improving thinking ability, kids are ready to begin solving some of their own issues of daily living. When appropriate, we even ask for their input on some issues of family concern. We become less the *boss* and more the *consultant*. Helping children see *themselves* as effective problem solvers is one of our greatest gifts to them. It is still our job, however, to balance the needs of the entire family.

Now that you have an overview of parents' roles in these early years, let's look in more detail at children themselves. The remainder of Part One (chapters 2–8) describes important changes in each phase of development. *Read the chapter that corresponds to your child's current age, then read ahead to see what's next along the road.*

Turn to Part Two when you wonder about any of the many topics listed there in alphabetical order (see Contents). This second section is not meant to be read from cover to cover. Keep the book handy on your bedside table, next to your favorite relaxing chair, with your coffee cup at work, or in your child's bedroom for *quick reference when concerns or questions come up.*

CHAPTER 2

Birth to 3 Months: Amazing Surprise Package

My baby watches me with such wide-eyed interest. When does she know I'm her mother?

I look into those big bright eyes—what's going on inside his head?

My baby cries so much. I'm so tired! What's wrong?

A Snapshot— What Newborns Are Like

When Does My Baby Know Me?

At birth, newborns can recognize their mothers by voice and smell. Two weeks later, they recognize familiar faces. Babies look at their parents twice as long as they do strangers. They prefer listening to their parents as well. By 5 weeks, they smile and make more sounds when their parents are around. By about 2 months, most can look at the face of a loving parent with spellbound attention for as long as two to three minutes.

Babies also arrive with an inborn attraction to other living things. From their earliest weeks (or even days), they seem to know that they are like us and can do what we do. When they are holding still, alert, and watching, we can stick out our tongue or open our mouth wide, and they may *copy* us. Babies' connection to human emotions also runs deep. By 6 weeks of age, babies appear more content when their parents smile.

How Does My Baby Communicate?

Newborns come from a dark and noisy place. It is as loud as the roar of a lawn mower inside Mom, with her heart, stomach, and voice contribut-

Family Goals

For newborns

- Adjust to nursing/drinking.
- Learn to trust that their needs will be met.
- Become comfortable in their new surroundings.
- Start to get interested in their new world.

For parents and caregivers

- Become interested in and attracted to *this* baby. This is the bonding process in action, the first step toward love.
- Rest and try to get enough sleep.
- See and respond warmly to the needs, likes, and dislikes of this particular baby.

The Colors *We* See

Brown-eyed babies keep their brown eyes. Blue eyes may become darker during the first 3 to 6 months or even the first year. This is due to increasing melanin in the iris. Darker skinned babies, over the early months or first few years, may become darker as their skin makes more melanin.

See page 150, "One Month to 12 Months."

ing to the din. Nonetheless, four days after birth, babies recognize their parents' native language because the sounds and rhythms are already familiar. They prefer listening to this language more than to any others.

Babies like it even more when parents talk baby talk (or "parent-ese"), which makes important sounds stronger and longer. "There's your HAAAP-py FAAAA-ce." Parent-ese is generally higher in pitch, and also exaggerates the difference between higher and lower sounds. Adults (and older siblings) around the world instinctively talk this way to babies.

One-week-old babies are ready to hold their first "conversations." Say a short sentence to your baby with high and low tones, such as, "I LOVE to look at Melody!" Now watch her. If she was still and listening, she will now answer by wiggling her arms and legs. (Newborns can't pay attention and wiggle their bodies at the same time.)

During the early months, our babies' bodies communicate their interest, surprise, anger, or fear at what they are experiencing. Though they can't speak in words yet, we gradually learn to understand them by observing their body language.

What and How Do Babies See?

To newborns, most of the world looks fuzzy, like a badly out-of-focus photograph. Things that are about 12 to 13 inches away from their face, however, pop into clear focus. Instinctively, most adults usually hold babies at this distance from their face when they pick them up.

Babies can also follow or track things that move nearby. They have an inborn sense of how things move through space. If a moving ball disappears behind a screen, they look to where the ball *should* reappear based on the direction it was moving.

By 3 months, most babies see colors much the way adults do.

Within the first month, it is important that a baby's eyes learn to move and work together. This may sound easy, but it is not. To imagine what this is like, think of using one computer mouse in your left hand *and* another in your right hand to move two separate dots across the computer screen as if they were a single dot.

During these early months, nerve cells are busy connecting the eyes with the part of the brain that records sight. In a few babies, the eyes continue to look off in different directions, so the brain gets two very different pictures, which is confusing. As a result, these babies' brains gradually start to ignore the view from one eye. If this problem is not corrected early, nerve cells stop connecting that eye to the brain. These babies can lose vision in one eye even though the eye itself was normal. If you think there could be a problem with your baby's eyes, check with your pediatrician.

29 JULY What's Happening Now?

Why Do Babies Cry?

According to pediatrician Dr. Harvey Karp, babies often cry because they aren't yet ready to be in the world. As he explains in *The Happiest Baby on the Block*, babies need another three months to get ready. For Mom's sake, they are born "early" before their heads get any bigger. Dr. Karp therefore calls the first three months after birth the "fourth trimester" because many babies still need the soothing sensations of the uterus.

Some healthy babies cry much more than others. Even-tempered Evan almost never fusses or cries. Spirited Shauna screams the moment she gets hungry. Spencer has strong feelings about everything and finds it hard to adjust to changes. After hours of coping with the newness of each day, he is often tired and out-of-sorts by late afternoon.

Babies who are sensitive or intense easily get overstimulated by all the new sights, sounds, smells, and skin sensations. Some of these babies suffer from colic, which affects 20% of babies. Colic has long been a medical mystery. Colicky babies cry three or more hours for three or more afternoons or evenings a week without any illness. Dr. Karp points out that in cultures where babies are constantly carried and can suck whenever they want, there is no colic. He therefore proposes that colicky babies in our culture are the ones who really still need the cues for calming that they had before birth.

To soothe all fussy babies (once they are fed and dry), Dr. Karp suggests the "five Ss," motions and sounds that kept babies calm before birth. These are:

- swaddling the baby snugly
- holding baby stomach or side down
- swinging or jiggling baby gently
- allowing baby to suck
- making "ssshhh-ssshhh" sounds, loud and slow like Mom's heartbeat

His book and video (both titled *The Happiest Baby on the Block*) give important details on how to use each of these calming strategies effectively.

Most babies, including colicky ones, cry less after 3 months. At that point, they have more control of their bodies. They can find and suck their thumbs or release muscle tension by wiggling and stretching. A few high energy babies are suddenly much happier once they can crawl.

Around the World

Mothers in **Holland** assume babies need much more rest than excitement. Their babies spend more time resting and sleeping in quiet, dark rooms than babies in other countries.

In **Japan,** mothers spend more time than American mothers soothing their babies. The Japanese believe that babies have lived before. Now, returning as babies again, they have to learn to accept dependence. As they grow up, they will gradually become *interdependent* (caring for others and being cared for).

In general, mothers in the **United States** spend more time than mothers in other countries stimulating their babies to help them learn quickly and grow into independence.

When Do Babies Eat and Sleep?

Breast-fed babies get hungry about every one and a half to two hours. Because formula made from cow's milk is digested more slowly, bottle-fed babies usually get hungry about every three to four hours. When parents are up during the night, daytime naps are extremely helpful. We need to sleep whenever we can! If we can't sleep during the day, we can still rest and relax while the baby naps.

See page 191, "Is It Daytime or Nighttime?"

Sleeping and eating schedules usually become more regular and predictable over time. Growth spurts and illness can throw them off, however, and a few babies never become really regular. In such situations, ignore the clock and pay attention to the baby's cues. Throughout most of human history, parents did not have clocks and their babies did fine.

Babies' brains develop continuously, both while they are awake and while they sleep. Throughout a baby's body, signals continuously travel from one nerve cell to another. This heavy traffic connects nerve cells more strongly and adds new ones to the network.

At night, babies dream half of the time they are asleep, which is far more than adults do. When we see their eyeballs move under their closed eyelids, they are dreaming. While they dream, arms and legs stretch and jerk, mouths suck or pucker, and breathing becomes irregular. The brain is sending practice signals to all those muscles, strengthening the nerve connections and helping the body work better.

Ways to Make Life Easier

Getting to Know Your Baby

Parents need time to *enjoy* their amazement and delight in their new baby and time to *get to know* what this baby is like. Every new baby is unique. What sound, sight, position, motion, or touch helps *this* baby relax and become wide-eyed with interest? Does this baby like high sounds or low sounds? Rocking or jiggling?

Some babies may be able to focus their attention more easily if we first soothe them with rocking, and then hold them still and upright. Try holding the baby in different positions. What works best with *this* baby?

Skin contact through infant massage is a powerful way to connect with babies and learn what they like. Gentle, responsive touch lowers stress and helps almost all babies relax. It also supports digestion, the immune system, and brain development. How and where does *this* baby like to be touched? Very lightly or firmly? Head? Feet? Tummy? Hands? There are many books, videos, and sometimes classes available on the gentle art of infant massage.

Realistic Expectations for New Parents

♦ Sometimes we simply don't know what babies want. We wait five or ten minutes, then we try again.

♦ Sometimes babies cry even when we do our best, and that is all right.

♦ It is hard to be with a baby who cries a great deal. Ask others for help.

Too much stimulation. Young babies may tire quickly of direct eye contact and will turn their head or eyes away to rest. When they are ready, they will look back for more contact. Adults need to invite, not demand, eye contact. When babies show they have had enough eye contact, it is time for us to go do something else and let them rest.

After Spencer gets over-stimulated, he screams from exhaustion. Sometimes he gets so wound up that he can't relax and needs to cry himself to sleep. Mom has learned to talk quietly and move gently. Other times Spencer just needs some quiet time alone. Mom keeps the daily exposure to new people and experiences to a minimum and sticks to the same quiet, familiar routine, especially in the late afternoon.

Some babies get hiccups when they feel stressed by too much stimulation.

Relaxing with baby. Every parent must find her or his own way to spend calm, contented time getting to know the new baby every day. Melody's mother, after the initial adjustment, feels most peaceful when nursing. Elena's mother, who often feels rushed, imagines herself in a calm, soothing place where it is easier for her to look at her daughter with warmth and love. Then they practice relaxing together. Because Spencer is a high need baby, *his* mother feels most comfortable when a family member or friend is nearby for support. We gradually discover what is most relaxing for us and our baby.

Soothing baby. What works depends on what is going on. Often babies want company. Some seem to like reminders of the good old days back in the womb. They like to be wrapped firmly in a blanket, rocked, and carried next to our body, or they want to lie on our chest so they can hear our heartbeat.

Melody is bothered by gas bubbles. She often fusses until she burps. Sometimes she cries when she starts to nurse because sucking stimulates her intestines and then she gets gas pains. Mom figured out that she passes gas more quickly if she lies on her *right* side (because of the shape of the intestines).

Malik gets bored. He likes tours around the house for close-up views of the sights. Sometimes he likes a particular sound, position, motion, or touch.

Active Shauna needs exercise. While she was tightly packed in the womb, she sucked her thumb. Now it flies out of reach and she won't be able to control it until she is about 3 months old. At first, Mom gave her a bottle every time she cried, but that overfilled her stomach, making her cry even more. Gradually, Mom learned to offer milk for hunger and a pacifier for sucking exercise. (Breast-fed babies automatically get milk first, then further exercise once the breast has emptied.)

Taking care of ourselves. With some babies, nothing seems to help at the moment. It is best if we take a five- to ten-minute break for ourselves, then go back and try again. By that time, our baby may be ready to notice what feels good.

Self-care is very important when babies cry a great deal. Someone else needs to take over baby care, if possible, while we take a break. If no one is available to help, we can step into the shower or listen to music in another room for a few minutes. If a baby's high-pitched crying hurts our ears, we can try earplugs: we can still hear the baby *and* we'll feel more comfortable.

When to Get Help

If your baby cries much of the time, it is best to call the pediatrician or clinic to be sure your baby is all right. Once you know your baby is healthy, talk with other parents or call a parents' hotline for more ideas about what to try and how to manage. Ask family members or friends to take over at times so you can get a break.

Feeling tired and overwhelmed for a few weeks is normal after a new baby arrives. If, however, you continue to feel overwhelmed and sad, are often in tears, or worry that you might hurt your baby, check with your doctor. The hormone changes and responsibility of motherhood sometimes trigger depression that will improve more quickly with professional help.

CHAPTER 3

2 to 9 Months: Falling in Love

I hear that you can't spoil a baby at this age. Are you sure?

They say that a baby's brain is growing like crazy. What's going on in there?

I know that attachment is important. What makes it happen? How will I know?

A Snapshot— Life with Young Babies

By 2 months, or maybe 3, most babies have settled in. We may still be short of sleep, but we understand them better, and many high need babies now cry less. Welcome to the golden age of parenthood! Never in our lives will we be more important to another human being than we are right now. Our babies are hardwired to adore us. Everything babies want at this age is good for them—food, sleep, tranquility, attention, and playtime. This is why responding to his or her cues is not going to spoil any baby.

We can safely indulge our desire to be the adoring, all-giving parent. Later, when our baby starts to crawl, we will have to deal with setting limits, and life will become more complicated. For now, we can focus our time and attention completely on building a responsive, loving relationship with this wonderful new being.

Of course, that doesn't mean our lives are simple. We struggle to get enough sleep, learn how to be a parent, and keep the rest of our lives going. The long-term commitment we've made to this child may feel frightening. The baby's health and temperament will make it easier or harder to provide peace and pleasure for everyone in the family.

What's Happening Now?

Growing Brains

A major growth spurt occurs in babies' brains when they are between 3 and 10 months old. At birth, a baby has billions of nerve cells (neurons). Each nerve cell has 500 to 3,000 connections to other nerves. During the early months of life, each nerve cell builds 7,000 to 10,000 *more* connections with other neurons. All the sights, sounds, and feelings babies experience will direct how the neurons connect. To accomplish this growth, the brain needs nourishing food and a variety of *ordinary* experiences.

The nerve cells are also growing covers, layers of fatty insulation called myelin, rather like the plastic insulation that covers the electrical wires in our houses. This insulation helps messages travel more directly and quickly from one part of the body or brain to another. Different parts of the brain and body will suddenly work much better after the nerve cells are insulated.

"Listen to me!" Between 6 and 8 months of age, babies begin to babble, which means they put two sounds together. They usually start by putting "b" or "d" or "m" sounds in front of their "oo" and "aa" sounds. That's why "dadada" or "mamama" are among the first words. We may hear another early sound that stands for something, "ga." Babies may announce "ga" when they discover that *they* have the ability to make their rubber ducky disappear: "All gone!"

"Look what I can do!" Gradually, as nerves grow, connect with each other, and become covered with myelin, babies gain more control over their bodies. By 3 months, most of them can see halfway across a room. They have also learned a neat trick of looking at the parent's eyes and then turning their gaze to look at what the parent is looking at. This shared attention provides a whole new way to learn. By 8 months, babies spend a good deal of time looking around their world, not just feeling and listening to it. As eyes become more important for learning, tasting things with the mouth gradually becomes less important.

As newborns, babies automatically grabbed on to things (like Dad's finger or Mom's hair), but didn't know how to let go. After several months, the muscles that open the hand get stronger. Now babies love to practice dropping things.

At about 3 months, babies see that the world responds to them. "When I cry, Mommy or Daddy comes to give me milk or a hug." "When I smile at Sister, she smiles back." A little older, between 6 and 10 months, babies suddenly *understand* that they make things happen. When they move their hands, the blocks bang together. When they shake the bell, it rings. Babies smile with delight and pride when they make things happen.

A world that magically comes and goes. When Melody looks at something, her brain compares it with memories in her head. Her brain then tells her,

See page 94–96, "Activities and Toys."

Family Goals

For babies

- Learn that they can make things happen. For example, "When I cry, someone comes," or "I can make my hands touch each other."
- Learn to trust that their needs will almost always be met by the same few loving caregivers. (Trust grows when feelings are understood, and unpleasant ones are soothed.)
- Experience the joy of taking turns, as when making sounds and faces with other people.

For parents and caregivers

- Rest and try to get enough sleep.
- Become more able to read baby's cues and calm her or him down.
- Enjoy leading and following at playtime.
- Enjoy playing with sounds together.

"This is familiar" or "This is brand new." In *The Scientist in the Crib*, Alison Gopnik, Ph.D., Andrew Meltzoff, Ph.D., and Patricia Kuhl, Ph.D., tell us that 3-month-olds recognize things they saw a week ago. When Mom brings Melody to the baby study center, the researcher ties a mobile to her foot. At some point, Melody kicks and the mobile moves. When Mom brings Melody back to the center in a week, she kicks immediately if she sees the *same* mobile tied to her foot. She doesn't kick so quickly if it is a different mobile.

In order to remember the pictures in their minds, however, young babies need to see the real object at the same time. While Malik watches, Mom puts a toy, such as a rubber ducky, under a washcloth. To Malik, it is "out of sight, out of mind." There are many other things to look at. He doesn't try to find the ducky.

Pretend for a moment that you, like a baby, can't see any pictures or hear any sounds inside your head. Your entire world is just what you see, hear, or feel at this very moment and nothing more. Nothing else exists. When you look to your left, you see the window; then you look to your right and see the sofa. You look to the left again. That window looks *familiar,* but while you weren't looking at it, it was *gone*. Things strangely appear and disappear.

Feeling fear. By about 8 to 9 months, the myelin insulation has grown on the nerve cells to the fear centers of the brain. Messages now travel there faster, causing babies to feel and react to anxiety and fear more quickly. Because of their newly insulated nerve fibers, crawling babies are now more ready to learn, remember, and react to danger.

Problem solving. Before they learn to walk, babies grow billions of nerve connections to the memory and problem-solving parts of the brain. At some point (researchers disagree on when), Malik can hold a picture of a rubber ducky in his *mind*, even though it isn't in his *sight*. Malik now thinks: Maybe the rubber ducky didn't dissolve into thin air; maybe it is just hiding. This is a huge step in problem-solving ability. Sometime between 8 and 12 months, he can make a plan to check out this possibility. Scientist that he is, he pulls off the washcloth—and there is the rubber ducky! "Look! I proved it," he beams. "Ducky was just *hiding*."

Spirited Shauna confirms her new discovery while in her high chair. She drops a cracker over the side; then she looks down to prove it fell on the floor. This is not about making a mess. She is doing scientific research. We can help her out by saying, "Is it gone? No, it's down on the floor!" Hungry scientists rarely drop food off a cliff, so we can take the dish away as soon as Shauna's tummy fills and give her some toys to drop. After a few weeks, Shauna will be so sure the toys are down on the floor that she won't want to drop things as often. Babies love to play peek-a-boo and other hiding games during this phase. They love to prove again and again that things just hide rather than cease to exist.

Developing self-confidence. As the years go by, people who believe they have considerable control over what happens in their lives are generally more self-confident and healthier than those who don't. We strengthen our babies' beliefs that they can affect their world when, during playtime, we follow their lead at least half the time. We copy their sounds, expressions, and movements. We play with the toys they choose, appreciating, describing, and copying what they do with them. Indeed, one of the greatest challenges as parents of children of any age is to slow down and enjoy being their appreciative audience.

Feelings: Our First Personal Guidance System

Culture in the United States often values thinking over feeling. Feelings, however, are older, more basic, and more important to the brain than many of us were taught. Our eyes, ears, skin, and nose flood our brain with information during every waking moment. Our brain has to continually sort through all this information. What to ignore? What to pay attention to? What to do next? Our feelings greatly simplify these choices. They give us a kind of yes-or-no "magnetic" guidance system. Emotions pull us toward things that make us feel happy and excited and push us away from things that make us feel anxious, afraid, or sad. Otherwise, our brain would be jammed by all the possibilities and unable to make timely decisions.

This push-pull guidance system is not just pleasant or unpleasant thoughts. *It is a physical reaction to chemicals released in the body.* When we smile lovingly at babies, their bodies release endorphins—the chemicals that make people feel good. When babies are worried, frightened, or in pain, adrenaline and cortisol (the stress hormones) flow through their bodies. High doses of these natural stress chemicals make the heart race, the body jittery, and the mind anxious.

How do babies learn about the positive and negative feelings that will guide them? During their early months, the brain is building the nerve pathways for feelings. Whether a baby *feels* an emotion or *sees* an emotion on another person's face, the same nerve path is used, similar to using the same telephone line or cell for talking and listening. If our baby shows us a feeling and we copy it, that same nerve pathway gets twice as much practice. The next time around, that emotion is easier for our baby to *feel* and *express*.

As newborns, our little ones could copy us when we stuck out our tongues or opened our mouths. Now at 3 months, they copy our smiles. With our help, babies practice feeling happy. In this way, a baby builds a strong "magnetic" signpost that says, "This is what 'happy' feels like." We help by mirroring our baby's feelings and naming them: "I see your happy smile! You're glad to see me! I'm glad to see you, too!"

Mixed messages are confusing. Babies appear to get confused when they send out one message to a parent or caregiver and a different one comes back. For example, when spirited Spencer is angry because the milk isn't coming yet, Mom tends to flash a reassuring smile to say, "It will be ready in

Around the World

In many traditional cultures, **from India to Mexico,** adults rarely look directly at babies, as we do in the United States. Because many young babies used to die of illness, there was fear that such attention could attract harmful evil spirits. Despite lack of eye contact, these mothers almost always carry babies against their bodies, and nurse dozens of times per day. It is a different, but nevertheless responsive world.

a minute." Spencer might understand his feelings better if Mom briefly copied his angry face, saying, "You don't like to wait." He would know by watching her face that she got his message. Those nerve pathways would also get more practice. Mom could then switch to her warm, reassuring face and say, "Milk will be here in just a minute, then you'll feel better."

Parents' feelings affect babies. Most babies are closely in tune with the emotions of their parents and caregivers. We may not realize that babies constantly react to the emotions we show them. If we are regularly depressed and distant, inattentive, frightened, angry, or resentful, our baby will likely respond with distance, fear, or upset. *For our sake and the baby's, it is important to get help if we often feel depressed or frightened, or unable to feel warm, content, and safe around our baby.*

The Long Road to Self-Regulation

Babies and children under 5 years often need our help in order to shift their attention or mood, especially when their feelings are strong. Babies usually can't *self*-regulate their emotions and attention. Even as adults, we know it is not always easy to self-regulate. We sometimes get too focused, or get stuck in an extreme mood and have trouble moving back to middle ground. As adults, we have more control than our little ones, so it is our job, as much as possible, to moderate our emotions for their benefit.

It helps to use a soothing voice and calm movements, especially around a sensitive or excitable baby. On the other hand, if the baby seems sleepy and uninterested in the world most of the time, we can speak louder with more changes in tone and act in a more animated way to get his or her attention.

As they grow, we continue to help our children shift their feelings, first acknowledging the current feeling and then leading them toward another: "Yes, it's cold with your diaper off. You don't like this, do you? Just a minute— I'm putting the warm, dry one on. Now that feels better, doesn't it?" We teach that feelings change, that upsets and anger don't last forever. With repeated help, little ones gradually learn how to shift their own emotions. *Learning how is a slow process that takes years to master.* Temperament plays a role, too. Babies who have strong feelings to begin with need more time to change those feelings and more help to calm down.

See page 31, "Why Do Babies Cry?"

How Do Babies Fall in Love?

An essential process in a baby's early months is to become attached to his or her parents. Babies connect with the people who hold them, smile at them, and play with them. When time after time the same face arrives, a baby gradually paints that face into a picture frame that has been ready and waiting to be filled by someone special. Blind babies fill in a voice recording. In this way a baby gradually connects "This person helps me feel better" with "I like having *this* person nearby!" Baby has begun to fall in love.

Attachment is deeply rooted in the survival of our species. It makes sense that attachment is normally in place by the time babies crawl. Babies who move on their own may face many dangers. Because they are attached, they automatically cry and reach for their first beloved whenever they feel worried or out of sorts. If their favorite adult isn't available, they will move on to the next favorite one. This way, babies waste no time deciding which adult to go to in an emergency. One research study found that two-thirds of toddlers turned to Mom first and one-third to Dad first.

Sense of security. While almost all babies become attached by 6 to 8 months, the *quality* of the attachment relationship can vary. *Secure attachment* grows when we repeatedly read babies' signals accurately, and warmly care for their social and emotional needs. We touch them with loving hands. We look sympathetically into their eyes. We usually are (and appear) content, pleased, or delighted to be near them. We take turns with them—trading smiles, sounds, and movements back and forth. We connect at a pace and level of emotional intensity that is comfortable for them. When they want a break, we back off. When they need us, we come back. In general, we make the things they like happen more often, and the things they don't like happen less often. Through hundreds of such experiences, babies feel understood and appreciated for who they are. We become the ones who light up their lives.

Of course, no parent is always warm and responsive. Babies may cry when we are in the shower or need a short break. Some babies regularly cry for a few minutes in order to get to sleep. At such times, we need to remember how often each day we do respond with loving attention. Secure attachment grows when babies *usually* get what they need. It is the *pattern* that counts.

It is not until much later, around 12 to 15 months of age, that we will be able to see clearly the fruits of our early work to build a secure attachment relationship. Only then will we be able to see that, depending on the quality of attachment, toddlers act differently when they are under stress.

A securely connected caregiver is a toddler's safe haven—someone to reach for and cling to without a second thought. Through this special relationship, toddlers are deeply comforted, and their sense of safety is quickly restored after minor stress. Recharged, they step out into the world again. As children grow, preschoolers who are securely attached find it easier to cooperate than those who are not.

On the other hand, when toddlers are not securely connected to us (called *in*secure attachment), they behave differently during times of stress. Some toddlers, during the moment of stress—such as when frightened by a dog, or scraping a knee, or being separated from us for a short time—pretend they are all right, and impressively tough it out. They appear to tell themselves, "I'm on my own to manage this." After the pressure is off, they become upset and fussy. Other children seem to hesitate when they want comfort but aren't sure it is available. As they toddle toward us they may suddenly freeze, refuse our open arms, pull away, or even turn and bang their heads. They seem to be reminding themselves, "No, I need to handle this myself." Still others can't easily regain their sense of safety. They appear to wonder, "If I go exploring again now, will comfort be here when I need it next time?" If you are concerned about your baby's attachment, look at "When to Get Help" on page 42.

Temperament and attachment. How can we tell the difference between temperament and attachment issues? The effects of temperament are almost always present. Emotionally intense babies regularly need extra time to calm down; cautious babies almost always take longer to set off exploring; sensitive babies get tired and fussy in any noisy environment; less sensitive toddlers routinely ignore minor discomforts. Attachment issues, on the other hand, more often show up at times of stress.

Ways to Make Life Easier

Why Does My Baby Cry When I Leave?

Left in the living room. Sometime between 7 and 12 months, babies begin to experience separation anxiety. Imagine babies growing up in an ancient jungle. As soon as they could crawl, they could get dangerously beyond Mom's watchful eye. To keep babies close by for their own safety, the fear centers of the brain get efficiently wired *before* babies crawl. Now, when Mom is out of sight, instinctive fear takes over, and Malik cries.

During this awkward period, Mom talks or sings to him whenever she steps into another room. At playtime, Mom hides behind furniture and doorways, then talks to him so that he gains more confidence that she, like rubber ducky, is just hiding. Within a few weeks, most babies become so sure we are nearby that they no longer cry when we step out of sight.

Child care and temperament. Separation anxiety, which starts between 7 and 12 months, generally peaks between 10 and 15 months and is usually much better by 3 or 3½ years. Some babies, especially very curious ones, separate without complaint. Some tots become comfortable within days; others need weeks. Don't judge by what happens as you walk out the door. Find out what happens after you leave. Many little ones settle down in three to five minutes, then enjoy their day. Until age 3 or 3½ and sometimes later, separation anxiety is likely to reappear when we leave little ones with a new caregiver.

Babies who are easily frustrated commonly have an especially difficult time because they depend heavily on their first beloved for help. They don't

Realistic Expectations for Parents

◆ It is still hard to know what babies want at times. We keep trying different things. Babies' wishes get much clearer as they learn to communicate more effectively.

◆ Expect to be up during the night. A backup plan to get extra rest during the day or on weekends is essential. (Appreciate your good luck if you get to sleep through!)

easily trust others to care for them as well. Babies who are cautious or have trouble with changes are more likely to be bothered by separation. The transition to child care is often easier if these babies get to know the provider before this phase begins. Or they may need a very gradual transition. Some youngsters need us to stay with them for *weeks* to get comfortable in a new situation. Or, we may leave them briefly, for half an hour or so, then gradually increase the time away. Tell caregivers about the special tricks that prevent and soothe frustration with your baby.

Some babies settle in more quickly if we hand them to the caregiver for a snuggle before we leave; others do not. Some babies wail for 30 minutes or more, day after day, if left. Some are too upset to eat or play until we return. These babies may not be ready for separation. Occasionally, caregiver and baby just don't hit it off, and a different caregiver will connect more easily.

My Baby Is Afraid of Strangers—Even Grandma!

Fear of strangers tends to start a month later than separation anxiety and just before or around the time babies start actively crawling. Fear centers in the brain have just been upgraded (with their new myelin insulation), so they work faster. Just when babies need it, Mother Nature gives them some healthy fear of the unknown, including strangers. Because babies' general memory is better now, they can more easily remember whom they have seen and whom they haven't.

Stranger anxiety is usually greatest around 15 months and commonly tapers off by 3 years. It may last longer in cautious children. On the other hand, some toddlers are very curious about everything, including new people, and they are not at all bothered by strangers.

Melody's dad understands her fear. He gives Grandma some interesting toys to hold. With Melody on his lap, all three sit on the sofa. After a while, Melody reaches out to Grandma and the toys she holds.

When to Get Help

Feel alone or overwhelmed? It can be harder to connect with babies when we are stressed or isolated. Some mothers often don't feel warm, content, or safe around their babies, or they may feel depressed. (Hormones that haven't yet returned to normal can increase risk of depression.) *Get help* for your baby's sake as well as your own. Talk with your doctor or clinic and ask about support groups and community resources. Attachment is a village affair.

Around the World

Research in **Uganda, East Africa** found that typical babies of African ancestry learn to crawl a month earlier than typical Caucasian babies in the United States. These early crawlers therefore become afraid of strangers a month earlier as well. Their developmental sequence is the same as Caucasian babies', just advanced by one month.

Baby is not doing his or her part? Some are harder to connect with than others—such as infants who cry a great deal or are hard to figure out. Most such babies become securely attached, but their parents often need information and support along the way. Some babies cannot do their part—despite our best efforts, they remain distant. Talk with your baby's doctor or clinic.

See page 150, "One Month to 12 Months."

Other concerns about attachment? Babies who have many different, short-term caregivers find life so confusing that they cannot paint a clear face of a *particular* responsive adult. Such babies often have trouble developing close, trusting relationships with others over time. Or, you may worry that your own losses (present or past) are a piece of the puzzle. With help, attachment can grow more secure over time. To find a therapist familiar with attachment, check with the social services department at the nearest children's hospital, or contact the World Association for Infant Mental Health at www.waimh.org.

CHAPTER 4

Crawling to 18 Months: Off to See the World

Setting limits is hard for me. Am I the only parent who has trouble?

When my son falls, he looks at me before he cries. Why does he do that?

My toddler is always on the move. Will she be this way the rest of her life?

A Snapshot— Babies on the Move

Into Everything: 9 Months

At 9 months, some babies already move about on their own. Within the next few months almost all will travel solo. They may scoot on their bottoms, crawl with their elbows, crawl on hands and knees, or toddle. No matter how they get around, they no longer stay where we put them. They have just moved out of the perfect Garden of Eden, where life was simple and free of limits. Life is forever changed for them and us. Now these curious little ones are into everything they can reach. They are messy and can hurt themselves. They are also delightful, and their sense of accomplishment is a joy to watch.

Look at Me! 12 Months

Confident that they can now move about, these babies are often calm and satisfied. They are very social around people they know and like. They love a small audience of supportive, favorite people.

A Motion Machine: 15 Months

A few mellow, low energy 15-month-olds are usually content to play with what is in reach. Most toddlers, however, are always up and about—busybodies in constant motion. The highly curious ones always head for whatever is new and different. Some toddlers get very frustrated by necessary limits, or because they can't yet tell us exactly what they want. For this reason, 15 months may be a rocky phase for some babies and parents.

 **What's Happening Now?**

Crawling into Trouble

Early on, babies pay a great deal of attention to the work of learning how to crawl and walk. Once they can get around easily, they focus on *where* they want to go. Their ability and need to explore now grow much stronger.

Like many her age who are securely attached to their parents, moderate Melody shows more curiosity when Mom is nearby. Melody trusts Mom to protect her if she gets into difficulty. All children are curious, but some are much more so than others. High energy Spencer roams far and wide to find interesting things to touch and taste. Cautious Evan looks carefully before he reaches for nearby toys or tastes a new food. Because easy Evan doesn't have a great deal of energy, he explores more with his hands than with his feet.

Sudden appearance of limits. Before babies crawl, we usually try to give them whatever they want. Once they are on the move, however, we can no longer support all their wishes. They have moved to the land of "yes" and "no." Now, Mom frowns and moves Malik away when he wants to explore the wastebasket or the bottom desk drawer. Even after we carefully childproof, there are things we don't want these explorers to take on. Our little ones can't know ahead of time when we will encourage and when we will halt their exploring. To them, we have become totally unpredictable.

Baby thinks:
- "I can poke the spots on the toy, why not the spots on the remote control?"
- "I can pound on the kitchen pans, why not on Daddy's nose?"
- "I can chew on rubber ducky, why not on this little button I found?"
- "I can pull teddy bear's leg, why not kitty's tail?"
- "I can climb up on the pillows, why not on the open dresser drawers?"
- "I can step on leaves, why not on doggie droppings?"

Around the World

Parents in the **United States** usually praise babies who crawl and walk early. Not so in **Java,** where crawling is considered animal-like and therefore not dignified. Whenever babies try to crawl, they are picked up and carried. Early walking, however, is encouraged.

In some traditional **Polynesian** cultures, family life cycles are seen as tightly interconnected. Parents believe that if a baby walks early (before one year), a grandparent will die early. Therefore, babies are actively discouraged from walking before one year. Clearly, there is no single "right" way to raise a human baby because all these children learn to walk.

Our unexpected limits make no sense to these little ones. (And they won't for years!) Over the coming months, as toddlers go from crawling to toddling, and eventually to walking and running, they bump into more and more of our necessary limits. Yet it is not until they turn 4 and 5 that they really understand *why* we set many such limits.

The roller coaster of life now carries children repeatedly through curiosity, frustration, and anxiety. Curiosity often feels terrific, then Mom stops Spencer's fun by saying, "Dog food goes in *this bowl*, not in the water bowl." Or Dad gets scared, yells "Stop! It can hurt you!" and pulls the electric cord from Elena's mouth. Because easy Elena's early months were so calm and quiet, this is the first time she encounters some of the harder feelings in life.

No wonder our little ones get frustrated! King Malik, Queen Melody, and their friends have been jolted from their thrones, and they object: "I thought *I* was in charge here. How dare you stop me!" Now there are suddenly two different Moms—one who helps and one who gets in the way. Babies who have intense, easily frustrated temperaments will protest especially strongly.

Like their children, most parents also feel a huge change once babies first crawl and then toddle off. We suddenly see that we cannot and should not always follow our babies' wishes and commands. This can be a difficult emotional shift from being only the Nurturing Parent during baby's earlier months. Now we are also the Bearer of Bad News. Sharing the challenge of this transition with others in parent-support groups can be very helpful. Check with your pediatrician, adult schools, and other parents in the park to find local support groups.

"Me" or "Them"?

Between 9 and 14 months, youngsters are still trying to figure out who is "me" and who is "them." Put a dot of lipstick on Evan's nose when he's 13 months old and set him in front of a mirror. He is likely to tap the rosy nose in the mirror. At 15 months, he'll probably tap his *own* bright red nose because he has figured out that the person in the mirror is "me."

In the baby study center, we can see when babies understand that other people think differently than they do. Fourteen-month-old Melody is given broccoli and animal crackers to taste. She prefers animal crackers. Then the researcher tastes while Melody watches. The researcher smiles while eating broccoli and makes a disgusted face at animal crackers. When the researcher holds out his hand, Melody passes him more animal crackers because that is what *Melody* likes best. Later, at 18 months, Melody passes broccoli to the researcher because that is what *he* seems to like.

Family Goals

For explorers

- Move around at will in order to learn about their world.
- Be understood by their caregivers.
- Get comfort when things don't go as they wish.

For parents and caregivers

- Figure out what children want.
- Encourage hand signs and sounds to help children express their wishes. (See page 111, "Communication with Signs and Sounds.")
- Keep explorers safe. Childproof, childproof, childproof!
- Encourage children's interests. Look for safe ways for them to explore. (See page 176, "Safety" and page 50, "Ways to Make Life Easier.")

See page 27, "Parents' Roles and How They Change."

New Ways to Learn

As toddlers begin to cruise around on their own, they also find more ways to learn about the world. Young babies know that what is important to their parents is important to them, so they notice where their parents look and turn their eyes to look in the same direction. By 12 months, Elena can look where Dad is *pointing*. In a room full of things, she can figure out which one thing he points to and calls "chair."

Copying. Around 9 to 12 months, babies can copy some hand movements as well as our facial expressions and some sounds. They love this new form of copycat. And they love to be the leader. They may make funny or odd hand movements just to be sure that Mom and Dad are really copying. By 15 months, they not only copy our hand movements, but they copy what we do with things. Fifteen-month-old Elena puts a toy telephone to her ear or swings a little broom back and forth because that's what Mom and Dad do. This is the beginning of imaginary play. More importantly, it is about learning crucial life skills by copying others. Think how long it might take us to figure out how to use a telephone or a broom if we'd never seen one used.

Feelings. Babies use their emotions to live more safely. If something hurtful happens, the strong emotion they feel helps them remember not to do the same thing again. Babies also use emotions to learn indirectly from others. In the baby study center, if Dad reaches into a box and smiles, Elena will also reach into the box. But if Dad reaches into the box and looks afraid, disgusted, or otherwise upset, Elena will not reach into the box. By 10 to 12 months of age, babies use their own emotions *and* their parents' emotions to learn about the world more quickly.

This emotional learning is an important tool for parents to use. Malik takes a little tumble and then quickly looks at Mom. If she looks frightened, he's more likely to cry. If she smiles with encouragement, he's more likely to get up and toddle on. (Some very sensitive toddlers will cry in either case.) Or imagine Melody reaching toward the safely covered electric socket. If Dad looks frightened and says, "Don't touch!" Melody is less likely to touch it. On the other hand, if Dad smiles and coos, "Don't touch it, sweetie," Melody is more likely to touch it. At this age, Melody pays much more attention to her parent's *facial expression and tone of voice* than to his words.

If Dad looks frightened or angry about many of the things Melody touches, she may learn that being curious is not a good idea. To avoid that, Dad puts the glass vases out of reach and locks the medicines in the cabinet.

A Body That Works Better and Better

See page 104, "Bilingual Babes and Beyond."

Speech. By 12 months, babies have learned to use their lips, mouth, and tongue to make many sounds according to the basic rhythms and speech patterns of their native language. By now, babies from different countries already sound quite different as they babble to themselves. Around 10 to 12 months, they stop paying attention to speech sounds they don't hear regularly. With time, it becomes harder for them to notice and copy different sounds from other languages.

3-D vision. Early on, babies often don't reach inside anything, such as a cup, because it looks flat, like a picture on paper. Only after they develop 3-D vision, depth perception, can babies see that the *inside* is farther away than the outside rim. Babies learn about depth perception as they begin to crawl. When they start crawling, they usually look first at one hand and then at the other. They practice looking at one thing with both eyes—first something that is to the left side of their nose and then something that is to the right side of their nose.

Usually after three weeks of crawling, the brain learns to use the slightly different views it gets from each eye. This tiny difference between sides is what creates 3-D vision. Researchers place a strong piece of glass over a space between two tables. Before babies learn depth perception, they crawl out onto the glass without concern. But a few weeks later, they stop at the edge of the table because it *looks* like they will fall if they crawl onto the glass. Babies now become more cautious of heights. They also see that there is space *inside* the cup they hold. With their new depth perception, they reach into the cup to see what's there.

Walking. The urge to stand and walk is one of our strongest drives. Even blind babies who have never seen anyone walk naturally take on this awesome task. Walking takes a great deal of work in the early months. It is hard for toddlers to keep their balance, especially when they turn corners. Those who can talk at this age can't yet talk *and* walk at the same moment. No wonder they tire so easily and often want to ride or be carried. Most 15- to 18-month-olds have more control over their big walking muscles than they do over smaller muscles in their arms and hands, so they spend most of their time toddling from one place to another.

Arms and hands. Controlling the arms and hands is more hard work. At first, it is easier to do the same thing with both hands. For example, toddlers often reach to take one cracker for each hand. Gradually, they learn to use their hands separately, but it is still not easy. When they try to hit their carpenter's bench with the head of the hammer, they may hit it with the side instead.

Toddlers still find it hard to control their fingers well. They want to explore, but may pull too hard at a book and tear the page they wanted to turn. Many things get dropped, torn, or broken unless there is an adult right there to help. Elena's mother holds Grandma's delicate figurine so that Elena can run her hand over its smooth form and shiny colors. In Spencer's house, thick-paged or cardboard books last longer at this age and are more relaxing for all.

One day toddlers discover that their arms can now throw things. Malik loves to practice this new skill. For safety, Mom shows him where to throw his blocks—first onto a blanket and then into a basket as his aim gets better.

Of course, all of the skills these explorers are learning—crawling, walking, using hands or words, and copying us—are improving at different rates. It is rather like the way we adults learn to use computers: we learn different parts of different programs at our own pace.

Temperament also affects the development of body control. Many high energy babies like Spencer naturally practice using big muscles early on, so they may crawl and walk earlier than others their age. On the other hand, low energy Evan spends more time sitting in one place. He naturally practices and becomes more skilled with his hands and fingers at an earlier age. These are some of the individual differences that make each toddler unique and special.

Problem Solving Is Still in Process

While toddlers at this age can find some things that hide, other things still magically disappear. Dad closes his hand around a key, and 15-month-old Elena now knows where to find it. She lifts his fingers and smiles because there it is. But then Dad closes his hand over the key, slides his hand under a blanket, leaves the key there, and shows Elena his hand again. She again looks under his fingers and is surprised the key isn't there, but she doesn't look under the blanket. Life still has many mysteries.

Ways to Make Life Easier

Safety

We obviously need to be careful about the safety of our little explorers who climb and crawl toward stairs, tabletops, bookcases, counters, and windows, from which they can fall greater distances. Toddlers have no idea what might fall on them or what else might happen because of their limited experience and lack of judgment during this phase. They are vulnerable and need our protection.

Realistic Expectations for Explorers

If we expect this phase to be all smooth and easy, we are likely to be disappointed. Expect explorers to:

- Ignore rules. (See page 117, "Discipline.")
- Study the world with feet, hands, and tongue. They need protection from danger, while being allowed to explore as much as is safe.
- Need cuddling, thumb, pacifier, breast or bottle when upset or tired. (See page 181, "Self-Soothing and Security Objects.")
- Get upset by separation—although some don't.
- Get a few bumps and bruises while learning to walk.

Fortunately, babies learn to walk while they are short and light, so normally, they don't fall far or hard. (A corner of something, such as a coffee table, can be a problem because the full force of the fall is concentrated on a small spot. Pad the corners or move the coffee table.) Toddlers get a few bumps and bruises while learning to walk, but serious injuries are rare.

The house, the yard, the garage and shed, the car—everywhere a small child may be, with or without supervision—needs to be looked at from the point of view of a low-to-the-ground (but able to climb and get almost anywhere) toddler. Neighbors' yards and friends' homes are also dangerous because these areas may not be childproofed. The street is particularly inviting for the younger toddler because he or she doesn't understand the danger of cars. For the older toddler, standing in the street, in spite of parents' rules, feels powerful.

See page 27, "Parents' Roles and How They Change."

What About Setting Limits?

At this age, safety is our top priority. That's why we put a baby gate on the stairway. In addition, we need to balance our role as nurturing, protective parent with our role as "life teacher." Therefore, put a baby gate a step or two *above* the bottom stair so that a baby can safely practice climbing at the bottom.

On the one hand, babies learn by exploring. On the other hand, we have limited energy to clean up behind them. Baby locks on drawers and cabinets are our easiest limits. Much exploring is best done together. For example, Mom holds a bowl of uncooked rice so that Malik can enjoy the texture, *and* she can remove the bowl before rice is splashed all around the kitchen.

We have to set limits with actions, not words. Mom can't simply tell Spencer to be gentle with his young cousin. She has to sit beside Spencer and guide his hand so that he strokes the baby's hair rather than pokes her eye. Mom first tells him what to do, "Stroke her hair gently." "Pat her hand gently," and then adds, "Don't hurt her." When active Spencer gets too rough, Mom picks him up and moves him elsewhere. At this age, it is *our* job to hold the line on limits.

Consistency pays off because little ones learn more quickly this way. If we often change the rules, they have to test constantly to see what the limits are *this time*. They feel more secure and confident when the rules remain the same. Depending on temperament, some little ones accept limits much more easily than others.

When to Get Help

As parents of a busy toddler, get breaks from family members or baby sitters. Check with your pediatrician or a family therapist for help if you often feel:

◆ Anger or exhaustion because your toddler still needs you so much.

◆ Little joy in watching your toddler learn and succeed. During this phase, toddlers really need us to cheer them on. They are working very hard and need our encouragement.

◆ Fear that your toddler will be harmed by minor disappointments. Such fear can make it extremely difficult to set appropriate limits.

◆ Extreme fear that your toddler will get hurt. Such fear may arise from your own experiences or because a child is dangerously adventuresome. In the second case, you'll need respite while others watch this fearless explorer.

CHAPTER 5

18 Months to 3 Years: Living in the Here and Now

How long will these tantrums and meltdowns last?

When can I start toilet learning?

Why can't she wait patiently, even for a minute?

A Snapshot— Life with Present-Timers

Don't Fence Me In: 18 Months

Toddlers live in the present moment. They hunt for all that is new and interesting in their world. Most are busy and constantly on the go—like restless sparrows that flit from branch to branch. All the moving from place to place takes most of their attention, so they may seem a little out of touch with us. For brief moments, they may even forget we're around. During their travels, they love closing things, such as books, drawers, and doors. Although most 18-month-olds toddle happily through these months, a few jump ahead early and react like demanding 2½s.

Me Do It! 2 Years

Despite the bad press, the months just after the second birthday often go quite smoothly. With better control of their bodies, these tykes may be calmer and more confident than they were a few months earlier. They are often gentle and delightful. We just can't expect them to hurry to the car or home from the park or anywhere else. They live in the present, with whatever is happening at the moment. And they are on their own time schedule, one that moves much slower than ours.

Me, Mine, My Way! 2½ Years

This is the classic era of the trying 2s. Our former little angels become bossy, demanding, contrary, and unreasonable. They may shout "No!" or "Mine!" or drop to the floor and refuse to budge. They may insist that we always serve things in the same order or sit in the same place at the table. Their emotions are often extreme—from loving hugs to screaming tantrums or from confident independence to limp helplessness. Some mellow, adaptable, low energy 2½s easily cooperate right through these months. For them, it is not until 3½ or so that "No!" may become their favorite word.

Present-timers are amazing to watch, and it is a privilege to help them figure out their world. They are often delightful, loving, and adorable. Even so, they are not always easy to manage. There are important challenges along the way as well.

29 What's Happening Now?

"Me" Versus "You"

Why are the time-intensive 2s so much more difficult than other ages? (This phase actually occurs at 18 months or 2½ or 3½ years, depending on the child.) Through daily experience, these toddlers gradually learn that "me" and "you" are different. Melody, "me," loves to splash water out of the bathtub, but Dad doesn't like that. There's a clue that "you" and "me" are different. Melody isn't hungry, but Mom says it is dinnertime. Another clue, after many others throughout her day. The experiences that are so necessary to toddlers' development of this new concept can be very trying for the whole family.

Back when Malik began to crawl, Mom seemed to split into two mothers—one who helped and one who hindered. Now Malik seems to split into a cooperative self and a defiant self. Before, there was only one way to do things. Now, there are two: Mom's and his. When Mom tells Malik to "come here," Malik "goes there." He has to do the opposite to know he's in charge of his own body.

One landmark day, Dad says to Melody, "Let's put on your jacket." She plants her feet and declares, "No!" For the first time, she's used a word to tell Dad that what he wants is not the same as what she wants. She's saying, "I'm me, not you." As toddlers start to separate from us, they often begin to refer to themselves as "me" or "I," or begin to use their own names. After some days or weeks of practicing "no," "yes" takes on a whole new meaning. "Yes" now means "*I* feel like 'yes,'" or "I *myself* prefer to do this!" Melody pays very close attention to her amazing new discovery. She now knows she is a separate person with likes and dislikes of her own. When Mom asks her to share or wait for someone else, it makes no sense at all to say "yes" unless "I, Melody, *want* to." For that reason, she says "No!" instead. No wonder life is suddenly much more difficult for parents.

Our 2½s are ready to strike out on their own in many ways. At the same time, they are intensely attached and still greatly dependent on us. Just because they are ready to leave us (for a moment) doesn't mean they want us to leave them. Consequently, they hate it when we talk on the telephone and are less attentive to them. If we ignore them, they know how to get our attention by grabbing the lamp cord or the knobs on the stove. Waiting is hard because they have no sense of future time. They interrupt again and again. As much as possible, we avoid important conversations while they are awake. The tug of war between being connected to us and being separate from us is why emotional outbursts are so common between 2½ and 3. As noted in chapter 1, it takes as much time to care for toddlers as for newborns.

Temperament also strongly affects how time-intensive 2s look, feel, and sound. The intense, high energy, easily frustrated toddlers may bite, hit, and scream when they run into life's barriers. The sensitive, cautious ones more often back off, whimper, or cry when things don't go their way. And the mellow, adaptable ones breeze past 2½ with ease.

See page 23, "How Does Children's Development Affect Parents' Time?"

Pictures in the Mind

Early on, Melody saw only one picture in her mind at a time. Mom handed her a red cup or a blue cup, and she was happy with either one. Then suddenly one day Melody could see two possibilities in her mind, a red cup *and* a blue one. Because more brain cells connect around 2, little ones suddenly realize there is more than one possibility in a given moment. They can now see what *is* and what *might be*.

There are things to choose and things to expect. Malik expects the top will fit on the pot, and he beams when he makes that happen. Even-tempered Elena whispers "Uh-oh" when she spills her cereal because she expected it to stay in the bowl. But when present-timers can't make the outside world match their inside picture, they may be flooded with disappointment. Spirited Shauna screams because Dad won't give her the cookie she sees in her mind. Pictures in the mind are the birth of imagination. What an advance! However, possibility brings the need for choice. Life has yet again become more complicated.

Future Heights?

Though present-minded now, children may later ask, "How tall will I grow?" If children are well nourished and healthy, height depends in large part on genes. Children may inherit height from either side of the family. As a *general* rule, girls reach about half their adult height at 18 months. Boys reach about half their adult height at 24 months. No guarantees. Only time will tell for sure!

Life Without Time

Toddlers are faced with choices long before they have a clear sense of time. They don't yet know there is a future. Melody can see the room she's in and see (in her mind) the sidewalk where she wants to walk. But she's not on the sidewalk *now*. Without a sense of the future, that walk is never going to happen if it doesn't happen now. Without a future, there's no reason for Melody to hurry to the park.

At 2, on the way to the corner store with Dad, Malik is delighted with the storm drain and old gum right here and now. Dad has to remind himself that the outing is more important than getting to the store.

Words and phrases such as *soon, later today, this afternoon, tomorrow,* and *next week* have no meaning. If it isn't *now,* it is *never.* No wonder these toddlers are so impatient and demand everything now.

Sometime after they turn 2, present-timers will understand *in a few minutes.* They'll actually understand this idea much more easily if they can look at an egg timer or listen to a familiar song. Not until 2½ can Melody think ahead and, therefore, want to hurry to the park so that she can ride on the swing. Not until they near 3 can toddlers divide the day into *before lunch* and *after lunch* or know that *tomorrow* is sooner than ten years from now.

Learning More Every Minute

A 2-year-old's brain uses as much oxygen and works as hard as an adult's does. By 3 most of the nerves have been insulated with myelin, a fatty covering, so the brain and body work more efficiently than before. (The *connections* among all those insulated neurons are what allow for mature thinking; these won't be complete until age 19 or 20 or even later.) Memory gradually lasts longer. Eighteen-month-olds can remember unusual events for up to four months. For example, a researcher shows Evan an unusual toy that lights up when the researcher puts it on top of her head. When Evan sees the same toy four months later, he remembers and puts it on top of his head.

Seeing. By 18 months to 2 years, most toddlers see almost as clearly as adults, though vision continues to improve throughout the early elementary school years. Toddlers begin to rely more and more on their eyes to guide their bodies and hands. At 18 months, Melody's feet were in the lead. She toddled around for a while and stopped. Then she looked at whatever was nearby. At 2, her eyes are in the lead. She sees the electric socket, then heads across the room to study it. Earlier, her fingers led. She explored the rubber ducky mainly with her fingers, as a blind person would. Now, she *looks* at ducky first. She sees the funny bump that is its beak, then she pokes the beak with her finger. Her eyes are not completely reliable yet. Melody may be afraid of an approaching train because she fears it will run into her instead of pass nearby.

Copying. Toddlers continue to watch and copy us in order to learn. As early as 18 months, they may feel upset when they *can't* copy adults. For example, if we swish around the floor in a dance step, they may watch sadly, feeling left out. When they *can* copy us, for instance, by "cooking" with some pots while we cook with others, they are often more content. The first time Malik pushes the doorbell, he flashes a delighted smile of success. Then for the next few weeks he insists on pushing the doorbell every time he arrives home. Practice makes perfect. For the rest of his life, copying and practicing will continue to be essential tools for learning.

See page 75, "Set Up Scaffolds."

Doing. Twos want to try things for themselves. "By self!" or "I do it!" are common exclamations. When we are in a hurry, we want to do things for them. They scream when they aren't allowed to put toothpaste on the brush, pour the milk, stir the pot, take off their shoes, open the car door, carry the cat, and so on. Not surprisingly, they resent it when we rob them of opportunities to feel successful. We need to slow down for them. It helps to remember that when we allow them to practice, they get better at things.

Present-timers continue to learn best from direct experience. They don't know that the kitty is soft or the needle is sharp until they touch both. Rather than say, "Don't touch the needle," Shauna's mother says, "The needle is sharp. I'll hold it still so you can feel it." This way Shauna can feel its point and learn what the word means without serious injury. Similarly, Spencer's mom puts cups of cold and hot water on the table so Spencer can touch them, feel the temperatures, and learn the difference.

One day, Elena pushes all her toy animals into one pile and all her crayons into another. She is demonstrating a new skill. Between 18 months and 3 years, toddlers learn to sort things into groups. This happens about the time they start asking for the names of many things—"What's sat?" But some groupings are still too hard to understand. Elena can't yet divide things into "alive" and "not alive." She waves "night-night" to the lamp, the chair, dolly, and to Dad.

Around 18 months, toddlers begin to learn more complicated problem solving. Imagine several toys on a table including a little rake. Also on the table, but beyond reach, is an especially interesting toy. Before 18 months, tots will only reach or cry for help. But after 18 months, they will use the rake to pull the fancy toy within reach.

Why Do They Test Limits So Often?

There are many reasons for all the limit testing during these months. Testing limits is a basic way to learn. Humans have pushed past obvious limits in order to live in Arctic snow, the Sahara Desert, and even outer space. In the same spirit, Spencer tries to pour his own milk, turn on the stove, and use the electric drill. When Dad necessarily takes some of these jobs away from him, he's angry. It is just like taking a bone from a hungry dog. Spencer's drive to learn is almost as strong as his instinct to eat.

Memory. Twos are still beginners at using mental pictures. They more easily *recognize* what is in front of them than *recall* pictures from memory. *After* Malik turns his cup over and spills the milk again, he *recognizes* that this upset Dad yesterday. (Even as adults we find it easier to recognize than to recall. For example, we may not recall our friend's front doorway, but we recognize it when we see it.)

Learning one by one. Before 3, children can't understand *general ideas* such as "No hitting." They have to learn specifically not to hit Mom or Dad or their friend or the window or the family dog. *Generalizing* is a skill that allows us to apply one bit of learning to many situations, but toddlers can't do this yet. They must go through the lengthy process of learning what to do in each individual situation. No wonder they need naps and we need breaks!

Learning cause and effect. When spirited Shauna snatches a block away from Spencer, Mom makes her give it back. When she hits Daddy's nose, he puts her down on the floor and won't hold her for several minutes. When Spencer reaches for the lamp cord, Mom says urgently, "Stop! Fingers away from the cord!" and she moves Spencer away.

But why does Spencer look right at Mom and then reach *again* for the lamp cord? This time Spencer is not nearly as interested in the lamp cord as he is in his mother's reaction when he reaches for it. He is interested *because* it upsets her. Spencer's peace of mind depends on figuring out what makes his parent upset and what doesn't. He does a scientific test to see whether she reacts the same way again. He must choose between his strong drive to understand people and his desire to live peacefully with his family. Scientist that he is, he picks understanding over happiness. As the authors explain in *The Scientist in the Crib*, Spencer's parents are his laboratory rats. He puts them through one trial after another until he's sure he can predict what they will do. The more consistently Mom takes him away from the lamp cord, the sooner he can move on to a different experiment.

Impulse control. We hear Melody tell her dolly, "No! No pick Gamma's fouwers." Obviously she understands the rule. But then she toddles to the flowerbed and pulls up Grandma's tulips. What is going on? One part of her brain says, "I want to hold the pretty flower." A different part of the brain puts on the brakes: "But I'm *not* going to grab it." Unfortunately, the part of the brain that stops us develops much more slowly. At 2, it doesn't yet work well or consistently. This is why we adults need to supply the control and stop 2s when they can't stop themselves.

Young brains think with pictures. Children have no mental picture for "don't." Therefore, when they hear, "Don't pull up Grandma's flowers," the picture they see is, "Pull up Grandma's flowers." "Don't go in the street" registers as "Go in the street." It is really important to tell these tots what *to do,* instead of what *not* to do. We need to train *our* brains to say, "Always hold Daddy's hand in the street," "Touch the flowers gently so they stay still," or "Hold your hands behind your back when you look at Grandma's flowers."

Why Do They Want Us to Do Everything a Certain Way?

Starting around 21 months, present-timers begin to figure out that one particular thing often follows another: "After Daddy fills my cup, then I can drink." They pay close attention to sequence: "After eating in my high chair, my face gets wiped. After lunch comes a nap. After my bath comes bedtime." *Sequence becomes their clock.* That's why they get so upset when we do things out of order. We'd get just as upset if someone kept resetting our clocks.

Without sequence, toddlers live in the middle of an overwhelming collection of disconnected events. Imagine giant space aliens telling us at odd times, "Eat now," "Exercise now," "Bathe now," "Get in the spaceship now." Life would feel completely out of our control, just as it does to toddlers.

By 2, and especially at 2½, toddlers are desperate to make sense of this confusing world. Shauna insists that Dad do many things in the same order each time. For example, she wants him to pour her cereal in the bowl *before* feeding the cat, put on her shirt *before* her pants, read the *same* bedtime story and tuck Dolly in beside her *before* the good night kiss.

If Dad tries to sneak past a few boring pages of the story or put on her pants first, Shauna screams until the whole routine is done over again, from the beginning. To avoid being overloaded by confusion, she needs the same rituals to remind her that there is order in the world. By 3 and 4 when the world is more familiar, most preschoolers will not depend so much on sequence and routine to feel secure. In the meantime, toddlers don't like surprises. They may not want their rocking horse moved to a different place, the new nanny to make their bed, or half a cookie instead of the usual whole one, and so on.

Memory experts say that routines can reduce stress for all of us. Most of us have adult routines, such as always putting our keys and wallet in the same place, so that we'll know where to find them. In the same way, routines help children.

Why Can't They Make Up Their Minds?

At 2 Shauna sees pictures in her mind, and there is no future. When Mom asks, "Do you want milk or juice?" Shauna has to decide, "Should I have juice now and give up milk forever?" or "Should I have milk now and give up juice forever?" No wonder she has trouble deciding! Seeing her frustration, Mom gives her a tiny glass of each and teaches a new word: "Both."

Why Won't They Accept Help from Mom or Dad?

Trying to make their world predictable, 2s commonly want the same person to bathe or get them dressed each day. If Mom has been the usual caretaker, they generally want her to continue. If Dad hasn't been very involved before now, it is a difficult time to change that. Age 3 will be easier. On the other hand, some 2s suddenly switch and demand Dad instead. At 2½, toddlers may cry for whoever is *not* there at the moment. This is about being in control and having trouble making choices. In this case, either Mom or Dad finishes the job quickly despite the protest. At this age, things often go better when only one familiar caregiver is nearby and there aren't any choices. Children in this phase continue to need a great deal of our relaxed and loving attention to balance out their difficult moments.

Ways to Make Life Easier

Look for Causes of Anger

Present-timers are famous for their crying, screaming, and tantrums. Sometimes they fall to the floor, scream, and kick their feet. Sometimes they hit whoever is near. Intense toddlers may start before 18 months. Mellow children may never have a single tantrum. Children have more tantrums at 2½ than at any other age.

Many tantrums at this age are caused by frustration. Because of the new pictures that are clearer in their minds, they often know exactly what they want. Frequently, however, they can't make it happen, so life is much harder than before. The crying and vigorous exercise of a tantrum eventually helps the body and mind settle down.

Body doesn't work well yet. Twos still stumble, fall, and drop things. Imagine trying to get through our day with our shoelaces tied to each other and boxing gloves on! That's what it feels like to be a toddler. Bodies will be much easier to live with once the brain has developed more and muscles do as they are told.

See page 61, "Offer Wise Choices."

Realistic Expectations for Present-Timers

We'll feel a lot more relaxed if we remember that these little ones are only 2, not 20. Don't take it personally that they aren't all grown up yet. Many, though not all, are likely to:

- Resist separation at childcare, bedtime, when we talk on the phone or with others.
- Need cuddling, thumb, pacifier, breast, bottle, or other security object to calm down or get to sleep. (See page 181, "Self-Soothing and Security Objects.")
- Entertain themselves for only a few minutes.
- Have tantrums and meltdowns. (See page 181, "Self-Soothing and Security Objects.")
- Break the rules.
- Refuse to share. Hit playmates and grab toys.
- Resist using the toilet.
- Refuse to say, "I'm sorry," "Please," or "Thank you." (See page 141, "Guilt/Regret" and "Gratitude.")
- Fuss in restaurants.
- Not understand *why* many things are important to adults.

Strong drive to learn and be in control. We stop children when they reach for the electric shaver, the computer, and the medicines. Toddlers wonder, "Why *can't* I jump in the bathtub or eat the gum I found on the sidewalk?" Our rules make no sense to them. We decide when they must leave the park, go to child care, or go to bed. There are constant conflicts between their instinct to learn and our instinct to keep them safe, protect our property, and care for our entire family.

Cannot solve problems well. When his tricycle gets stuck in the sand, Spencer pushes and pushes. He can't yet figure out that it would be better to back up onto the sidewalk. He works hard without success. Depending on inborn temperament, a youngster may give up quickly, keep at it doggedly, or scream in frustration.

Not understood. Think of living in a country where no one understands us. Even our simplest wishes would be hard to satisfy. Similarly, our 2s get frustrated when *we* don't understand. The sooner they are able to show us or tell us what they want, the less frustrated they are. Not surprisingly, late talkers are more likely to have more meltdowns than early talkers. Mellow toddlers may freeze when they don't know what word to use next, while more intense ones may bite, scream, or drop to the floor.

See page 111, "Communication with Signs and Sounds."

Jealous. Our 18-month-olds are good observers. They notice that Mom's attention is drawn away from them when Dad or brother is around. They feel jealous and left out when others have our attention.

Offer Wise Choices

Choices can help us get around the natural resistance of 2s. If Dad says, "It is time to go to bed," Malik will likely answer, "No!" Instead, Dad asks, "Do you want to walk to your room or be carried?" Dad gets his way, and Malik feels powerful in deciding how it will happen. Similarly, with 2s, we also use choices to narrow the options and *keep life simple:* If Mom asks, "What do you want to drink for breakfast?" Shauna might reply "milkshake" or "coffee." To keep life really simple one day, Mom asked, "Do you want milk or do you want your glass empty?" Shauna answered, "Empty." Mom realized that Shauna usually said "No!" to the first option, no matter what it was. So the next day, when Mom wanted Shauna to drink some milk, Mom asked, "Do you want your glass empty? or do you want milk?" Shauna answered, "Milk."

Choices may be overwhelming in new, unfamiliar situations or when children are tired. Around 2½, choices may be especially difficult. Shauna simply doesn't know what she wants at this age. She switches back and forth, screaming, "Blue pants! No! Green pants! No! Blue pants." Dad then picks her up and changes the scene. He takes her along while he brushes his teeth.

Returning to the bedroom, he calmly announces, "It's time for your blue pants." For a few weeks, Dad stopped offering choices and just said, "Now we are going to . . . " even though Shauna often yelled.

At 3, Shauna will be much more able to handle complicated choices, such as "Do you want to wear the blue pants or the green pants?" As children get older, they want to be part of the planning. They may propose their own options. Mom asked Malik, almost 3, "Do you want to walk or be carried to your room?" Malik grinned and announced, "I want pulled." He flopped on his back and stuck his feet in the air. Malik giggled all the way as Mom gently pulled him to his room. Malik's surprising suggestion was easy for Mom and accomplished her goal, so she wisely accepted. She would not have agreed if he'd said, "Go to park." At 4, Malik will be able to handle a wide-open choice, such as "Which friend do you want to invite over today?'

How to Manage Anger and Upsets

Give information and alternatives. Redirect toddlers' energy with alternatives: "Hit pillows, not people." "Stamp your feet when you're angry." (Feet are always nearby.) Tell them what *to do*. "Hug and hum." (Some energetic toddlers bite because of excitement, not anger, but they can't bite while they hum.) "Bite your bracelet, not people." (Find a soft plastic bracelet for them to wear.) "Use your words." "Touch gently."

When everyone is in good spirits, practice what to do with anger. Take turns pretending to be angry. Play the "Angry Games": stomp feet, hit pillows, or blow out "the angries." Stuff a paper bag with newspaper, close it with tape, and kick "the angries" around. Eventually, young children will be able to remember to redirect their anger.

Let toddlers stay nearby at this age, if time-out makes things worse. Some calm more quickly when held. Others do better if we just sit nearby and wait. Sometimes it is useful to say, "Tell me when you've finished crying." Some calm more quickly if we go to a nearby room where they can join us when they feel ready. Forcing them often to go to another room may teach that anger causes separation beyond their control.

Let toddlers cry. Tantrums and meltdowns release tension from the body. Toddlers will stop when their bodies are able to relax. Most older children, at 4 and 5, may be able to stop themselves from crying after 5 to 15 minutes. In the meantime, it helps us to notice how long these reactions last, so that we'll know what to expect next time.

Separate meltdowns from tantrums. Meltdowns and tantrums look the same. Toddlers typically drop to the floor where they may cry, scream, or kick. They may bang their heads or bite. Older children may cry, scream, hit, kick, or throw things. While meltdowns and tantrums look the same, their meanings are different. Sometimes it is easy to tell one from the other, sometimes not. Make your best guess.

Meltdowns occur when children are overwhelmed. They are hungry, tired, or undone by too much excitement, too many changes, or a world that is too confusing. Children may be frightened or frustrated. In general, offer patient help and compromise; then try to avoid the next meltdown by bringing food along, going home sooner, allowing more time, or whatever makes sense for the situation.

Tantrums are emotional power plays to get us to back down. Children, especially 2s, demand any number of things that are not possible, not appropriate, or not reasonable. With their words or behavior they declare, "I want to: stay up all night . . . go to the store without my clothes . . . never leave the park . . . eat my ice cream on the sofa!" Hold the line with a firm and kind tone of voice. Ignore these complaints or pick up your unhappy child and do what you need to do next. Tantrums, especially with older children, may stop suddenly when children see they aren't working.

When toddlers are ready for contact, offer a hug and sympathy. "It is hard when you can't do the things you want to do."

Help with Friendships

Think of how eager puppies are to jump on visitors. Some 2s get just as excited. They don't know that people are different from things and that people feel pain. Shauna walks across Evan's body as casually as she walks on a pillow. She pokes, pinches, and pushes him just like any other toy. Two-year-olds don't understand yet that people are different from furniture. We can stop them more patiently when we know they don't intend to hurt others.

Conflicts increase between 2 and 2½. Also, toddlers can now use words to report problems to us: "She hit me" or "He took my truck." And they try to change their playmates' actions with words: "No! Leave it alone," "Don't push me," or "You go there!" They don't ask politely yet.

Toddlers don't understand the difference between *accidental* and *on purpose.* Malik accidentally stumbles into Melody. Melody believes he deliberately attacked her, so she hits him back.

With our help, present-timers will begin to play more smoothly around 3 because they will understand more about intention ("on purpose"). Later they will also become better problem solvers. In the meantime, we stop them, restrain them, and model how to talk through problems politely. We continue to model good behavior even though they won't be able to copy us just yet. Fortunately, poor social skills at this age do not mean they are headed for Juvenile Hall.

How to help. To help toddlers treat family and friends nicely, we stop aggression each and every time. When Melody starts to grab or hit, Dad claps his thighs and says, "Stop!" Hold the hand that hits. Separate the children. Put down, walk away from, or restrain the child who strikes or bites *us*. Some sensitive, intense toddlers and preschoolers may hit people who crowd into their personal space. Help them find a safe, private space when they need one.

Report what we see. Mom tells Shauna: "You want the bear and Evan wants it, too. What can you do now?"

Teach assertiveness. More-aggressive toddlers often choose the same mellow victim. Mom tells even-tempered Elena, "Say, 'No!' in a loud voice so Shauna won't grab your doll," or "Tell Shauna, 'Don't push me.'" Then Mom pretends to be Shauna, and Elena practices being assertive. Dad and Elena take turns practicing a strong voice.

Most time-intensive 2s need constant supervision when playing with friends as well as brothers and sisters. Sometimes, two toddlers of equal strength can tug, push, and learn from each other that force doesn't work. Otherwise, we need to step in to prevent and settle conflicts. Late talkers need even more help and close watching.

Sharing Takes Time to Learn

Sharing doesn't come naturally to present-timers. Without a future, turns don't make sense. "If I can't have it now, I never will." We say, "You can have the rubber ducky when Evan is finished." But Shauna learns by copying Evan, so she is most interested in rubber ducky *when and because* Evan is holding it. When Evan puts the duck down, Shauna is no longer interested. Now she wants the *block* Evan is holding. Another identical duck or block doesn't solve this sharing problem. Only time will help. Mom intervenes to prevent hitting and remembers to comment on the process, "You really want to see what Evan is holding, don't you?"

Around 18 months, Malik begins to connect things he often sees together: Daddy and his hat, Mommy and her purse, and Doggie and her bone. But Malik doesn't understand the *idea* of ownership. He doesn't understand that this will always be Mommy's purse. Malik's parents, however, want him to learn about ownership. That's because today, next week, and next month, they want him to not touch Mom's computer, Dad's briefcase, or the dog's food. At 2, though, Malik is busy figuring out what he can touch. He's delighted that he can touch and control his shoes, his pacifier, and his teddy bear. He calls these "Mine!"

When Malik picks up Evan's truck, Malik also says "Mine!" He doesn't mean he owns it. He means, "I *control* this truck right now." It must confuse Malik when we say, "No, that's Evan's truck," because Evan is not holding the truck right now. Instead, it would be more helpful if we said, "Yes, you have the truck right now."

We can demonstrate solutions for conflicts. For example, when spirited Shauna tries to grab Evan's shovel, Mom stops her and tells her, "It will be your turn in a few minutes." Shauna doesn't understand this yet and screams. As she approaches 3, taking turns will begin to make sense, especially if we mark turns with a song, an egg timer, or other visible sign that time is passing. For now, adults need to step in again and again.

Separation: How to Help

When 2s feel separated from the trusted caregivers they are attached to, they become anxious. Some children become more anxious than others. Researchers can measure higher levels of stress hormones in their saliva. Even if our 2s are left with familiar people, they don't understand when we will be back. A night in the crib or day with the sitter are clear to us, but not to them. Good-byes would upset us, too, if we didn't know whether a loved one would return tonight or next year.

By 2½, most toddlers carry a picture of loved ones in their minds. Mental pictures of parents and connections are still delicate and seem to disappear when toddlers are frightened or angry. They can recognize familiar adults in a photograph, so this may be a good time to post a picture above their crib and in their cubby at daycare and beside their bed at home. In addition, some parents point out, "There is a magic rope that always ties us together. Can you see it? What does it look like to you?"

Good-bye songs that tell the day's events, including Mom's return, remind toddlers of the sequence. Mom picks up Evan after lunch. Dad picks up Melody after her nap. As children approach 3 and understand that a day has a morning, an afternoon, and an evening, these transitions will be easier. Not surprisingly, if we leave for several days, our toddlers are likely to become extremely clingy upon our return.

When to Get Help

Life is often difficult with time-intensive 2s. Look for a support group or parenting class during this phase—you will find that you are not alone. Definitely get help if:

- Your anger and resentment of your present-timer make it hard for you to have fun together.
- You worry that you might hurt your child.
- You find it hard to give your toddler the age-appropriate control he or she is ready for.
- You have trouble setting reasonable limits and sticking to them.

CHAPTER 6

3 Years: Mostly Sunny Skies with Some Showers

Does my child have to be in child care to make friends?

Why is my child so whiny? Will this last forever?

Everyone says 3s are so easy. Why isn't it easy at my house?

 ## A Snapshot— What 3s Are Like

Around the World

Dressing **in many countries around the world** is so easy that 3s can manage on their own. Many children wear nothing at all at this age. Others wear pull-on clothes, without underpants for easy toileting. Most have only one or two outfits for daily wear, and maybe one extra for special occasions. Whatever children wear to bed, they wear through the next day. In **rural Mexico,** little boys just add their hats in the morning, and little girls pull their shawls around their shoulders.

Differences in both temperament and development affect how children move through their third year. This chapter is shorter than those about 2s and 4s because 3s are generally easier for adults to understand. The topics in Part Two describe the tremendous growth during this third year.

Let's Do It: 3 Years

Threes love to please and are more able to share and cooperate than before. They are more able to accept suggestions and follow directions rather than always wanting to do things their way. They often say "we" instead of "I." They are more comfortable with language, which allows them to express their needs and wishes more easily. They begin to enjoy rhyming sounds, like *bam slam, squishy wishy,* or *yucky mucky.*

They cry and hit less, but whine more, especially when they are tired, bored, or lonely. Some proudly dress themselves in easy clothes, while others still find it too difficult, particularly when they are rushed. Overall, for most families, this year is delightful and fairly peaceful.

Don't Look at Me: 3½ Years

Many 3½s aren't in full control of their rapidly growing bodies. They may stumble or fall more often. Their hands may tremble. They may avoid activities that look easy to us. Feeling less sure of themselves than earlier, they may seem worried or fearful. They may keep to themselves more. They may blink, stutter, return to baby talk, suck their thumbs, bite their nails, pick their noses, or masturbate. They express their insecurity with commands, questions, and accusations: "Don't look at me," "Don't talk to me," "Don't laugh," "Do you love me?" or "You don't love me!" Given their insecurity, they are less likely to try new things. They are prone to jealousy when others in the family get attention. With reassurance, these moments of upset usually pass quickly.

What's Happening Now?

Family Goals

For 3s
- Learn by doing things with adults.
- Gradually learn to talk more easily.
- Gradually gain more physical skills.
- Enjoy playing with a friend.

For parents and caregivers
- Enjoy time together.
- Support and appreciate child's growing competence in all areas.
- Appreciate this particular child's emerging personality.
- Arrange time with a playmate.
- Work with nightmares and fears about scary creatures.

Brain Growth

Between 3 and 10, children's brains are twice as active as adults' and use twice as much oxygen. There are many more connections from one brain cell to another, making their thinking more flexible and creative. During the coming years, especially between 10 and puberty, connections that aren't used slowly dissolve. This leaves each person with an efficient brain that is fine-tuned to what he or she needs and uses most. Many of us remember very little that happened before 4 or 5. This may be because so many early connections were trimmed away from our busy young brains.

What Is Real?

All this creative thinking can make it hard to separate reality from fantasy. The shadow in the closet shifts easily into a fearsome monster. Melody's mother still remembers walking into the bathroom as a little girl and seeing "a real alligator" draped over the towel rack. Her dad said it was just a rumpled up towel, but it looked truly alive and terrifying to her!

Gaining Emotional Control

As we know all too well, circumstances occasionally push *us* over our emotional edge. We lose control and yell or sob. How can we be surprised that young children also lose control at times? Between 3 and 7, however, they gradually gain much more control. Between 3½ and 4, they begin to ignore minor mood swings. Consequently, their general mood, positive or negative, becomes more stable. They gradually find more specific ways to manage stronger emotions.

The Family Connection

Often around 3½ or 4, preschoolers who have been tightly connected to just one parent now want a closer connection to the other parent as well. Spirited Shauna began to demand that Dad, not Mom, put on her coat and buckle her seat belt. Melody's dad noticed that Melody still preferred to be with Mom. His feelings were hurt, so he started to spend more time with Melody. Soon she enjoyed being with him as much as with Mom.

Friends

At 3, children begin to play *with*, rather than *beside*, other children. They can now really enjoy each other's company. This is a good year to arrange playtimes with another child, either informally with a neighbor, another family, or child care. Outgoing 3s especially enjoy time with other children.

Ways to Make Life Easier

Feelings and How to Handle Them

Whining is more common at 3 than at any other year. When they were younger, children cried more. When they get older, they will use words more effectively. In the meantime, many whine.

Temperament also plays a role. Of children with strong, intense feelings, some are also high in energy while others are low in energy. These low energy kids are more likely to whine when upset. High energy kids may whine and then tantrum when things don't go their way.

Parents may demonstrate a whiny tone to help children understand. Then say, "Tell me in your strong voice. I can hear you better that way." Use your own strong voice to state the child's feelings and wishes: "You're really disappointed that Malik can't play with you today, aren't you?" It can also help to notice our own tone of voice. We may catch ourselves whining, "Come on. Pleeeease come here." *We* may need to model a strong voice.

Young children continue to learn about emotions, which are the fabric of human relationships. Infants and toddlers unconsciously use emotions and notice the effect on others and themselves: "I smile at Daddy, he smiles

Realistic Expectations for 3s

◆ Expect tears at parting. Many 3s can't separate from parents easily unless they are with very familiar people. This will improve by 3½ or 4.

◆ Some 3s still have trouble sleeping because they are intense, or high energy, or easily frustrated.

back, and I feel happy." Twos noticed that their actions affected the emotions of others: "I kicked the dog, and Daddy is angry." Threes (if we teach them the words) can understand and talk about how emotions affect themselves and others: "I'm mad. Shauna broke my castle." "Evan is sad. His mommy left."

When to Get Help

If life is hard at 3, parents often wonder if something is wrong and whether to get help. Your child's temperament may be a factor, or it may be your family's circumstances.

Mellow temperament. Even-tempered Elena breezed through 2½ with hardly a protest. Around 3½, she began to speak up. Her parents were surprised because they had come to expect easy cooperation, not demands or resistance. Once they adjusted to Elena's occasional new assertiveness, Elena, for the most part, settled back to her old mellow self. No outside help was needed.

Challenging temperament. If this year is harder than you expected, consider your child's temperament. Understanding temperament allows you to work *with* rather than *against* your child's inborn nature. If you need more help with a challenging child, talk with your doctor or a temperament counselor.

Family stress. There are many sources of family stress, including good ones such as the arrival of a new baby. Your 3 may clamor for needed attention when it is hardest for you to give it. Ask for help from family, friends, or professionals.

Special circumstances. Life may be difficult for your 3 because he or she needs some special help. For example, a child may be frustrated because language is still a challenge. Or a child with very sensitive hearing may be distressed by sounds that don't bother anyone else. Your doctor and other specialists can help discover individual needs and show you how to work with them.

CHAPTER 7

4 Years: The Next Declaration of Independence

Why do they have more trouble with friends than they did last year?

Why can't my child be a better sport? Why is he such a poor loser?

I told my son to tell the truth. Then he said, "You're fat!" What do I say now?

 A Snapshot— What 4s Are Like

Development affects *when* children strive for more independence. Temperament affects *how* they go about it. Because no two preschoolers are the same, the following description of 4s is a general picture.

I Can Do Anything! 4 Years

Happy 4s are often noisy and bouncy. They may talk constantly, say silly things, laugh, and sing. With their new self-confidence, most are curious and love to try new things. (About 10% of children are still quite cautious.) They delight in the excitement of life and believe anything is possible. They love to hear how strong they are. This blooming self-confidence causes 4s to show off and brag: "I can run faster than anyone." "I've got more than you."

You're Not the Boss of Me! 4½ Years

Especially around 4½, these powerful, self-confident, determined beings want more decision-making power. At 2, they wanted to run their own

Family Goals

For 4s

- Gradually take more control of their immediate world.
- Understand rules by testing them.
- Begin to learn about cause and effect of things, including emotions.
- Gradually gain more control over strong feelings; learn to see when they reacted too strongly.
- Gradually learn to play with two friends at the same time.
- Learn about the adult world.

For parents and caregivers

- Catch 4s being good and praise them.
- Have fun together.
- Support independence and learning as child is ready.
- Choose battles wisely. Set clear limits in a calm, firm way. See page 117, "Discipline."
- Teach about cause and effect as well as responsibility. See page 159, "Independence and Responsibility."
- Start holding family meetings.
- Set up playtime with a compatible friend or two.

lives; at 4 to 4½, they want to run *our* lives, too. They push harder to get their own way. They speak up, challenge authority, talk back, and negotiate.

Fours may test limits to learn how the rules work and who is in charge. Many don't yet have enough self-control to follow the rules all the time, especially the hard ones, such as "Ask before you go to play next door at Malik's house."

When angry, most 4s can now use angry words instead of hitting. They call others names, swear, and make threats, such as "I won't invite you to my birthday party." They may also make faces, stick out their tongues, or spit.

They behave worst with the parents they trust, because they believe we will love them regardless. They need our patience, not pressure, and rules that are both kindly stated and backed up with consequences.

Fours don't appreciate what we do for them. Spencer announced, "I'm moving out!" Mom helped him pack his bag, even as she sighed about how much she would miss him. Spencer marched off the front porch (while Mom watched just out of sight). He soon returned, saying that he would stay home "until tomorrow."

What's Happening Now?

Gaining Emotional Control

Fours can now hold in their mind a comforting picture of their parents, even when they are flooded with strong feelings of anger or loneliness. They can also talk to themselves: "Daddy comes home from his trip tomorrow." They can sometimes shift to a different goal: "I don't want to ride Elena's trike anyway." When a monster appears on television, they may hide behind the sofa or cover their eyes to protect themselves from feeling afraid. They may cover their ears to protect themselves from a sense of failure when we complain to them or tell them how they should behave. The curiosity that drives 4s out into the world introduces more uncertainty, fear, and confusion than before. It is helpful that they now have more ways to handle their emotions.

Most 4s have strong feelings. Each moment of life is either wonderful or terrible. Fours learn that angry words are different from angry actions. Even-tempered Evan can remember, "Hold your lips closed with your fingers when you're angry." But others shout, "I hate you!" or "I'll scratch her eyes out!" or "I'll kill him." This is frightening for parents, but hopefully we can see their progress from hitting and kicking to using words. Our most useful response is, "You are *really* angry, aren't you? What are you angry about? What can we do that will help?"

Sometime between 4 and 5, most preschoolers become able to self-reflect—to think about, describe, and evaluate their own actions. By using self-reflection, we can compare how we *did* behave with how we *should* behave: "I was mean when I pushed Elena," or "I wasn't fair when I took all the cookies." Children between 4 and 5 automatically combine self-reflection with their all-or-nothing thinking. When Melody misbehaves, she feels like a total failure. Then she's afraid no one will love her. No wonder 4s find it hard to admit mistakes. Fours need a great deal of encouragement.

Self-reflection also allows us to compare ourselves with others. This is hard on spirited Spencer who, because of his temperament, gets easily frustrated. When Spencer's friend Evan was 3, he often practiced building and drawing. When Spencer was 3, however, many activities frustrated him. Unless he felt immediate success, he moved on to try something else. Now at 4, Spencer notices that Evan can do things he can't do. He judges himself and thinks, "I must be stupid." Spencer could become sad and withdrawn or angry and aggressive because of this self-reflection. Fortunately, his parents and teacher help him practice and succeed at one activity after another. He soon starts to feel better about himself.

What Is Real?

Once children turn 4, expect the common question, "Is it real?" Our answers are hard for children to figure out. Are things that move real—the puppy *and* the wind-up doggie? Elena can close her eyes and see a picture of Daddy inside her head, and Daddy is real. Then why aren't nightmares real? At 4, children expect real things to have fronts and backs. However, Mom says the weather forecaster on television is real, even though Melody can't see his back when she looks behind the television. Dad says the television basketball players are real and the movie actors are real. However, actors pretend to be people who aren't real—unless they pretend to be other people who *are* real. No wonder it is confusing! With time, experience, and our patient explanations, children will gradually figure it all out.

Cause, Effect, and Confusion

A main goal of 4s is to figure out how the world works, what *causes* things to happen. When younger, they noticed that one thing followed another. Now they want to know why. Why does it rain after clouds fill the sky? Fours gradually learn to predict, plan, and make things happen: "Mommy is grouchy. I will tell her something funny, and that will make her smile."

In their effort to make sense of the world, 4s often think events are connected when they aren't. This morning, Malik pulled the cat's tail and was scolded. He feels bad and expects something bad to happen. This afternoon, he falls on the sidewalk. Malik now thinks the sidewalk hit his nose because he pulled the cat's tail this morning. When bad things happen, 4s assume it is because of something *they* did. Dad tells Malik, "Sometimes accidents just happen." Gradually Malik will learn the difference.

The Family Connection

When he was younger, Malik felt left out when Mom and Dad talked with each other. Now, at 4, he's been studying cause and effect. He knows that if he can get Mom's attention, Dad will be left out instead of him. He also knows that Dad gets annoyed with this tactic. He wants to stay on Dad's good side, too. He needs *both* Mom and Dad. Malik used to think about just himself and one other person. Now he is learning about three-way relationships. Fortunately, Dad understands what's going on and says, "You and I *both* like having Mom's attention, don't we? I love you even though you want all Mom's attention." Malik feels relieved that Dad understands.

Now is a wonderful time to share family dinners together (in case we didn't start earlier)—even if it is only part of the meal. Family is important to 4s. Most like to tell about their day and enjoy hearing something interesting from ours. This is valuable time to enjoy and appreciate one another, without distractions.

Fours understand that families go back in time. They love to hear stories from parents or grandparents about their parents' childhoods. Because it is hard work for 4s to always be "good," they love to hear that we misbehaved in similar ways. It gives them hope that they too will turn out all right. With their newfound sense of family, 4s love family traditions and rituals. They want to be included in important family events.

Ways to Make Life Easier

Build Self-Esteem

Follow personal interests. We encourage children to notice, follow, and practice what *they* are interested in, whether it is art, music, dinosaurs, dance, building with blocks, playing ball, or making up stories. Supporting them can be hard when their interests are very different from our own. For most children, interests change rapidly in the preschool years. If we enroll 4s in a class, it needs to be a short one, a few weeks or several months at most. If they love it and want to continue, then we can sign them up for more. We arrange for cautious children to observe new activities before signing up. We invite them to begin slowly, so that they can learn what they like.

Teach problem solving. This is especially important for 4s as well as older children. Research shows that good problem solvers talk themselves through problems. We can demonstrate this process. When we make or fix something, we can talk out loud in order for children to hear our step-by-step process. When they ask for help, instead of completing the task for them,

---

Realistic Expectations for 4s

Even though we repeatedly teach them what to do, remember that 4s aren't completely civilized yet. Relax and keep teaching. Many need more time to develop the ability to:

◆ Dress themselves quickly, if clothing is difficult, or if they are tired.
◆ Sit and pay attention for more than 10 to 15 minutes.
◆ Write (print). Many aren't yet interested or able.
◆ Use appropriate language. (They enjoy bathroom language.)
◆ Be kind and considerate of others. (They are still self-centered.)

Until their impulse control grows stronger, 4s are still likely to:

◆ Break the rules when we are out of sight.
◆ Say mean things when they are angry.
◆ Need help solving problems with friends and siblings.
◆ Speak bluntly even when we wish they would be more tactful.
◆ Tell tall tales and some outright lies.

we can ask, "What do you think we should do next?" or "I wonder what would happen if you . . . " Of course, if they really can't figure out what to do, they will want our instructions, not our questions. Sometimes questions just cause more frustration and discouragement. Nevertheless, we can still describe the steps we use.

Set up scaffolds. When we build a new building, we put a scaffold around it, so that it is easier to get the job done. We can use the same concept to help children learn. We can do things to make it easier for them to succeed. Spencer wants to wash dishes. Mom lets him wash the pots and plastic dishes, not breakable glasses. Dad holds the nail with pliers while Elena learns to hammer. Then *Elena* holds the pliers and pounds with the hammer. Once she's ready, she holds the nail with her fingers. Melody, at 5, wants to cut fruit with a sharp kitchen knife, but has trouble telling whether the cutting edge is up or down. Mom paints red nail polish on the underside of the handle and says, "Stop if you see red."

Use imagination. In imaginary play, we set up problems to be solved: "Evan, let's drive this truck to the store and get some food. Uh-oh, the store is closed. What shall we do now?" "Spencer, both of these firefighters want to drive the truck. What could they do now?"

Ask 4s for their help. Now that they are 4, we need to add another parenting role. At this age, if we haven't done so earlier, we need to shift from usually telling them what to do to brainstorming with them. Fours are ready to start solving problems in daily life. If they are unhappy about what's usually for breakfast, what to wear, or the amount of time they have with playmates, it is time to consult them to help find solutions. This does not mean asking them about adult issues, such as where to go for vacation, what relatives to visit, how much money to spend, or where we will live.

See page 27, "Parents' Roles and How They Change."

See page 133, "Family Meetings."

Help 4s Handle Feelings

At 4 and 5, the face often reveals true feelings. Four-year-old Spencer tests his growing sense of power by frightening even-tempered Elena with a loud roar. The teacher reports, "Soooo, you succeeded in scaring Elena." Spencer, knowing he was being mean, instinctively defends himself, "No, I didn't scare her." But a tiny smile of success curls at the corners of his mouth before his poker face returns.

The key is to talk about feelings. It is easy to talk with some 4s about their feelings. With others, it is a challenge. Mom was startled when emotionally intense, high energy Shauna announced, "There's a bad witch inside me." This is spirited Shauna's way of saying she has strong, unpredictable impulses that she can't yet control. Mom replied, "I don't think there's a bad

Fascination with Fire

Many 4s—especially boys—want to learn about the powerful natural force of fire. To start, we tell children that fires are *always, always* made *with* grown-ups. Then we make safe fires *together*, so they will be less tempted to experiment on their own. We light matches and candles together. We make magic writing: Write on a piece of paper with lemon juice and then carefully hold the paper above a candle flame. Once the paper warms, the words will appear. We roast marshmallows in the fireplace, the barbecue, or over a tiny campfire in the driveway. We roast hotdogs in the park. And we keep matches and lighters out of reach, even locked up if necessary!

witch in there. I think there's a team of wild horses. As you get bigger and stronger, you'll get better and better at keeping that team under control." Parents continue these conversations with their children over time. We can ask later, "How can we know when the horses are about to run out of control?" "What helps the horses calm down?"

Spencer said he had a volcano inside him. His dad asked, "What things can we do next time *before* the volcano blows?"

Emotions have causes. Starting at this age, we can ask a series of important questions: 1. What happened? 2. What did you think about that? 3. Then how did you feel? One day Malik walks away from Evan. Evan thinks, "Malik doesn't like me any more." Then Evan feels hurt and lonely. Professionals tell us that step 2 is very important. The thought in step 2 (usually a quick, silent judgment in our head) causes our next feeling. Unless Evan notices this inner thought, feelings often seem to come out of nowhere. On the other hand, remembering that inner thought or judgment helps Evan make a good decision about what to do next.

Information and actions can change feelings. Mom tells Evan, "Let's go ask Malik why he walked away from you." After they talk with Malik, Mom says, "It is a good thing we talked to Malik. He wants to play with Spencer now, and with you after lunch. What do you want to do before lunch?"

Thoughts are different from actions. Children can't control their thoughts. Dad reminds Malik, "It's what you *do* that counts." Mom reminds Spencer, "It is okay to be angry at your friends, and it is not okay to hurt their feelings." (*Note:* We often use "but" in situations like this; however, when both statements are true, using "and" makes our meaning clearer.) When Spencer turns 5, he may more easily remember to use kinder words. For now, Mom is relieved that he hits less often.

Talk about feelings indirectly. Our 4s want to please us, but their emotions and impulses get in the way. They misbehave and we get annoyed. Children may see this pattern and think their strong emotions put them at risk of losing the love they need. Therefore, it may be hard for them to talk about troublesome feelings. We can often help if we guess and then express these feelings *indirectly*. Mom says to Melody, "This dolly is jealous because Mommy spends so much time with the new baby. Do you think other little girls feel that way, too?" Mom tells Evan, "I'd feel sad if my friend wouldn't play with me. Do you think other little boys feel that way, too?" Dad describes how Malik plays with his toys: "That truck crashed into the train so hard that he might be angry. I wonder what the truck might be angry about. What do you think?" Sometimes Mom simply reports, "When I was your age, I felt . . . " She knows this will help Evan feel understood, even if he can't talk about his own feelings.

Parents wonder if conversations like these make matters worse by "putting feelings into a child's head." Psychologists tell us this is rarely the case if we casually and occasionally mention possible feelings. Generally, preschoolers are interested in the emotions they experience personally and ignore those they don't feel. On the other hand, if we worriedly and repeatedly ask about their feelings, they may start to react to *our* worry. Researchers tell us that young children who act out their upset feelings in imaginary play are generally better at managing their feelings appropriately in the real world.

 See page 135, "Feelings."

Communication:
Truth, Tact, and Wishful Thinking

Why do 4s stretch the truth and just plain lie? Fours exaggerate because they are enthusiastic. They are also a little fuzzy about what is fantasy and what is reality. Malik and Evan played as firefighters this afternoon. When Dad gets home, Malik reports, "Evan's house burned down today." Having just seen Evan's undamaged house, Dad asks calmly, "Is that so? Tell me about it." Sometimes Malik's dad tells an even bigger story, and they both get a good laugh. Malik reported, "We caught a dinosaur in the backyard today." Dad replied, "My car wasn't working today, so I rode a dinosaur to work!"

When Mom visits preschool, Evan points to a picture he likes. Despite Elena's name in the corner, he announces, "*I* made it!" Mom thinks, "Evan would like to be able to make a picture like that." She simply replies, "I like the bright colors in that picture, too."

The most common reason children lie is to protect their relationship with us. They know what we want them to do, so they *pretend* they are the kid we want. When Mom asks, "Who spilled the milk on the carpet?" spirited Shauna answers, "A monster came out of the TV and spilled it." There's no point in arguing with Shauna. Mom simply replies, "The milk needs to be cleaned up. I'd really appreciate your help. I'll get two sponges." Children are relieved to know that mistakes can be fixed.

When Melody was 3, a researcher had shown her what looked like a box of candy. When Melody had opened it, she had been surprised to find pencils. After closing the box, the researcher had asked, "If your friend, Elena, came and looked at this box, what would she think is inside it?" Melody answered, "Pencils." She assumed that Elena knew everything she knew. She could not imagine fooling her friend. Now at 4, Melody giggles, "Elena will think there's candy in it. She'll be *surprised*." One has to be 4 to trick others or to lie.

Do other preschoolers steal things? Many preschoolers cross this line. They sneak something from day care, a friend's home, or a store. They are still learning about ownership *and* how to control impulses. Calmly go with them to return it because "It belongs to . . ." This usually solves the problem after a time or two.

Around the World

Bragging can also express the emphasis on individual accomplishment in American culture. In some **Native American cultures,** such as the **Hopi,** it is acceptable to express pride in things accomplished by your group. Showing off or bragging about individual success, however, is strongly discouraged.

Why can't 4s use more tact? "Grandpa, you have hairs coming out of your nose!" "Grandma, I wanted a pink shirt for my birthday, not this ugly green one." "I don't like you!"

We've been encouraging our little ones to use their words and express their feelings—and then they do it. It can be embarrassing! We're also teaching our 4s to tell the truth. Tact is knowing when to skip the *whole* truth. Understanding the ways our words can affect others is complicated and takes time. Fortunately, 4s can understand, once we explain, that it would be painful to receive comments on appearance or complaints about gifts. After several such mishaps and gentle explanations, things usually smooth out. In the meantime, Mom says simply to Grandpa, "I'm sorry," or "We're still working on tact."

Why do 4s brag so much? Fours are all-or-nothing thinkers. When they feel good about themselves, they are the best! They tell everyone how great they are. In general, 4s, 5s, and 6s tend to see themselves as terrific at everything they do. If we ask, "Who can jump the highest?" all children raise their hands. It is this confidence that helps 4s to keep on trying in spite of all their youthful mistakes and shortcomings.

Boys brag more than girls: "I'm *strong.*" "My daddy is bigger than yours." "I have more cars than you do." Boys, more than girls, establish a pecking order. Bragging gets you to the top for a while. As long as no one is getting hurt, it is probably best that we ignore the behavior. In the coming years, it is our job to help children find a place where they each shine. Personal success builds self-esteem despite the ups and downs of the pecking order.

What can I do about the terrible words my 4 uses? Fours love to experiment with words. They commonly use bathroom language, and it is best ignored. Such phrases as "you pooh-pooh head" or "you butt head" usually pass if we don't make a big deal of them. Unfortunately, 4s also try *whatever* language they hear, including personally or culturally offensive language used in the media or heard at child care. Adults understand when and why certain words are a problem, but 4s usually don't. Their lack of judgment is the problem.

Because 4s love silly language, Dad and Melody made a list of words to use when upset: "You're a potato-puzzle-head!" "You're a soggy salamander." "Oh, piddly posh!" "Oh, dandelions!"

Help children express their emotions in direct but respectful ways. It helps if we pretend we're not surprised or upset when we hear them use an offensive word. Otherwise, they are bound to use it again when they are bored or angry at us. Beyond this, parents use different approaches: "Use a different word to tell me what you mean." "Our family doesn't use that word." "Children don't say that word to adults." "Grandma doesn't like to hear that word." "We don't use words that hurt feelings." "We tell what the problem is." "That word is not respectful." "I don't listen to people who use that word."

Foster Friendships

Why do 4s argue so much with their friends? Twos play mainly by themselves. Threes play one-on-one and aren't very choosy about playmates. Fours often select playmates who suit their own temperaments and interests. They are also learning about more complicated three-way relationships. As groups of friends form and shift, a child is sometimes ignored. It is hard work to share friends and play in groups.

At the same time, 4s notice three-way relationships at home. We parents naturally focus on other adults at times, and preschoolers feel left out. Sometimes they unconsciously try to manage their lonely feelings by reversing roles and leaving out another child at school. A good way to deal with these issues is to ask children how they feel at home and at school. Then we can encourage them to brainstorm about what might work better in the future.

Fours commonly shout, "You aren't my friend anymore!" We are shocked to hear such cruel words. It is not until 7 that children understand the abstract idea that friendship means a long-term connection. At 4, a friend is someone you want to play with right now. That means that if Shauna wants to play with Malik instead of Elena, Elena isn't her friend. Similarly, in any moment of loneliness, 4s are likely to complain, "Nobody is my friend." We can teach children more accurate language: "I want to play with Elena right now," or "I want someone to play with." And we can relax, knowing that they will eventually understand friendship as we do.

Now that 4s understand the difference between *accidental* and *on purpose*, they often react strongly to intentional aggression. Spencer pushes Shauna away from the slide because he wants to use it first. Shauna knows the push was on purpose, so she pushes back and shouts, "You're mean!" Dad interrupts, saying, "You both want to slide at the same time. What can you do?" Without our help and tools to settle disputes, intentional aggression gets worse between 4 and 7. In spite of our fears, the vast majority of aggressive 4s do not become permanently antisocial. Their best protection is loving support in learning how to develop friendships, and limits upon antisocial behavior when necessary.

While intense children more often express anger directly, mellow children may be indirect. Elena is mad at Evan, so she hides his truck when he isn't looking. Encourage easy-going children to speak up. First, Dad role-plays with Elena: "I'll pretend I'm Evan. What do you want to tell me?"

To help settle fights, we're tempted to ask, "What happened?" We're not likely to hear the truth, let alone the whole truth. Instead, it is usually more effective to ask each child, "What do you want *now*?" Like newspaper reporters, we then report back what we've learned. "Malik says he wants to be a dinosaur. And Melody, you want him to be the mail carrier." Next we invite them to brainstorm solutions: "What do you think you two might do?" If we were lucky enough to see the very beginning of the disagreement, we can start by reporting exactly what we saw. Stay nearby until they find an answer they can both accept. This takes time and patience at first. If we model this process repeatedly, children gradually learn to settle their own disputes.

Why all this aggressive play from 4s? Many fours, more often boys than girls, are fascinated by the good, the bad, and the powerful; this includes dinosaurs, firefighters, police, and action figures. Why? Because they struggle to gain control over their own strong feelings and impulses. Yesterday, Malik was frightened by a loud fire engine and by his angry mother. Today it is a relief to pretend he is a noisy dinosaur that scares other creatures. Spencer couldn't stop his impulse to hit his brother, but he can stop other "bad guys" in their tracks with his gun. (For safety, do not let children play with realistic-looking guns. Children cannot tell the difference between a real gun and a play one, and won't know to stay away from the real one.)

Why do many boys play more aggressively than many girls? At 4, a typical boy has more pounds of muscle than a girl does. Like other male mammals, boys have a strong biological need to exercise and tone their muscles by running, bumping, hitting, pushing, shoving, and throwing. For this reason, they may more often be in conflict with the environment. Imagine them in a field or forest where there is nothing they will damage! The more we can find safe ways for both boys and girls to exercise all their muscles, the less conflict there will be. Make sure high energy children get *hours* of exercise each day. This helps them be happier, more agreeable, and more cooperative.

See page 144, "Friends," and page 182, "Differences Between Boys and Girls."

Fairness Is Frustrating

Why do 4s often complain, "That's not fair!"? We've taught fairness, such as sharing, taking turns, and dividing the cupcake into equal parts. Fours have learned the lesson well. At this age, *fair* means *exactly the same*. For example, Elena believes she shouldn't have to take out the trash if no one else does. She should be able to cross the street alone because her older sister does. She and her sister should get the same size and number of presents. As adults, we know that to be fair we must respond to individual differences. Children won't understand this complex idea until age 7 to 9.

Here are some ways we can help in the meantime. Dad explained to Elena, "When you are 6 like your sister is now, you will be able to cross the street alone." Some families rotate chores so everyone takes turns with different jobs. As for the birthday presents, Elena could sort of understand that she and her sister each received the gift they wanted most. But it still won't be easy. Fairness is also about shades of gray that make no sense in Elena's all-or-nothing world.

Why can't 4s be good sports? When things go well, 4s feel like queens and kings. When things go badly, they feel like garbage. That's why they are such poor losers. When they lose a board game, they feel like losers in *life*. To avoid this problem, Dad asks Malik if he wants to play by "his" rules or the "game" rules. Malik usually prefers his rules, which help him win. Mom avoids games where there are winners and losers. Malik will begin to outgrow his all-or-nothing thinking around 5½ or 6. Then he'll begin to understand that *what he does* is different from *who he is*. At that point, he won't be such a sore loser, and it will be easier for him to play fair.

When to Get Help

For some parents, it is very difficult to give 4s more control of their own lives. For other parents, it is hard to set reasonable limits and stick to them. Because of who they are, some children are much more difficult to manage than others at this age. If, day after day, you are often yelling or feel like hitting your child, get help. Connecting with others in a parenting class may be just what is needed. You can also check with your pediatrician, a temperament counselor, family therapist, occupational therapist, or learning specialist.

CHAPTER 8

5 Years: Kindergarten, Ready or Not?

Should my child start kindergarten now or wait a year? How do I decide?

I want my kids to feel part of a community and value helping others. What can I do?

Why is my child so worried about my safety?

A Snapshot— What 5s Are Like

As in earlier phases, each child is unique. Most 5s, however, are showing more maturity more of the time, which leads to the following picture of typically developing 5s.

Competent and Confident: 5 Years

Fives are quieter, more secure, and more dependable. Not only do they want to please and cooperate, they usually can. They report their feelings more calmly. They wait more easily for their turn or for something to happen because they understand time and have more impulse control. There are good reasons why kindergarten starts at this age. Those who still find self-control hard may find it easier at 6.

Who Will Take Care of Me? 5½ Years

At 5½, children may be somewhat more worried and anxious than before. They feel more competent in familiar places and may prefer staying

See page 143, "Fears About Safety."

home to going on unfamiliar outings. Even though they gradually spend more time with friends, parents are still the center of their world and will be until 12 to 13. At the same time, with their wider awareness of the world, they now understand that bad things *can* happen. At 5½, they may need reassurance that they will be cared for.

What's Happening Now?

Brain Growth

At 5, children's brains are growing at different rates. In general, the more complicated a skill, the wider the range during which typical children learn it. Most babies learn the same simple skill, such as reaching out and grabbing our finger, within the same few weeks. Many months may pass, though, between the time Evan and Spencer can each copy letters. This natural range in normal development is not a problem unless we expect all children to succeed at the same tasks at the same age. (More about kindergarten readiness later in this chapter.)

What Is Real?

Many 5s still believe there are little people inside the television. After all, there are little fish inside the fish tank. If there are monsters *in* the television, they may get *out* and grow big and dangerous. At a child study center, 5s and 6s were given a small box that made the sound of a baby. Most of these children *insisted* that there was a real baby inside. Belief in the tooth fairy and other magical beings generally remains until 7, unless an older brother or sister tells the secret.

The Community Connection

As 5s notice the world around them, they are delighted to learn that they are a significant part of it. They love to slip into adult roles, and blossom when they actively contribute. These roles were automatic when children regularly helped care for younger brothers and sisters, and the family farm or farm animals. With today's small families, age-segregated playgroups, and livelihoods that take most parents out of the home daily, it can be hard for children to feel significant in the real world.

Today's families take many different approaches to community involvement. With their parents, children may help with family chores, or remodeling, or building projects. They can also help "take care of" a younger child

Family Goals

For 5s
- Enjoy learning; feel successful in their learning environment.
- Learn more about the big wide world.
- Know that their parents are safe.
- Strengthen friendships.

For parents and caregivers
- Share relaxed, pleasant times together.
- Help children feel part of a larger family or community.
- Make wise choices about kindergarten. (See page 86, "What About Kindergarten?")
- When possible, protect young children from too much of the frightening side of life. (See page 143, "Fears About Safety.")
- Encourage children to explore their interests.

on the block, take food to relatives in a nursing home, make decorations for family and cultural events, join environmental clean-up days, or give out-grown toys to other children. The goal is to find ways for children to feel pleasure and pride in their ability to contribute to society.

Ways to Make Life Easier

Communication and Feelings

Choice of words. This is a good time to ask ourselves, "Do we want our children to talk to their future partners as they talk to us now? Do their words build understanding, trust, respect, and cooperation?"

The issue of word choice when angry is a special challenge for intense children—and adults—because their feelings are so strong. We can sit down and write a family list of words that are acceptable, as well as those that are not. We can talk about how people think and feel when they hear each word. Children or adults who later use an unacceptable word might be asked to practice a better one by saying it out loud five times—after the tension has subsided. For some children, the impulse to say mean words may still be beyond their control.

Double standard? Sometimes it is realistic to have two standards for word choices. First, we need to be clear about respectful language within the family and with people we don't know well. On the other hand, sometimes buddies (usually boys) who are *equals* and *good* friends exchange insults in a good-hearted manner. It is often best to ignore such games as long as we are sure that no one's feelings are hurt.

Ups and downs of feelings. At 5, as at 4, children are still all-or-nothing thinkers. At any given moment, Shauna feels she is either wonderful or worthless. She believes that friends love her or hate her. Not until 5½ or 6 does thinking become more flexible, and even more so at 7 and 8. Then she will more easily be able to see shades of gray—a range of feelings and possibilities.

Feelings come in different sizes. Around 5½ to 6, we can encourage children to notice and express a wider range of feelings. All the reactions of low energy, mellow children seem mild. Intense children tend to use just a few words to describe their strong emotions. Our goal is to help children of both temperament types to recognize the levels in their feelings and to teach them the words to describe what they are feeling. We can help by asking such questions as: "Which was a bigger disappointment—when your paper tore or when we couldn't go to the zoo?" "Did that pinprick hurt a little, a lot?" "If a 1 means not too bad and a 5 means very bad, was it a 1 or a 5, or somewhere in between?"

See page 136, "When Do Children Feel Gratitude" and page 157, "Impulse Control."

Realistic Expectations for 5s

Fives have made so much progress, but they aren't all grown up yet. Don't be surprised that most still:

◆ Need our help to complete common household tasks and chores—and will until age 8.

◆ Need reminders to start common household tasks and chores—and will until age 8-10.

◆ Confuse what is real from imaginary.

◆ Can't walk confidently into a new classroom if they have a cautious temperament. They may need several weeks (or more) to feel comfortable.

What Happened at School Today? Nothin'

Psychologist Mike Riera suggests we ask more specific questions, such as "Who did you sit with at lunch today?" or "What was new today?" (or interesting? or funny?) "What did the teacher read about today?" "What interesting question did you hear or ask?" Sometimes it helps if we start by saying a *few* words about our own day: what was new, interesting, hard, scary, or funny. Then ask about your child's day.

Thoughts are different from actions. Children cannot control what thoughts enter their heads. We continue to teach, as we did at 4, that "It's what you *do* that counts." Given spirited Shauna's strong feelings, Mom still reminds her at times, "It is okay to be angry at your friends, and it is not okay to hurt their feelings." Now at 5, Shauna can more often explain her upsets without saying hurtful things. She can't always do this immediately, but once she's calmer, she's more able to go back, apologize, and talk about the problem with kinder words.

Bragging. Bragging usually lessens at 5. If it doesn't, try this explanation: "Feeling proud is good. Parents and grandparents want to hear about your success. But if you tell Evan, 'I can climb to the top of the high slide, and you can't,' he may feel bad about himself. Then he'll probably get angry at you because you reminded him of what he can't do."

Lying. If lack of honesty is still a problem at 5, we may need to pay attention to how we react: "If you promise to tell me the truth, I'll promise to stay calm." Of course, we then have to keep our word. One day spirited Shauna told yet another lie. Afterwards, every time she said anything, Mom replied, "I don't know if you're telling me the truth or not." After a morning of this, Shauna understood the importance of telling the truth. Spencer, who is easily frustrated and distractible, is especially likely to lie to protect his self-esteem. He gets distracted on his way to the bathroom to brush his teeth. When Dad calls, "Did you brush your teeth?" he answers, "Yes." Now, instead of asking, Dad says, "Spencer, it is time to come to the bathroom so we can brush our teeth."

What About Kindergarten?

In traditional kindergartens of the recent past, children moved around quite freely as they learned social skills and enjoyed small muscle activities, such as coloring and puzzles. Almost all 5s are ready for such classrooms. Now, expectations vary widely. Some kindergartens remain child centered. Others require a lot of sitting and formal academic work, such as printing. Fewer 5s, especially younger ones, can feel and be successful in such environments, so the decision of when to start kindergarten is more difficult for parents.

When Waiting Is *Not* a Good Idea

If children need special help with learning, the sooner they get it, the better. Simply waiting another year won't make school easier. Many learning differences are addressed most effectively at the beginning of kindergarten, if not earlier. If you (or others who know your child well) are concerned about your child's learning, it is very important to get more information.

See page 91, "When to Get Help."

Children who haven't been in preschool may need a little extra time to settle in to kindergarten. They may be leaving their parents for the first time or may not yet have learned to take turns or follow a fixed schedule. However, most 5s make these adjustments quite quickly. A background of poverty or a different language at home are not good reasons for delaying kindergarten. According to the National Association of School Psychologists, careful comparison studies show that these children do best when they get the extra services they need along the way so they can move through school with their age mates.

Signs of Kindergarten Readiness

Physical readiness
- Toileting: Rarely, if ever, has accidents, even under moderate stress.
- Eating and dressing: Can eat and get dressed with little or no help.
- Sleep: If an afternoon nap is still needed, try to schedule a morning kindergarten.
- Balance: Stands on each foot for 5 seconds, a very general measure of large muscle skill.

Small muscle skills
- Traces along a line fairly well.
- Copies a square fairly well after watching an adult draw one.
- Colors inside a square.
- Holds scissors and cuts fairly well along a straight line.

(Most 5s who have never done these things before learn quickly at this age.)

Learning readiness
- Speech: Other adults and children can usually understand what the child says. Usually speaks in complete sentences, such as "I want the ball."
- Follows directions: Easily and quickly understands simple directions, such as "Go to the cabinet and get a pencil."
- Identifies (by pointing or naming) basic colors and shapes.
- Says the numbers one through ten. Names eight body parts.
- Tells left hand from right hand.
- Remembers information, such as playground safety rules.

Social skills
- Easily separates from parents after some time to adjust.
- Usually accepts teacher's directions without protest.
- Moves on to the next activity and adjusts to kindergarten routines fairly easily.
- Usually waits for turns and listens while others talk.
- Tries new things without a great deal of personal reassurance.
- Asks for help when needed.
- Can do activities with a partner.

Around the World

Given the range of normal development at this age, many countries in **Europe and elsewhere** don't begin formal schooling until 6. At 7, most late developers now have the needed small-muscle skills and are also ready for teacher-directed lessons. Their self-esteem is not put at risk by expectations that may be too high for them to meet. In the **United States,** the age at which a child must start formal schooling varies from state to state. The range is from 5 to 8 years.

See page 157, "Impulse Control."

When Waiting May Be a Good Idea

When children have mid-year birthdays, parents frequently ask, "Will it be better to be 6 months older or 6 months younger than many classmates?" Spencer's father was concerned about him waiting a year while his friends moved ahead. He felt better when he thought far ahead to high school. There, being 6 months older would make it easier for Spencer to get on sports teams, and he'd be proud to be able to drive sooner than his classmates.

Some parents face public or private schools with rigidly high academic expectations more suited to 6s or even 7s than to 4s and 5s. If your child must take kindergarten entrance exams, remember that children can be pushed to memorize answers to possible test questions, but such memorized answers cannot accurately predict school success.

Children often aren't interested in things until they are *able* to learn them. Mother Nature protects them from hopeless discouragement. Furthermore, general attention span grows with age. For this reason, it is not surprising that when they are older, more children are able to pay attention and learn from a classroom teacher.

5. Age and Classroom Readiness

Child's Attitude	Almost 5 yr.	Almost 6 yr.
Eager to learn new things from the teacher	66%	80%
Able to pay attention to the teacher	57%	73%

From Entering Kindergarten—A Portrait of American Children When They Begin School *by Nicholas Zill and Jerry West*

Temperament. Some high energy 4½s who love to run and jump are not ready to sit and practice printing. Very shy or cautious 4½s may do fine in a small kindergarten with a sensitive, available teacher. However, in a large class they may find it hard to speak up when they need help or to get started on new things. In another year, many events of daily living will be more familiar and routine. Cautious children are more likely to be followers when they are with older children and more likely to be leaders when they are with younger ones.

Boys and girls in contrast. Boys and girls generally have quite different interests at 4 and 5. Unfortunately, many kindergartens emphasize activities that are more interesting to—and therefore easier—for girls. In many school-related tasks, the *average* young girl is 6 months or even a year ahead of the *average* young boy. Boys gradually catch up and are on an equal level by age 10.

In years past, when boys and girls went to separate schools (or girls didn't go to school at all), these differences were not a problem. Now, however, when boys and girls start in the same class at the same age, some boys are

See page 182, "Differences Between Boys and Girls."

unable to do as well as girls in the early grades. Given the average learning differences between young boys and girls, it can be especially hard for boys who are the youngest in their class. Ideally, many boys would get 6 extra months to get ready for kindergarten.

6. Learning Differences Between Boys and Girls

Task	Half of Girls Can Do This at:	Half of Boys Can Do This at:
Tell own sex.	2½ yr.	3 yr.
Point to and count three objects.	3 yr.	3½ yr.
Tell own age.	3 yr.	4 yr.
Hop on one foot.	3½ yr.	4½ yr.
Copy a triangle.	4 yr.	4½ yr.
Print first name.	4½ yr.	5 yr.
Tell month of own birthday.	5 yr.	6 yr.

From The Child from Five to Ten *by Arnold Gesell, M.D., Frances L. Ilg, M.D., and Louise Bates Ames, Ph.D.*

How to explain, "We are waiting for kindergarten."
Here are positive ways to talk to children about the situation:
- "You get to stay another year with a teacher you like."
- "Kindergarten is for *older* children. You are just 4½, and most of your friends are 5."
- "When you are older, kindergarten will be easier and more fun."
- "Yes, it will be hard at first not to be with your friends in school. We'll set up play dates so you can see them," or "With time, you will make new friends like you did before."

Medical Issues That Can Affect Learning

Vision problems may cause children to tire easily or avoid close-up work. The standard vision test in the pediatrician's office checks only distance vision because distance problems are more common at this age. A few children, mostly boys, may have trouble learning colors because of color blindness. Talk with the doctor, clinic, optometrist, or ophthalmologist.

Hearing difficulty can make classroom learning harder. Check with your doctor or clinic.

Muscles that don't yet work smoothly can make it hard to kick a ball, hold a pencil, or coordinate eye and hand movements. Check with your doctor or clinic.

Sensory processing, how we take in and use information from all our senses, from hearing to sense of balance, may be a problem. Children may get too much or too little information from their senses. For example, they may be overwhelmed because sounds are so loud, or they may bump into things because they are unsure exactly where their body is. Occupational therapists who specialize in sensory processing may be helpful.

See page 104, "Attention Deficit Disorder."

Attention Deficit Disorder (ADD or ADHD) is a medical problem in which children may be *unable* to pay attention or control their impulses. Talk with your pediatrician.

Learning Differences

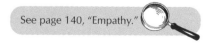

Most of us learn through listening (auditory learning), seeing (visual learning), and moving (kinesthetic learning). Some people find it *much* easier to learn one way rather than another. With a new story book, is your child equally interested in hearing the story and looking at the pictures? Does your child strongly prefer to be in motion, as in playing ball, building, or painting? These are clues about learning style. Learning style is affected by temperament. For example, many high energy children learn most easily through movement. It is important that the teaching style accommodates the child's learning style. If you are concerned about your child's learning style, talk with the teacher or a learning specialist.

Most of our important skills are managed by small clumps of brain cells. Given the amazing complexity of the brain, it is not surprising that we aren't all wired in the same way. Skills that you and I take for granted can be extremely difficult for others. Children who are smart or even very smart can have specific learning differences, or disabilities, when it comes to a particular kind of learning.

Some examples of learning difficulties are:

- Language processing: A child hears and understands the meaning of individual words, but has trouble understanding a *group* of words, such as "Go get a yellow pencil from the drawer and give it to Daddy."

See page 140, "Empathy."

- Emotions: A child cannot read the emotions on other people's faces or know how to respond to their emotions. This is part of the diagnosis of Asperger's syndrome.
- Organization: A child has difficulty sorting things into groups, thinking step-by-step to get something done, keeping track of things, or setting priorities. These children may need help keeping their rooms in order.
- Math, memory, music pitch, spelling, or writing: Some of these very specific learning difficulties may not show up until elementary school when your child first encounters the need for the skill.

Children with learning differences need teaching methods that work with and *around* their specific difficulty. Learning specialists and educational therapists are needed. Holding your child back to repeat the same class in the same way usually does not help.

Other Factors that May Affect School Success

Fast learners. Children who learn quickly and easily can become painfully bored while waiting for their classmates. Rather than doing more easy work to fill the time, they need *more interesting and challenging work.* Otherwise, they may act out in class or drift away in day dreams. Work closely with the classroom teacher if boredom affects your child's learning. Consider testing for the school or district's gifted program.

Stress or emotional difficulty at home, in the classroom, or on the playground can distract children from learning. Frequent school absences, whether due to illness, family problems, or avoidance of schoolwork, make problems worse because your child misses out on instruction. Talk with teachers, school nurses and counselors, doctors, or therapists about how best to get help for your child.

 ## When to Get Help

If you are unsure about when to start kindergarten, ask for more information. Start with the following:

- Ask preschool teachers, "Is my child ready to move on?"
- Ask teachers or school officials what will be expected in kindergarten and what help will be available.
- Ask for a second opinion from an impartial, qualified professional if you disagree with a teacher's pressure for your child to begin now or to wait.
- Ask about testing. Educational testing (through the school or privately) can help sort out whether it is better to start now or wait. If it is still unclear after the first tests, ask about more detailed testing with a learning specialist, speech therapist, or occupational therapist.

"Spencer, keep your feet inside *the treehouse," called Mom from nearby.*

PART TWO

TOPICS OVER TIME

An Alphabetical Reference for Dealing with Child Development in Daily Life

Activities and Toys

Activities and toys develop abilities and skills. Children like different activities according to their age, personal interests, and body development. Buy things that can be used in many different ways and that invite wide-open imagination, rather than those that encourage repetition of narrow television or video roles.

The charts that follow offer activities for different ages. Start with the age your child is now. Also, look a little behind and ahead to find other interesting things your child may enjoy. Even after children seem to have learned or outgrown an activity, they often enjoy returning to it weeks later when they can use it in a different way.

7. Birth to 4 Months: Activities for Fun and Learning

Muscles	Senses	Language
◆ Offer things to hold. ◆ For neck exercise: place baby on tummy several times a day *while awake and alert.* Start early. See p. 163, "Tummy Time." ◆ After 1 month, start another neck exercise. With baby lying on back, gently pull hands to raise shoulders several inches. Wait so baby can try to lift head. Repeat 2 or 3 times.	◆ Touch, stroke, and rock baby. See p. 32, "Getting to Know Your Baby." ◆ Show baby around his/her home. ◆ Set baby on different textures to feel (fuzzy, bumpy, smooth) during tummy playtime. ◆ Offer pieces of cloth or stuffed animals to feel. ◆ Make rattles: put rice in a plastic bottle, then glue on the top. ◆ Hold baby while you dance gently and support baby's neck.	◆ Make faces at baby and copy baby's faces. ◆ Tell baby what you love about him/her. ◆ Describe what you're doing as you carry baby around. ◆ See p. 111, "Communication with Signs and Sounds."

Compiled by Helen F. Neville

8. Four Months to Crawling: Activities for Fun and Learning

Muscles	Senses	Mind/Imagination	Language
◆ Continue as above. ◆ Give baby containers to fill and empty. ◆ Play drop-the-toy from the sofa and other low places. ◆ Give baby rattles, wooden or plastic spoons and cups, bowls, pans to play with. ◆ Provide wooden, plastic, foam, and/or cloth blocks to play with. ◆ Fill a small plastic bottle halfway with colored water and glue the top on for baby to shake. ◆ Give baby float toys for the bath. ◆ Provide a "busy box" with parts that squeak, move, open, rattle, shine, etc. ◆ Once baby can hold head and body up straight (often at about 5 mo.), try a doorway "bouncer."*	◆ Continue as above. ◆ Explore motion with baby, always supporting baby's neck: gentle swinging up and down, back and forth, side to side. ◆ Once baby has good head control, bounce baby on your lap in different rhythms. ◆ Sing the names of things baby touches or sees. ◆ Sing songs that have hand motions. ◆ Play pat-a-cake. ◆ Play with bells, maracas, tambourines, see-through rattles, drums. ◆ Look at old magazines with bright pictures—expect ripped pages.	◆ Take baby out to watch people, other babies, and animals. ◆ Attach an unbreakable mirror to a wall where baby can see into it. ◆ Play hide-and-seek with baby, using blanket, clothing, towel, and later hiding behind a door, wall, or piece of furniture. ◆ Look together at books with thick pages. ◆ Hide toys under a blanket or inside pans or boxes while baby watches.	◆ Continue as above. ◆ Say names of things baby sees and touches. ◆ Play give-and-take: "I have the spoon; you have the spoon." ◆ Make funny sounds: high, low; fast, slow; loud, soft. ◆ See p. 111, "Communication with Signs and Sounds."

* Baby bouncers may not be allowed in some child care settings.

Compiled by Helen F. Neville

9. Crawling: Activities for Fun and Learning

Muscles	Senses	Mind/Imagination	Language
◆ Continue as above. ◆ Play crawl-and-chase together. ◆ Roll and chase soft balls together. ◆ Provide plastic bowls that fit inside each other. ◆ Provide things that float and pour: a sponge, cup. ◆ Provide egg cartons, paper tubes, small empty boxes, and plastic bottles to stack and knock over. ◆ Provide a peg bench with toy hammer.	◆ Continue as above. ◆ Shake bells and other things that have interesting sounds. ◆ Crawl through dry leaves in the fall.	◆ Continue as above. ◆ Take turns hiding from each other or hiding toys. Ask, "Where's ____?"	◆ Continue as above. ◆ Look together at books. Ask, "Do you see ____?" "What does ____ say?"

Compiled by Helen F. Neville

10. Walking to 2 Years: Activities for Fun and Learning

Large Muscles	Small Muscles	Senses	Mind/Imagination	Language
◆ Continue as above. ◆ Walk in the neighborhood. ◆ Play chase and hide-and-seek with your child. ◆ Throw and kick balls together. ◆ Play cowboy with adult as horse. ◆ Climb on anything safe: pillows, sofa, up and down several stairs. ◆ Make pull toys, made from boxes with short strings attached. ◆ Make push toys using a laundry basket or cardboard box to fill and push around the floor. ◆ Provide a small wagon. ◆ Provide a wheel toy for child to ride (push with feet, no pedals).	◆ Continue as above. ◆ Provide a sandbox or use a large, shallow, plastic, under-the-bed storage container outdoors filled with sand, with old spoons, strainers, small toys for play. ◆ Provide smooth building blocks for stacking and building. ◆ Provide colored stacking ring toys and stacking boxes that fit inside each other.	◆ Continue as above. ◆ Enjoy bedtime snuggles and back rubs or leg massages. ◆ Rock with your child in a rocking chair; provide a rocking horse. ◆ Swing your child on a swing or glider. ◆ Allow child to stomp in water puddles, play in the mud, romp through dry leaves. ◆ Provide water toys, plastic cups, strainers, sponges, etc. for water play. ◆ Listen to all kinds of music. ◆ Provide a wind-up music box. ◆ Look at old magazines with colorful pictures, especially of babies and animals. ◆ Offer things to smell: flowers, soap, spices.	◆ Continue as above. ◆ Provide cardboard boxes large enough to crawl inside. ◆ Save milk cartons to make large, lightweight stacking blocks. ◆ Provide trucks, cars, bulldozers, etc.; plastic toy dishes, dress-up hats, shoes, and clothes, small unbreakable mirror; dolls and stuffed animals, doll buggy; farm and zoo animals, toy people. ◆ Talk together on a toy telephone.	◆ Continue as above. ◆ Look at books together. Ask, "What's that?" In some books, change the child's name to match your child's name. ◆ Show child his/her baby pictures and tell the stories that go with them. ◆ Act out and name different feelings. Ask child to act out different feelings. See p. 135, "Feelings." ◆ Recite/read nursery rhymes and poems. ◆ Play games with directions, such as, "Point to the kitty," "Get the ball," "Pat the sofa," "Put the doll on the chair." ◆ Make up finger-play stories. ◆ Use puppets to act out and tell stories or experiences. ◆ Take turns acting out different feelings.

Compiled by Helen F. Neville

11. Two Years: Activities for Fun and Learning

Large Muscles	Small Muscles	Senses/Music/Art	Mind/Imagination	Language
◆ Continue as above. ◆ Provide small broom, garden rake, and other tools. ◆ Play games that increase balance: walk on tiptoe, walk a narrow (6 in.) wooden beam or concrete curb. ◆ Take child to a park where there are slides and swings.	◆ Continue as above. ◆ Provide wind-up toys, Jack-in-the-Box, large beads and string, connecting toys, shape sorters; household items such as hair brush, plastic jars with screw tops, very large buttons, large zippers, switches, knobs; play dough with cookie cutters and garlic presses; puzzles with lift-out pieces each fitting in its own hole.	◆ Continue as above. ◆ Move with music. ◆ Provide large crayons, paper, and sidewalk chalk. ◆ Provide finger paints and bathtub crayons for tub time. ◆ Provide a footstool or chair so child can reach the sink. ◆ Make a drum, tie bells on wrist, play xylophone, harmonica. ◆ Clap the rhythm of familiar music and nursery rhymes. ◆ Sing songs together.	◆ Continue as above. ◆ Encourage child to watch people do things (cook, garden, paint) and pretend to help. (Child can "paint" nearby with a brush and a bucket of water.)	◆ Continue as above. ◆ Play games that teach opposites. Make a big circle with your arms, small circle with fingers; make a happy face, make a sad face; close your eyes, open your eyes, etc.

Compiled by Helen F. Neville.

12. Three Years: Activities for Fun and Learning

Large Muscles	Small Muscles	Sensory/Music/Art	Mind/Imagination	Language
◆ Continue as above. ◆ Wrestle together. ◆ Do daily exercises together. ◆ Fill sock with rice, tie top, and throw at cardboard box for target practice. ◆ Practice coordination on a variety of smooth boards for balancing and sliding on. ◆ Practice balancing on one foot; when that is easy, try hopping on one foot. ◆ Push, pull, and ride in a wagon or wheelbarrow. ◆ Ride a push or pedal toy (tricycle, "big wheel"). ◆ Bounce on a mini-trampoline with bar to hold onto or on a mattress on the floor. ◆ Invite child to jump over lines on the sidewalk. ◆ Swing and climb on a play structure.	◆ Continue as above. ◆ Build with building sets. ◆ Play with doll clothes. ◆ Provide large buttons, snaps, and zippers to open and close. ◆ String large beads on pipe cleaners or shoelaces. ◆ Use small, real hammer and large nails on soft wood or plastic foam.	◆ Continue as above. ◆ Dance and march to music. ◆ Draw and paint with markers and large brushes. ◆ Try block printing. (Cut designs on potatoes and dip in poster watercolors, apply to paper or cloth.) ◆ Glue scraps of material, bits of torn paper, leaves, buttons, etc. to paper to make collages. ◆ Place shapes of felt on a felt board. ◆ Make soap bubbles in a dishpan, make or buy wands of different shapes and sizes. ◆ See p. 100, "Art and Artists."	◆ Continue as above. ◆ Sort things: large buttons, macaroni, silverware, poker chips, socks, spools of thread, pens vs. pencils, etc. ◆ Use hand puppets to tell stories and replay experiences. ◆ Play with small cars, boats, airplanes, spaceships, or a block train. ◆ Play with doll furniture, dishes, pots, pans, small mop, clothespins; make play food and appliances from cardboard. ◆ Play with dress-up clothes, jewelry, wigs, bracelets, purse, briefcase, small suitcase, old telephone, etc. (Many items for make-believe can be purchased from secondhand or thrift stores.) ◆ Build a tent with a table and a sheet.	◆ Continue as above. ◆ Enjoy nursery rhymes, stories and songs with rhymes. Make up rhymes for your 3.

Compiled by Helen F. Neville

13. Four Years: Activities for Fun and Learning

Large Muscles	Small Muscles	Music/Art	Mind/Imagination	Language
◆ Continue as above. ◆ Play hugging games. ◆ Exchange back rubs or shoulder rubs, especially at bedtime. ◆ Roughhouse and wrestle. Set clear rules: Play on this rug, take off shoes or jewelry, don't push face or genitals, don't pull hair. If needed, set a timer for "rounds" to keep intensity under control. ◆ Fight with long, skinny pillows. (Avoid faces.) ◆ Hang a pillow in a doorway as a punching bag. ◆ Provide low-key lessons in tumbling, dance, or swimming.	◆ Continue as above. ◆ Put together puzzles with 4 to 10 large pieces; work up to more pieces if your child is comfortable. ◆ Provide squirt bottles for water play on hot days. ◆ Use large screws and real screwdriver on soft wood or plastic foam. A Phillips screwdriver is easier for beginners to use. ◆ Play with building sets; gradually challenge your child with smaller and more numerous pieces. ◆ Take apart old clocks, radios, and other mechanical devices that don't have sharp pieces.	◆ Continue as above. ◆ Play singing games, such as "Ring Around the Rosy." ◆ Make up new words to old songs your child knows. ◆ Take turns matching each other's pitch. ◆ Provide blank paper for drawing and painting. ◆ Provide coloring books and tracing paper. ◆ Cut old magazines with blunt-tipped scissors. ◆ Glue collages of paper, cloth, buttons, sticks, leaves, string, yarn, etc. ◆ Listen to music and dance or draw to it.	◆ Continue as above. ◆ Take turns making up stories about people, places, and things; write down your child's stories and invite him/her to decorate with crayons or pictures cut from magazines. ◆ Go to the library, parks, and learning centers. ◆ Invite your child to join you in grocery shopping, cooking, housekeeping, projects, etc. ◆ Take frequent trips to the adult world: construction site, hardware store, zoo, waterfront, nature walk, farm, firehouse, museum, bus stop, train station, ferry terminal, airport, etc. ◆ Create a playhouse with sheets or blankets draped over furniture; make and paint a house from an empty stove or refrigerator box. ◆ Play job-related dress-up: cook, firefighter, astronaut, etc. ◆ Experiment with flashlights and magnets. ◆ Create a doctor/nurse set. ◆ Make sand castles and mud pies. ◆ Play with dinosaurs and action figures.	◆ Continue as above. ◆ Answer child's questions. Ask a few, too, and balance listening and talking. ◆ Tell child real stories about your childhood (and theirs) and about the mistakes you made. ◆ Read books together every day: fours love funny books with made-up words and rhymes. Read books about mischievous or frustrated children/animals. Fours try very hard to be good and often can't, so they like to hear how others get along. Change characters or events or endings to suit your child's situation; read a familiar story backward, word for word.

Compiled by Helen F. Neville

14. Five Years: Activities for Fun and Learning

Large Muscles	Small Muscles	Mind/Imagination	Music/Art	Language
◆ Continue as above. ◆ Play on/with scooter, stilts, jump rope, roller skates, ice skates, bicycle with training wheels. ◆ Dig big holes in the ground. ◆ Build a fort from tree trimmings. ◆ Kick and throw balls; begin to learn rules of play for ball games.	◆ Continue as above. ◆ Put together jigsaw puzzles with 6 to 12 pieces. Work up to more pieces if your child is comfortable. ◆ Color coloring books. ◆ Connect the dots and do simple mazes in activity books. ◆ Use a workbench with a saw, vise, wrench, hammer, etc. ◆ Try weaving, spool knitting, or simple sewing. ◆ Create and play with dollhouse and miniature furniture and people. ◆ Play with building sets with small pieces.	◆ Continue as above. ◆ Play "I spy" games: "Find something yellow…" "You're getting hotter. You're getting colder. You're getting warmer. You found it!" ◆ Draw simple maps to follow. ◆ Play simple card games, dominos, board games, and picture lotto. ◆ Play store with empty food cans and boxes from the kitchen; use play money. ◆ Provide a magnifying glass; get a library book of easy science experiments. ◆ Look at simple picture books about the human body. ◆ Play in a homemade playhouse or a safe tree house.	◆ Continue as above. ◆ Skip to music; beat out rhythms in time to music. ◆ Take turns conducting songs. ◆ Sing group songs such as, "Here We Go Loopy-Lou." ◆ Play a keyboard or piano. ◆ Take photos with an easy-to-use camera. ◆ Make designs out of home-made clay and bake them in the oven.	◆ Continue as above. ◆ Look at books with drawings and photos full of detail and talk about what you see. ◆ Read stories about relationships between parents and children. ◆ Read stories about real or imaginary things. (Keep in mind that some children are still frightened by scary stories.) ◆ Read simple nonfiction about the natural world.

Compiled by Helen F. Neville

Art and Artists

Hand a crayon or marker to a child. What is likely to happen next depends, in large part, on the child's age and developmental level.

Between 13 mo. and 2 yr., toddler art begins as a dance. Crayons glide, swing, loop, hop, and pounce across the paper with the sheer joy of motion. Gradually 2s begin to notice the *results* that show up. They realize that *they* can make different kinds of lines and dots. They now watch their dots, wiggles, lopsided spirals, and zigzags appear. In time, they may become interested in results they can *repeat*. Drawing is now intentional, rather than an accidental side effect of the dance.

Some tots make the same scribble again and again, just as they once practiced the first steps of walking. Then they move on to something else. Others practice everything at once. When they can repeat results, they may compare big swirls with dots, straight lines with zigzags, or empty space with colored space. They may practice their forms on different parts of the paper or one on top of the other.

Between 2 and 4 yr., they find that a loop can go around, come back, and meet its beginning. A whole new world of circles and ovals is now possible. Then they can contrast circles, overlapping circles, and spirals.

As far as we know, children this age do not set out to

draw grass or flowers or anything else in particular. However, sometimes when they are finished, they may notice that what appeared on the page *reminds* them of grass or raindrops or spaghetti or worms. Then they may name it.

As they approach 3 and until about 4 yr., children around the world commonly make circles with designs in the middle, such as smaller circles, crosses, or Xs. They have an automatic interest in symmetry—in making one part of a circle look the same as another. Having now drawn the *outside edge* of something, many more shapes become possible. As they approach 4, many gain ever more skill with their crayon, marker, or pencil. Children this age commonly make sun or daisy-like designs that become more and more detailed.

Child psychologist Howard Gardner reports that there are two general types of 3-year-old artists. One group is fascinated by color and design. They enjoy the process and the visual results. They have little to say about their work. The other group talks a lot about everything. Drawing is almost an afterthought or adds to what they talk about. There are, of course, some young artists in both camps.

Sometime between 3 and 4 yr., preschoolers often start to draw people. Around the world, these first figures often look like tadpoles. They have big heads and eyes, long legs, and no body. The big heads may reflect how important faces are to young children. These figures may or may not have arms sprouting from their heads. They may be right side up or upside down. The body parts may or may not connect.

Preschoolers now know their drawings can represent something in the world. For example, an animal might look similar to a person, except that it has four legs instead of two. Such figures gradually progress to more lifelike, though still stick-like figures. Some 3s and 4s now draw geometric shapes: circles, rectangles, and triangles. Gradually these shapes combine into objects. Just as they combined words into sentences, they now combine shapes into things.

4s draw very differently from each other. Some rarely sit long enough to draw at all. Others show little interest because the small-muscle control needed to draw easily just isn't in place yet. Still others love to practice for hours. Not surprisingly, those who happily spend more time drawing generally have more detailed pictures.

Around 4, we may begin to recognize the pictures they draw—houses, trains, dogs, superheroes, furniture, and more. For most preschoolers, human figures continue to be a special interest. They may still draw rather large heads and eyes. They may not yet draw ears, fingers, or even arms. Many draw the same thing in the same way for months at a time. Children this age are learning that things come in *general classes,* such as animals, food, and plants. Therefore, they draw *general* things. They usually draw a dog that represents all dogs or a person that represents all people. (Boys usually draw boys first, and girls usually draw girls first.) Not until about 8 will most children draw a particular cat, tree, or house.

Two more types of artists emerge around 4 based on temperament. Most children this age quickly change their expectations to match what appears on their paper. They may start to draw a dog but notice it looks more like a cat, so they add whiskers to make it even more like a cat and add a mouse to finish off the scene. For these artists, blank paper is wonderful.

Spirited Shauna, however, screamed and ripped up her drawings when the dog on the page began to look different from the picture in her head. As a natural planner she couldn't quickly shift her mental picture. Dad told Shauna that it took him a long time to learn to draw. Mom offered stencils and suggested drawing easier things, but Shauna refused. Mom got tracing paper so Shauna could trace pictures of dogs. When Shauna was still unhappy, Mom bought a coloring book. When Shauna couldn't draw a doll, Aunt Adriana, an artist, brought Shauna's doll from the bedroom to look at as she drew. When Shauna still had trouble, Aunt Adriana said, "Let's go back to where you had trouble and

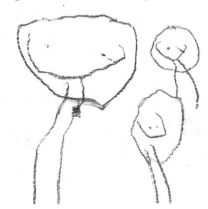

Tristan, age 3, and his friends

see if we can figure it out." Gradually Shauna's ability to draw caught up with her mind's eye.

From 4 through 7 yr., children typically draw with X-ray vision. They draw what they know is there, rather than what they see. For example, if asked to draw a nail sticking into a board, they draw the *entire* nail. They may draw the chimney that is outside the house *and* the furniture that is inside. Similarly, they may draw the man inside the elevator or even the banana inside the monkey's stomach. Sometimes they creatively include both the front side *and* the back of what they draw.

5s create a variety of interesting and expressive art. Most can clearly draw subjects that interest them. Many of their drawings have color that shows balance, rhythm, and joy. Their scenes may now suggest action. They often draw to illustrate stories in their heads (not just a single thought or scene). They may have *a great deal* to say about what they draw.

To draw realistically, professional artists can set aside ideas, such as "draw a dog," and pay attention to exact shape, direction, angle and length of line. We can trick our minds into thinking this way by turning a simple picture upside down (top edge to the bottom). Now copy lines and angles just as they appear. The results are often surprisingly realistic. Some 5s will enjoy this game, and it may later help them see the shapes that make up everything we see.

Symbols of power, such as trains, airplanes, spaceships, and superheroes are common, especially in boys' drawings. These drawings may represent boys' desire to keep control over their own impulses. Or these drawings may help the artists feel more powerful in a world where most important people are much bigger than they are. Fives draw houses, cars, princesses, and castles. It is also common for 5s, both boys and girls, to draw scenes of violence and destruction. These violent drawings may show children's wishes to act out angry impulses. They also show that children are aware that the world isn't always a safe place. Such scenes may also relate to the violence children have seen on television (real and pretend), videos, and computer games.

"What a Pretty Picture!"

When Elena has drawn her best, it is discouraging if we ask, "What is it?" It is better that we adjust what we say according to how each child draws. This is a more effective way to acknowledge his or her pleasure and skill. See the chart below for specific suggestions.

15. Appreciating Children's Art

When	What to Say
All ages	◆ *Let's hang it up so we can see it!*
1 to 2 yr.	◆ *What fun! Those lines are swinging, bouncing.*
2 to 4 yr.	◆ *You chose a strong blue color.* ◆ *This design flows all across the page.* ◆ *You filled the whole paper with red.* ◆ *Those circles look just the same. . . . Those lines are different.* ◆ *Look at all those tiny lines you drew so carefully!*
4 to 6 yr.	◆ *I see two people.* ◆ *That looks like a dog to me.* ◆ *Would you like to tell me about your picture?*

Compiled by Helen F. Neville

Attention Span: How It Grows

There are three kinds of attention. First, our ears, eyes, nose, and skin are always checking around to be sure we are safe. Babies and adults automatically turn to check out the unfamiliar bark of a dog or a loud crash. Some people are more aware of this process than others, and some more quickly ignore unimportant distractions.

Second, we are pulled along by our own interests when we are hungry and look for something to eat or work on a

16. Attention Span at Different Ages

Age	Time and Activity	How to Help Attention Spans Grow
2 to 7 mo.	**With us:** 2–3 min. May watch us, copy the expressions on our faces, trade sounds with us, etc. By 7 mo., they can do this for 5 min. or so.	◆ Take turns leading and following. Be warm, interested, and interesting to look at. Let babies rest when they turn away.
18 mo.	**Alone, one activity:** 30 seconds. **Alone, several activities:** 1–2 min. before returning to caregiver.	◆ Keep adult expectations realistic.
2 yr.	**Alone, one activity:** 30–60 sec. **With us:** 2–3 min. when we actively encourage their interest.	◆ Toddlers pay attention longer with our help than when they are alone. Therefore, point out more interesting things about whatever they are playing with: "Do you see the black dot on it?" "Will it fit in the cup?" "Can you push it over here?"
2½ yr.	**Alone, one activity:** about 2 min. but prefer almost constant attention from Mom if she is around. **Small group of children:** 10 min. May play peacefully near others.	
3 yr.	**Alone, one activity:** 3–8 min. if they are personally interested. May finish a task on their own if it is easy and interesting.	◆ Support activities children are interested in. Look for ways to keep them interested in activities they start. In general, encourage and follow their interests. Try not to change the subject or take over.
3½ yr.	**Alone, several activities:** 15 min. with interesting things to choose from.	
4 yr.	When they are very interested, they can begin to tune out some distractions (including our call to dinner). **Alone, one activity:** 7–8 min. if it is personally interesting. **Single activity if new and interesting:** 15 min., as an eye exam for glasses. **Small group of children:** 5–10 min.	◆ Attention grows from the inside and is fueled by the emotion of interest. Feeling comfortable and successful encourages continued interest. At this age, few children are interested in perfection. However, some need help to meet their own high standard of success. ◆ Fours understand that it is harder to pay attention when they aren't interested, or when they are distracted by outside noise or their own thoughts. Use games and humor to keep things interesting.
4½ yr.	**Alone, adult chosen activity:** 2–3 min. for things we want (get dressed or pick up some toys).	
5 yr.	Most can ignore minor distractions. **Alone, one activity:** 10–15 min. if interesting free play. **Small group of children:** 10–25 min. of work or play. **Adult chosen activity:** 4–6 min. for something we ask, if easy and interesting.	◆ Personal interest is still the main motivator. 5s can pay attention to something that is personally interesting twice as long as to other things. Look for each child's passion and support it.
6 yr.	**Alone, one activity:** 30 min. if easy and interesting work or play.	◆ Build on children's interests. Pay attention to what makes tasks hard, so you can help.

Compiled by Helen F. Neville

project we love. For a child to keep paying attention, the materials at hand have to be personally interesting.

Third, adults pay attention because other people ask us to, which is why we read the same story *again* to our toddler or finish a dull task for the boss. Only gradually do children learn to pay attention because we adults want them to.

Just as it takes years for children to grow taller, it takes years to grow their attention spans. Understanding this process helps us hold realistic expectations and plan realistic activities. Caregivers can help children develop longer attention spans. Television and videos, on the other hand, encourage short attention spans. The chart on page 103 shows the *growth* of attention span in typical young children.

See page 179, "Screen Time: Television, Videos, and Computers."

Attention Deficit Disorder

About 3–5% of children have Attention Deficit Disorder—they *can't* pay attention. Some children only have trouble with attention: ADD. Others have ADHD (Attention Deficit Hyperactive Disorder), which includes trouble with energy level and impulse control. The parts of the brain that focus attention and stop impulses are less active than normal. ADD and ADHD may be inherited, or caused by early birth, brain injury, or other factors.

Most of us can think of a time when we wanted to remember a name or fact. The harder we tried, the less our brain worked. Similarly for these children, the harder they try, the less their brain is *able* to focus attention. Many, therefore, have trouble with chores at home or school. Some find it hard to make and keep friends because they are so distractible. A child with ADHD may get teased by others because they enjoy how quickly this kid gets upset.

Most high energy kids are simply "active." They are not "hyperactive," which means "overly active." They just need plenty of exercise or maybe a learning situation that suits them better. If there is concern, careful and complete evaluation for ADD and ADHD is essential because the disorder can be confused with many other issues, from depression to learning differences.

In order to succeed, most children with true ADHD or ADD need medicine as much as some kids need glasses. (Most also need some extra help with behavior.) These medicines *wake-up or stimulate* the parts of the brain that automatically focus attention and stop impulses for other children. A few *extreme* children are diagnosed as early as 4. Most are diagnosed at 6, 7, or later. If these children don't get the help they need while in elementary school, they are at risk for poor self-esteem, depression, anxiety, and other behavioral problems. If concerned, talk with your child's teacher and doctor.

See page 90, "Learning Differences" and page 157, "Impulse Control."

Bilingual Babes and Beyond

Many parents wonder which is better: one language or two? Logically, children who don't speak English at home do better in elementary school if they are in bilingual programs early on. What many people don't know is that native-English speakers (persons who start out life with English as their first language) also test better when they are in bilingual programs—better than classmates in English-only programs. Learning with two languages improves general knowledge by expanding vocabulary and exposing students to broader ideas. Bilingual learning is a big and complicated topic. Here are some of the basics.

As explained in chapter 4, babies listen for small differences in language sounds. If sounds are so similar that they might be confused easily, they are sent to widely separate places on the "sound map" in the brain. The distance between these areas in the brain makes it easy to recognize and later say sounds that are similar but different.

Early nerve connections to the sound map are in place at 12 months, but are easy to rewire until 8 years. By 10 years, it gets harder to hear new, slightly different sounds. After puberty, it is nearly impossible for many people to hear small differences. For example, Japanese adults learning English don't hear the difference between *L* and *R*. Similarly, American adults learning the Thai language have trouble with another sound that is similar to, but different from, the English *L* and *R*. If we can't hear those small differences, we can't say them. For this reason, when we learn a new language after puberty, we are likely to speak with an accent.

Young children (and adults) learn language best when adults speak in their native tongue. It is important for children to hear speech that is comfortable and detailed, including all kinds of thoughts, ideas, and feelings. It is better to hear correct Spanish or Vietnamese grammar from parents than *incorrect* English grammar, which children have to relearn later. A full and rich understanding of *any* language helps children learn another one.

Children learn language most easily when it is part of their everyday experience with people they feel emotionally close to. If both parents are really fluent in two languages, it is recommended that each parent speak to the child in only one. This helps keep the two separate. For example, if parents speak both Russian and English well, one parent speaks to the child in Russian and the other in English. Some English-only families deliberately hire non-English speaking caregivers to give an early start in a second language. Toddlers and preschoolers *seem* to mix the languages up at first. However, they just borrow a word they know in one language when they don't yet know it in the other. They rarely mix up the words they know in both languages.

According to Edith Harding-Esch and Philip Riley in *The Bilingual Family*, babies who hear two languages from birth usually start talking a few weeks later than children who hear just one. This is not a problem. (Similarly, the typical boy begins to talk a few weeks later than the typical girl.) Other factors have a much larger affect on whether or not children develop a rich language base: how much we talk with them, the number of different words we use, and individual learning differences. If an infant's early language development is much slower than expected, check with a speech or language specialist about language disabilities and the pros and cons of one language or two under those circumstances.

Children's Experiences at School

Preschoolers who speak their native language fluently at home commonly stop talking at school if no one understands and talks to them in their language. These preschoolers may remain silent for several weeks or up to one year while they listen and learn English. When ready, they start speaking. (In the meantime, some whisper to themselves in English.)

Unfortunately, many Americans lose their gift of a second language. Once nonnative-English speakers are exposed to English-speaking schoolmates and culture, many stop speaking their native language. This is especially so if one adult at home speaks English. Studies show that the earlier children are surrounded by the language of the dominant culture, the more likely they are to lose their native language. The same pattern occurs around the world when the home language is different from the main language of the country. Children as young as 3 may refuse to speak their native language, though others refuse in junior high or after. Years later, *many* adults regret that they can't talk directly to grandparents or even one of their own parents.

Among the most common reasons children stop speaking their own language is that schoolmates tease them. If children taunt others because of language, it is essential that adults step in and speak positively about the value of knowing another language. It is also important that native English-speaking teachers acknowledge and appreciate other languages. Teachers can learn a few words or invite second language students to teach songs, games, or words in their languages. This helps all the children know that the adults value language diversity.

Non-English speakers learn math, social studies, and science more easily in their own language. After all, how many of us would be ready to take a regular math or social studies class in Spanish if we'd started Spanish two months or even two years ago? When non-English speakers start kindergarten, they can't say in English what they already know in their native language. Such students commonly score three years behind their age mates. To close this gap, they need to learn course material in their native language while they learn English. With effective help they do well. Without it they stay behind, get discouraged, and are at high risk for dropping out before high school graduation.

Bilingual Learning

In the past, immigrants attended English-only schools. Why should we do things differently now? Good blue-collar jobs used to be available to those who dropped out of high school. Now, with few blue collar jobs, high school graduation is important for all. Furthermore, we now know that *early* language learning is more efficient. Unfortunately, we waste a great deal of money trying to teach our English-speaking student another language when the window for easy learning has already passed. This money would be better spent on early bilingual programs that would benefit both English-speaking and non-English-speaking students.

About half of the school districts in the United States have students whose native language is not English. Not all bilingual education works well. Here are two approaches that do. When at least 30% of a class are native speakers of different languages, students help each other learn. Elementary age children learn another language best when they spend time with native speakers their own age. Teaching time is equally divided with a native speaker in each language who speaks his or her own language.

Alternatively, if, for example, almost all the children are native-Spanish speakers, 90% of teaching, during the first year, is in Spanish with native-Spanish-speaking teachers. In each year that follows, more is taught in English by native-English-speaking teachers. By 4th or 5th grade, teaching is half in English and half in Spanish. The children are now comfortably bilingual and ready to continue learning in either language. Teaching early for success makes more sense than picking up the pieces after high school failure.

Planning is obviously more complicated when children in a single classroom come from several different language backgrounds. For more information, see the National Association for Bilingual Education at www.nabe.org.

Around the World

Half the people in the **world** use our human ability to speak more than one language. Some speak several different dialects of the same language, while others speak two or more entirely separate languages.

In *The Nurture Assumption*, Judith Rich Harris points out that most children ultimately speak the language of, and with the accent of, their age mates, not their parents. When opportunity sits on our doorstep, the most efficient route to bilingual adulthood is for young children to share bilingual learning.

Child Care and Preschool

Children's needs change over time, both at home and in child care. The younger the child is in child care, the more important is a *warm, interactive* relationship with the caregiver. Also, the more hours per week in child care, the more important that relationship is.

Chart 17, opposite, shows how the children's needs in childcare change over time. In each age column, the bigger the space, the more time is ideally spent in that activity. Notice how time relating directly to the caregiver changes as the child grows (shaded area).

Choosing Child Care

Parents have many questions and concerns about child care. Here are things to look for and think about in general order of importance:

1. Caregiver who is warm, responsive, and available to your child.
2. Same caregiver over time; the fewer changes, the better.
3. Number of children per caregiver. See chart 19, page 109.

17. Child Care and Learning Needs

	Under 3 yr.*	3 yr.	4 yr.	5 yr.	
Independent Time	**Activities and space** that suit the child's energy level, interests, and abilities.	**Activities and space** that suit the child's energy level, interests, and abilities. **Children** to talk, play, and explore with.	**Activities and space** that suit the child's energy level, interests, and abilities. Enough activity to tire out high energy children, and interesting small-motor activities for low energy ones. **Children** to talk, play, explore, imagine, and create things with.	**Activities and space** that suit the child's energy level, interests, and abilities. **Children** to talk, play, explore, imagine, and create things with. **Preprinting activities** such as painting and drawing. **Prereading activities** with sounds and books.	**Independent Time**
Caregiver Time	**Caregiver protects** toddlers from each other as much as possible. **One-on-one relationship** with a warm, responsive caregiver. Caregiver spends as much time following as leading. Includes lots of play with sounds and words.	**Caregiver helps** children learn to share space and toys, as well as listen to playmates. **One-on-one relationship** with a warm, responsive caregiver. Lots of practice talking one-on-one with caregiver. Enjoy sounds and nursery rhymes together.	**Caregiver helps** children talk, listen to each other, and solve problems. **Circle time**, optional.** **Warm relationship** with a responsive caregiver. Explore, sing, imagine, make rhymes, and problem solve. Talk about life and books together.	**Caregiver helps** children talk, listen to each other, and solve problems together. **Circle time** for group activities. **Warm relationship** with a responsive caregiver.	**Caregiver Time**
All Ages: Kind, firm limits and consistent expectations. The more parents and caregivers agree on discipline, feeding, toilet training, etc., the easier it is for children.					

* Children under 3 may enjoy watching other kids, but they rarely play with them.

** During circle time, children may be expected to sit still, listen to others, or follow directions right away. Some shy, high energy, or slow-to-adapt kids are not ready for such formal situations until age 5 or older.

Compiled by Helen F. Neville

4. Total number of children in the home or center. See chart 19, page 109.
5. Caregiver who understands and is committed to young children, their emotional needs, and how they learn. She or he may be trained in Early Childhood Education.
6. Enough space.
7. Toys and activities suited to your child's interests.

Children benefit from relaxed time to build relationships with us. In the United States, many parents, however, work long hours. With a standard workweek of 40 hours or more plus commute time, many parents are away from home more than 50 hours a week. As loving parents, we use the time we have to build warm, close relationships with our children. Parenting experts T. Berry Brazelton, M.D., and Stanley Greenspan, M.D., among others, are encouraging policy changes that would allow parents more time with their young children. Ideally, Drs. Brazelton and Greenspan say, every baby would be with his or her loving, responsive parent for the first year. Between 1 and 6 years, little ones

Around the World

Extended family members are the most common caregivers **everywhere**—brothers, sisters, grandparents, aunts, and uncles. Thus, little ones have the same caretakers year after year.

In these less structured environments, children naturally pick friends with similar energy levels, interests, and language skills, regardless of their age.

Around the World

Parental leave varies widely **around the globe.** A few countries have no legal parental leave, while others offer several years. When at home with children, 50–80% of regular pay is commonly replaced by countries with parental leave. For current numbers, see www.childpolicyintl.org/maternity.html.

would be away from their parents for no more than 30 hours per week.

Does my child need child care or preschool? At-home parents sometimes wonder, "Does my child *need* child care?" Children under 3 don't *need* child care as long as they get plenty of personal interaction and interesting, hands-on activities at home. At 3, and especially 4, children benefit greatly from play with other children, but it can be informal, at home and the park. Good homes, like good preschools, can provide similar learning experiences to prepare for kindergarten.

Preschool advocates point out that adjustment to kindergarten is faster and smoother for children who have been in preschool than for those who have not. While that is true, to say *earlier is therefore better* is to forget that for any individual child, the adjustment to out-of-home-care is easier and faster with each added year of maturity. (A few children aren't ready for routine group care at 4, and even when they turn 5 may still have some difficulty adjusting to kindergarten routines.)

18. With Whom Do Young Children Talk?

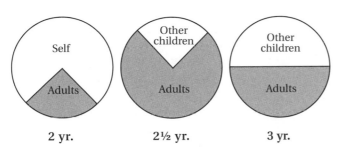

2 yr.   2½ yr.   3 yr.

From Your Two-Year-Old *by Louise Bates Ames, Ph.D., and Frances L. Ilg, M.D.*

With Whom Do Children Choose to Practice Talking?

Young language learners are particular about with whom they talk. It is important to keep this in mind when choosing childcare. Before 2½, toddlers speak only with adults, not children their age. Between 2½ and 3½, children continue to practice speaking mainly with adults (or much older children). This makes sense. When we learn a new language, we look for a teacher who speaks well and easily. Only after 3½ do children speak with their age mates more than with adults. Without interested adults, younger children don't get the language practice they need. These changing patterns are shown above in diagram 18.

How Many Children Should a Caregiver Have?

Several factors affect the ideal number of children per caregiver. Babies obviously need a great deal of personal care. Babies and toddlers depend on the warm, interactive relationship with caregivers for both emotional growth and language development. Preschoolers benefit from relationships with their caregiver and with each other. The caregiver ratios below reflect these developmental changes.

How Do Preschoolers Learn?

Most children learn mainly by *doing*. They learn more quickly when they touch, move, and ask questions rather than just watch or listen. (This is the reason television and computers are not good teachers for young children.) They learn more quickly when they are personally *interested or excited* by the learning at hand. The more children (and adults) are *personally* interested, the more they are able to tune out distractions in their environment.

Through 3, children learn mainly through sharing their world with adults. They also learn from their day-to-day environment and a few well-chosen toys and books. In previous generations, children 4 and older used to learn from being part of the adult world. Now, most adults work out of sight. Fours still need *activities* that connect them to the real world, as well as encourage imagination and creativity. They don't need many different or expensive toys.

19. Ideal Number of Children per Caregiver

Children per Caregiver	Under 1 yr.	1yr.	2 yr.	3 yr.	4 yr.	5 yr.
Number that make it possible to respond well to individual needs and differences.	3	4	4	5	6	7
Number that may be more realistic since a caregiver can't make a living with only the ideal number of children in care.	3	4	6–8	8–10	8–10	12–14
Maximum number of children per room, with two adults.	6	12	12	12	12	14

From The Irreducible Needs of Children *by T. Berry Brazelton, M.D., and Stanley I. Greenspan, M.D.*

Types of Child Care and Preschool Programs

Location, schedules, and cost are obvious considerations in picking child care. Parents also choose between the generally smaller, informal, home-based programs, and larger, center-based care. It is important to remember that children are *always* learning, whether we call it "play" or "work." Programs do, however, reflect different values and beliefs about how children learn. Programs may combine several of the following approaches:

Teacher directed. These are often called "academic" preschools. They offer an early start to formal, traditional school subjects, such as reading, printing, and math. The schedule, activities, and projects are preset and often focus on specific content and skills. All children are expected to sit, learn letters, count, practice printing, and so forth. Time is also spent with music, art, and free play. Teachers often give directions and encouragement.

Child choice. Maria Montessori has come to symbolize this "developmental" approach. She believed that children will learn when they are ready to learn. All they need are time, choice, and interesting materials that suit their level of development. In reality, child-choice programs vary tremendously in terms of what is available for climbing, building, art, make-believe, and pre-reading. Indoor-outdoor time may be flexible or scheduled. "Circle time" may be required or optional. Teachers often encourage children and help them solve problems.

In teacher-directed programs, children more often ask for help and follow directions. In child-choice programs, children more often show leadership and assertiveness, as well as use materials in creative ways. Given a choice of either teacher-directed activities or child-choice activities, girls more often seek teacher direction and boys more often head for child-choice activities.

Project-based or Negotiated learning. This newest approach, like Maria Montessori's before it, is from Italy and

What About Reading and Writing in Preschool?

There is much controversy about how preschools should prepare children for later reading and writing. Discussion will likely get more heated as we hear more about "Universal Pre-K" or "universal preschool." See page 172, "Reading and Writing."

builds on the "developmental" approach. It is named after the town of its origin: Reggio Emilia. In addition to activity centers, teachers note children's interests, such as the rain, birds, the mail, or bread. With ongoing input from children, teachers plan a small-group project that follows an interest and may last for weeks. Teachers carefully observe children so they can introduce new materials that deepen and expand children's understanding of the topic. Children can move in and out of the project, as interest dictates. Teachers often encourage problem solving by asking open-ended questions, such as "What do you think we could try next?"

Adjustment to Child Care and Preschool

Adjustment to child care is affected by age, temperament, time, and other factors.

For separation issues, see page 41, "Why Does My Baby Cry When I Leave?"

Good fit. Child care goes more smoothly when we find a situation that suits the individual needs of each child. A sensitive child may do better in a calmer, quieter situation. Those who are quite slow to adapt usually do better when there is a small number of children and adults. High energy kids need plenty of space and time to run and climb.

Intense, high energy children generally cooperate more easily with somewhat older playmates. They are attracted by the physical skill of the older children and learn social skills more quickly with the older group. Shy, cautious children may be followers with their age mates, but leaders with younger children. Early talkers may get frustrated with age mates who don't yet talk.

Large, age-segregated child care centers work well for many children. However, such artificial age boundaries may separate kids from their ideal playmates. Small, in-home centers may have more flexibility.

Without a good fit, child care is more stressful. Children may hold things together while they are there, but regularly fall apart when they come home. (Of course, they may also have meltdowns because they missed us, are tired or hungry, and so forth.)

Communication with Signs and Sounds

Young children understand many words months before they use them. In general, they talk sooner if we talk to them a great deal and appreciate their efforts in return. In fact, the only way they will learn to talk is if we talk to them. Boys tend to say their first words several weeks later than girls. In addition, cautious children, twins, and the youngest children in big families tend to start somewhat later. Many tots work on either walking *or* talking first because both skills require a great deal of energy to learn. For this reason, less active babies may talk sooner and more active ones may talk later.

20. Children's Communication

Age	What Children Say	What Children Understand
2 to 3 mo.	◆ Say single vowel sounds, like "oo."	◆ Expression on our face and tone in our voice.
6 to 8 mo.	◆ Babble. Put two sounds together, like "ba-ba" or "da-da."	◆ Some words: If we ask, "Where's Mommy?" the child will look at Mommy.
8 to 18 mo.	◆ Say first words.	◆ They learn new words very quickly during these months. By 2 years, they understand 1,000 to 2,000 words.
8 to 21 mo.	◆ Use body signals: nod head, wave bye-bye, point, etc.	
18 to 26 mo.	◆ Say 10 to 300 words. Once toddlers can say about 50 words, they start putting two together, as in "Mommy, up!"	◆ Almost all we say if we speak clearly, use easy words, and only one- or two-part sentences.
3 to 4 yr.	◆ Say two-part sentences, such as "The glass broke because . . ." or "I can do it if . . ." ◆ May say one thing to mean another: "I've got a fire in my tummy" for stomachache.	
4½ yr.	◆ Have more control over whether their voice is loud or soft.	◆ Three separate commands, such as "Open the door, find the ball, and bring it to me."
6 yr.	◆ Most children can now say all the hardest sounds of English: l as in little, r as in right, ng as in ring, ch as in chicken, j as in jump, sh as in should, s as in sad, th as in through, th as in them, v as in very, z as in zebra, and zh as in measure. (The most difficult sounds are listed last.)	◆ 10,000 words.

Compiled by Helen F. Neville

How Parents Can Help Language Develop

Language basics. Talk to babies in baby talk or "parent-ese." The exaggerated tones of parent-ese help babies learn the sounds of our language; for example, "LOOOK at the BAAAL." However, use real words and say them correctly because mispronounced words make learning harder. For example, "You're a schweet wittle baby" would confuse any language student. At 1 year, most babies have already learned to hear all the different sounds of our language, so they no longer need parent-ese. However, continue to talk slowly and clearly.

Repeat slowly, clearly, and often the words that little ones will find useful. The words might include *eat, more, sleep, all gone,* and names of important people. Use words that will help children be clear about what they want: "Do you want *milk* or *water*?" "Do you want the *big* one or the *little* one?" Use short, complete sentences. Repeat new words and say them slightly louder: "Here is your *sock*. Let's put this *sock* on this foot. And this *sock* goes on the other foot."

Look at little ones when talking to them. Get down on their level. They learn more easily when they can see how our mouth moves to make different sounds. Once they know the sounds, the emotional connection of eye contact continues to be important.

Take turns smiling and make sounds and funny faces. After we say something, we need to pause so they have time to "answer" with a look or a wiggle. Communication begins long before babies say their first words. We trade sounds, movements, and feelings back and forth. Sometimes we lead, and sometimes we follow or copy. Touching and stroking babies encourages them to "talk" to us. Show appreciation for their effort. With infants, smile and repeat back the sounds they make so they know we notice.

From birth, talk about what's going on. Tell them what we are *going to do* and what *we* are *doing* and what *they* are *doing*. For example, "I'm going to change your diaper. Here we go—over to the diaper table. You're wiggling your legs."

Signs and sounds. Once they start to babble (as in ba-ba or da-da), smile and repeat back their sounds. Then try a different sound and see if they can copy. Take turns leading and following. Use sound effects for dogs, the family car, or other things of interest. Some sound effects are easier than words for babies to copy.

Babies can use movements or gestures before they can talk. Respond to the hand signals or other body signs that babies use, such as raising their arms to be picked up. Copy any signals they use. Mom noticed that Elena puckered her lips whenever she smelled a flower or food, so Mom always puckered her lips just after she said the word "smell." Soon they had a sign and meaning they could share.

Make up hand or body signals. The sooner babies can communicate, the more content they will be. The easiest signs to learn are similar to the action itself. For example, when you say "eat" or "hungry," touch your fingertips to your mouth. When you say "drink" or "thirsty," tip your fist up by your mouth.

We can make up other simple signals for important words or ideas. Malik's mom pats the back of her hand whenever she says "more." When Elena finishes eating, her parents always pat the side of the high chair just before they set her down on the floor. Elena soon learned to pat the side of the chair when she wanted to get down.

Have fun with signs. Babies will naturally switch to words as soon they are able.

Babies this age also love songs with hand actions (for example, "The Itsy, Bitsy Spider" or "The Wheels on the Bus Go Round and Round") because they can join in with their hands. We can make up our own words, too. They will continue to enjoy such songs long after they can sing along with us.

Add new words. Once children say their first words, smile and repeat the important word so they know we understand. Then add something new. Evan says to Mom, "Kitty." Mom answers, "Yes, *kitty*. The kitty is *soft*."

Once children say two- or three-word sentences, make short conversations that continue the same topic. Evan says, "Kitty!" Mom answers, "Yes, the *kitty* is under the table." Then she asks, "Can you see the kitty's ears?" Evan nods and says, "Kitty sit." Mom answers, "Yes, the kitty is *sitting* with his tail over his feet. Do you have a tail like the kitty?"

Help children understand the world by using words.

Use easy words to explain why we do what we do: "Walk slowly so the kitty doesn't get scared." "Put the cup here so your milk won't spill."

Answer their questions. If they keep asking the same question, try to guess what else they may want to know or tell us. *"Where's Daddy?"* "At work." *"Where's Daddy?"* "At work." *"Where's Daddy?"* "Do you miss Daddy?" *"Yes!"* If we can't answer a question, we can tell them why: "I have to pay attention to driving now. I'll answer later," "I don't know the answer to that," or "I will have to think about it and tell you later."

See page 109, "With Whom Do Children Choose to Practice Talking?"

Teach the words of emotions. Name the feeling when it happens, "You look sad." As children grow, keep adding to this important vocabulary—excited, angry, disappointed, frustrated, etc.

Words that confuse. Young children think in pictures. To them, words therefore have exact, literal meaning. No won-

der our world sounds strange and sometimes scary to them, as when we say: Keep your eye on the baby; let's put the candle out; Grandpa lost his hair; he stole third base and ran home; they'll drop these letters at the post office; she'll beat the eggs and whip the cream; she's a real witch; Grandma was run down after her trip. One little girl always cried in fear when her parents said, "We're going to drive over the bridge." Finally they understood the problem and told her instead, "We're going to drive *to the other side* of the bridge, not *over* the edge of the bridge."

Finer points of talking. Children often don't master certain sounds and grammar until kindergarten age. Chart 21 below shows ways we can help them.

Future language. At a certain point, school children will pay more attention to their age mates than to us. Judith Rich Harris points out in *The Nurture Assumption* that in the long run, children will be most comfortable using the accent and vocabulary of their friends, not their parents.

See page 104, "Bilingual Babes and Beyond."

21. Common Speech Concerns

Difficulty for Preschoolers	How We Can Help
Children don't say all the sounds correctly.	◆ Say sounds clearly when we talk to the child ◆ Don't ask the child to repeat sounds. ◆ Most children will learn all the sounds by 5 or 6.
They say some words we can't understand.	◆ Say, "Show me," "Point to what you want," or "Tell me again," rather than "I don't understand."
They repeat words. This is common for 2 to 5.	◆ Wait patiently.
They stutter. This is common at 3 when the mind works faster than the mouth for a few weeks.	◆ We can speak more slowly ourselves. Sit down and say, "I have time to listen to you. Take the time you need to get the words out."
99% of their speech can be understood: for girls, at 3 and for boys, at 4½.	◆ Explain to others what our children mean.
Children naturally use easier grammar between age 2 and 6, such as "My foots is cold," instead of "My feet are cold."	◆ Don't make the child say it differently. Repeat the idea with your preferred grammar: "Your feet are cold? Let's get your socks." Children will naturally learn with time as they regularly hear your grammar.

Compiled by Helen F. Neville

Death: Helping Children Cope

Not surprisingly, age affects how children understand death. Elena, 3, and her mother buried the dead sparrow they found on their front sidewalk. The next day, Elena saw a sparrow sitting on the fence and said, "There's the bird we buried yesterday!" Young children simply don't believe in death. When Melody's grandpa stopped visiting, Melody got angry. Being dead was simply not a reason she could understand. She was angry at Grandpa and her parents because the delightful visits had stopped.

When Evan was 4, his grandmother died. Evan was sure Grandma was alive *somewhere.* Maybe she was sleeping most of the time or maybe she was on a trip to that place called heaven. It hurt his feelings that Grandma didn't come to visit him.

Overhearing the word *reincarnation* at 4, Melody asked what it meant. Her dad explained, "Some people believe that when you die your body stops working, but part of you, your soul, keeps on living and comes back in another body." Melody replied, "Well, of course!"

When Elena was 5½, her uncle died and she missed him. At this age she understood that he couldn't come back. Gradually, between 5 and 9, children come to understand that breathing and physical feelings stop with death. They realize that the body's death is permanent and that all living things will die someday.

Children have three primary fears when someone close to them dies:

- Who else might die?
- Then who will take care of me?
- What did I do to cause this person to die?

How Children Grieve

Children mix grieving with life. They grieve in their own time and way. At one moment they are sad or upset, and at another they run, sing, and play. They may keep looking for the person who is missing. They not only feel sad, but they often strike out at family and friends for no reason that we can see. They may act out what they understand of death, such as lying still, burying a toy, or breaking something. They

may study death around them by touching a dead bird or killing an insect and watching for it to come back to life. Imagining that the dead person will come back can soothe their loneliness and their fear that they are responsible.

With the loss of a parent or other close relative, children often regress to bed-wetting or thumb sucking. They may have physical symptoms such as loss of appetite, tiredness, or trouble sleeping. Recovering from the loss of an important pet may take several months. After losing a close family member, the whole first year will be especially hard, as each season and family event passes without this loved one. For adults, the intensity of grief often peaks about 4 months after the loss. Grief is usually more varied and spread out for children, who end up reprocessing important losses with each new phase of development and understanding.

How to Help Grieving Children

What we do and say during times of grief depend on our personal beliefs as well as the child's age and relationship to the person who died. Here are some basic guidelines.

Give reassurance with confidence. After a loss, children commonly worry about what may happen next, "Will Mommy die, or will Daddy, or will I?" We're unsure about how to answer these questions because we know anything could happen tomorrow. However, at this moment most children simply want reassurance. They want us to take away their worry. Unless we're aware of other likely losses in the near future, give reassurance *with a tone of confidence:* "No, we're all going to be fine." Most young children will then be able to relax.

On the other hand, if they keep asking questions, continue the conversation. Children also feel reassured when we keep daily life the same as before—in as many ways as we can.

Give information. If children have lost a parent, give honest, realistic information about who else will care for them.

22. Death—Children's Questions

Children's Questions	Simple, Honest Answers	Confusing or Frightening Answers to Avoid
Will you die, Daddy?	◆ *I'll stay here with you for a long, long time.* ◆ *When you grow up and have children of your own, I want to be here to play with them.*	◆ *No, not until after you grow up.* (Child may think, "I'd better not grow up—I'll act like a baby.") ◆ *Not as long as you need me.* (Child may think, "I'd better show him how much I need him.")
Will I die?	◆ *Not for a long, long time.*	
Will I die in a car/plane crash?	◆ *I will keep you safe. And lots of other people also work to keep you safe.*	◆ *I hope not. I don't think so.* (This child is asking for reassurance. To be helpful, our answer needs to feel solid and in control.)
What will happen to me if you die?	◆ *You would stay with ____. They would take good care of you.*	◆ *I won't die for a long time.* (Child may think, "But Grandma just died, so I know people die. I don't believe that answer. I'm still scared.")
Why didn't Lisa's mother pick her up at school?	◆ *Lisa's mother died.*	◆ *Lisa lost her mother.* (Child may think, "Will my mother get lost? I'd better watch her every second!")
What does dead mean/look like?	◆ *Dead means people can't see, breathe, feel, or move. They never see, breathe, feel, or move again.*	◆ *It looks like the person is sleeping.* (Child may think, "Then Grandma will wake up again!" or "I'd better not go to sleep, because I might die.")
Why did he die?	◆ *He was very old and sick. Most people who get sick get better. People who have lived a long, long time sometimes don't get better.*	◆ *He was sick.* (Child may worry, "Mommy's going to take me to the doctor today because I'm sick. Am I going to die?") ◆ *He was old.* (Children don't understand the meaning of old and young until about 9.)
Why did he die now?	◆ *We often don't know why people die when they do.* ◆ *He was ready to die—he'd done everything he wanted to do.*	◆ *It was his time to die.* (Child may worry, "Is it Mommy's time now? Is it Daddy's time? When will my time be? I'd better watch carefully for signs!")
Where is Mommy/Grandma?	◆ *In heaven.* ◆ *She's with God. God keeps people safe after they die.* ◆ *Everything good about Grandma is right here with us. What is something you especially liked about her?*	◆ *In heaven—watching over you.* (Child may think, "What if I'm not good enough and she doesn't like what she sees?") ◆ *She is with God because she was such a good person.* (Child may think, "I'd better not be good because I don't want to go stay with God. I want to stay here with Mommy and Daddy.") ◆ *He's around, we just can't see him.* (Child may think, "He must be hiding. I wonder when he will jump out. That's scary.")

Continued on next page

22. Death—Children's Questions *(continued)*

Children's Questions	Simple, Honest Answers	Confusing or Frightening Answers to Avoid
Won't Grandpa get hungry in there?	◆ *No. People who are dead don't feel anything and don't get hungry.*	
Where is heaven?	◆ *No one knows for sure. I wonder about that, too.*	◆ *It's up in the sky.* (Child may wonder, "Will she fall down and hurt herself when it rains? Can I go up in an airplane to see her?")
Why doesn't Daddy come to see me?	◆ *People who are dead can't come back. Daddy can't, even though he loved you and wanted to stay with you.*	
When can I see her again?	◆ *We have pictures of her. Sometimes people have nice dreams or visions of people who have died. Maybe you will too.*	◆ Children are sometimes frightened by such dreams. If they know we are willing to listen, they will feel more able to talk about their dreams.
What are ashes?	◆ *After she died, we dried out Auntie's body in a special drying machine. Ashes are what's left of her body.*	◆ *We burned her body.* (Child may think, "That must have hurt Auntie a great deal!")

Compiled by Helen F. Neville

Answer children's questions. Children may have many questions about death. Straightforward, simple answers usually work best. Even so, because children take our answers very literally, common explanations about death may cause confusion, worry, or fear. After Elena's grandmother died, Elena and her friend Malik asked, "Where is she?" Elena's dad said, "Her body is in a box." Elena wondered, "Where is her head?" and Malik wondered, "How can she breathe in there?"

Sometimes children need to ask the same question several times. If they *keep* asking, we probably haven't figured out yet what worries them. We may learn a great deal about how children think if we ask, "Do you have a guess? Then I'll tell you what I think." Before leaving the conversation, ask again, "Is there anything else you wonder about—or worry about?" Correct any misunderstandings and check back in a few days or weeks with this same question.

Show children that they are not alone. Hold them and give lots of hugs. Our tears show that we, too, feel sad: "We both miss him!" On the other hand, children also react to *our* distress. They can feel deserted when we are too overcome by

our own feelings to respond to theirs. Ideally, we'll have time to grieve while others take care of our children.

Tell children that death is not their fault. The cat didn't die because Shauna pulled its tail. Grandpa didn't die because Spencer refused to talk to him on the phone. Tots as young as 2 can feel responsible when their family experiences significant pain. If we can find out what children think, then our reassurance can be more helpful: "Sometimes people worry that something they did or didn't do caused another person to die. Do you think kids might worry about that? Do you think kids would worry that something should have been done differently?"

Encourage the expression of feelings. Cry, talk, and read relevant stories. Help children express anger with pounding a pillow, yelling, scribbling, or tearing paper. Set aside a regular time each day or week to talk about memories, feelings, and how things are going. Show your confidence that they can survive grief. For example, to immediately replace a pet suggests that the child can't survive grief and that loved ones can be replaced easily. In fact, it is often difficult to build new connections when we are grieving old ones. Also, let them know it is still acceptable to have fun.

Encourage children to participate in good-bye ceremonies. Cultural practices vary widely. You may light a candle, say a prayer, plant a memorial flower or tree. Because some children are very frightened by funerals, it's better not to pressure them to attend such services if they do not want to. On the other hand, family events are important to many 4s, so they may feel resentful about being left out. Even 3s may later express regret at not being included.

Tell children ahead of time what they would see at the funeral. "Grandpa will be dressed in his good suit and lying perfectly still. His eyes will be closed. He won't move or breathe." Without details, children's fantasies of what a body may look like can be much more frightening than the reality. If possible, take them to view the body and/or cemetery before the funeral when we can pay full attention to their feelings and questions. Then decide together whether to attend the formal events.

For adults, the presence and energy of children at a funeral can be reassuring proof that life goes on. If a parent dies, consider asking a friend to take some photos of the ceremony. Pictures may also help children revisit the events and emotions days, weeks, or even years later.

Elena found it hard, but comforting, to dictate a good-bye letter to her grandmother. She listed things they had enjoyed together. Mom then suggested words that were hard for Elena to say: "I'm sad you aren't here. I miss you a lot." Elena agreed to the additions. She couldn't decide whether to slip her letter inside Grandma's coffin or to keep it, so Mom made an extra copy for her to keep.

Keep memories. Collect a few favorite photos. Write down children's memories of what they loved about this person and things they did together. When the child is ready, also write how this individual was difficult at times. Remembering only the good, especially in a close relationship, can create unrealistic expectations and make it hard for anyone else to ever fit comfortably into a similar role.

Advance preparation. Sometimes when parents (or grandparents) know that death will separate them from their children, they tape-record or write thoughts and wishes for their children to hear, read, and save.

Get professional help when needed. After the death of a parent or major caretaker, it is always wise to consult a professional. This is even more important if the child shows little sign of grieving.

To be able to help our children, *we* also need to experience our grief and may benefit from professional help. Most local hospitals can help locate bereavement support. With time and help, we and our children will be able to move on with life.

Discipline: What Works Now?

Babies are born self-centered, not socialized. Over the next six years, it is our job to teach them a great deal about how to stay safe, manage their emotions, get along with others, and take care of things in their world. No wonder being a parent is such hard work!

How Do We Teach Children Appropriate Behavior?

Model what we want them to do. Say "please" and "thank you." Cross the street at the corner. Listen when others talk. (Yes, it is hard to be a parent!) Children are most likely to copy models who are warm, show affection, and look competent. Modeling is necessary, but it is often not enough. Children are more likely to copy when two adults model the same behavior. If we're single parents, we can ask friends and relatives to help. Around 4, children start to notice whether we practice what we preach.

Talk about what to do, instead of what *not* to do. Young minds work in pictures, so describe the pictures you *want*. "Food stays on the plate." "Touch gently." "Stay on the sidewalk." When Melody starts to grab or hit, Dad folds his hands together and says, "Stop!"

Children learn even faster if we give at least two "yeses"

for each "no." "You may jump on the floor or outside (not on the sofa)." "You may splash or pour water in the bathtub (not outside the tub)." "You may kick the ball or pat the dog (not kick the dog)." "You may smell the flowers or touch them gently (not pick them)." "Leave the cookie on the sidewalk. You can look at it or jump over it." Notice and appreciate what children do that is good and helpful.

Give clear, specific information ahead of time when possible. If we don't want to hear "no" for an answer, it is better to skip the question. We invite resistance when we ask, "Do you want to leave the park and go home now?" Instead, we can say, "We have to go home. Do you want to slide two more times before we go?"

Connect facial expression and words. If we mean business, we must look serious. Toddlers pay more attention to faces than to words. Tell children what to expect *beforehand*: "We talk quietly in the library." Children often surprise us with actions we didn't expect—Evan carefully picked all the green tomatoes from Granddad's tomato plant. Next time, however, we can remind them *before* the mistake gets repeated. Once kids turn 4, keep a list on the refrigerator of positive family rules that say what to do.

Vague rules get tested more often. Think of family rules as stoplights:

- ◆ Red rules are clear. "Always hold my hand in the street." "We don't bite people."
- ◆ Green rules are clear. It is okay to play with toys and run in the park.
- ◆ Yellow rules are not clear. Bedtime stories, sodas, and videos are sometimes okay, so why not more now? To get out of the fuzzy yellow zone, make rules more exact: "We read two stories at bedtime," "We drink soda just at picnics," or "We only watch one video each day."

Practice what to do. "Let's pretend we're angry. We can stomp our feet because that doesn't hurt anyone." Or role play with stuffed animals: "This bunny wants to play with the bear's truck. What can the bunny do?"

Use teachable moments and set up learning situations when necessary. While Mom was driving, a ball rolled under the car. Mom asked Malik, "What could have happened if a kid had chased that ball into the street?"

If trips to the grocery store have been difficult, take an extra trip or two when you don't *need* groceries, so you can leave immediately when a child misbehaves.

Find a balance between control and flexibility. After a family picnic, Elena said she was too tired to take a bath, so Mom skipped the bath that night. If we change a rule for a special situation, explain why: "We are having a special dessert today because we have company." Most 4s understand such changes. Expect 2s to fuss when we return to the usual plan.

Offer rewards when children work hard to *learn* a new behavior or try hard to do the right thing. For most children, rewards don't get them to *continue* familiar behaviors. As actions get more automatic, gradually taper off the reward.

What Kind of Discipline Works at Different Ages?

Crawling babies and toddlers. If *we* aren't in charge, *they* aren't safe. Because they think only of themselves, we need to look out for both them and others.

Discipline is the long, slow process of teaching and learning appropriate ways to behave in the world. We begin the lessons many times each day. Some harmless things we *ignore*, as when Melody at 10 months bangs the cupboard door. Eventually she will tire of it.

As far as discipline is concerned, children under 3 pay less attention to our words than to our tone of voice, facial expressions, and *actions*. Spencer's mom *childproofed* the refrigerator with a bungee cord. Dad *distracted* Elena from Grandmother's potted plant by *offering* his keys.

Toddlers often do just the opposite of what we ask; for example, they go away when we ask them to come. Fortunately, we are bigger and stronger. When spirited Spencer gets rough with Grandpa's dog, Mom simply picks Spencer up and *moves* him, saying, "Hitting hurts."

2s love *routines and sequence*, which we can use to our advantage: "First we wash hands, then we eat dinner." "Once you're in bed, we can read a story."

See page 61, "Offer Wise Choices."

23. Rewards to Encourage Cooperation

3 yr. and Older	◆ Things you would purchase anyway: clothing, art supplies, doll clothes, a little car, a ball, or pieces for a building set.
	◆ Stickers and star charts as their own reward or leading to another reward.
	◆ "Extra" activities, such as another story or special walk. Occasional special treats: ice cream cone, dinner out.
Crawling and Older	◆ Desired activities, time with parents, favorite toy, play with playmate.
	◆ The next planned activity: wash hands, then eat; in bed, then story; pick up toys, then go out.

Compiled by Helen F. Neville

3s understand and respond to language better than 2s. Continue to keep explanations short and simple. Sequence is still important and choices may be more helpful than they were at 2½. Sometimes we say, "This is what we need to do now." Occasionally, we have to ignore their protest or pick them up and carry them where we need to go.

4s and 5s are learning how the real world works. They learn more quickly when there is a direct connection between their misbehavior and what happens next. *Natural consequences* teach when we simply let life happen. Malik refused to hang up his bathing suit, so it was wet and cold for the next day's swimming lesson. After that, he hung it up.

When there is no obvious or appropriate natural consequence, we make up a *logical consequence*. A logical consequence has some obvious relationship to the issue at hand. Melody and her sister were fighting in the car, so Dad pulled off the road and said, "I can't drive safely when there is yelling in the car." When spirited Spencer spit at Mom *again*, Mom took him to the bathroom and said, "We spit in the sink. You can come out when you have finished spitting." It often helps to remind 4s ahead of time; and that they are making a *choice*: "If you choose to pour water out of the bathtub, what will happen next?" (Malik remembers that his bath will be over.)

At 4, and especially 4½, children want to be in charge, so they don't take well to our demands. We often get better results if we *question* rather than command: "What has to happen before we read a bedtime story?" "We walk in the library. What do you think we do at Grandma's new apartment?" The phrase, "I wonder … " is very useful this year: "I wonder what toys might be easier to share with your brother?"

Mature 4s can understand that rules change with the situation: "At our house … " "At Grandma's house … " "When we are a guest, we ask before we open the refrigerator." "When we are the host, we let the guest take the first turn." Recall from chapter 5 that 2s use sequence to understand the world. Fours use rules. We still need to keep rules and explanations short: "Because it can break easily." "Because it hurts people's feelings."

With 4s and 5s we can often talk about issues, especially away from the heat of the moment. Children can now generalize rules and brainstorm solutions. "How can we make mornings go better?" Some 4s want to argue about all the rules all the time. A weekly family meeting avoids the need to discuss every rule every day: "Let's figure that out at our next family meeting."

See page 133, "Family Meetings."

We can often win cooperation from fun-loving 4s with humor: "Let's chase all these blocks into their box so they can't get out," or "Ted picks up red toys and Bean picks up green toys. Do you want to be Ted the Red or Bean the Green?"

Our goals are to teach important behaviors and set necessary limits while we build a positive relationship and support children's self-esteem. The key to success is to discipline according to their age and development.

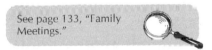

See page 120, "Discipline Strategies for Different Ages" chart and page 122, "Why *Do* Children Follow Our Rules?"

The chart below shows that effective discipline changes as children grow. In each age column, the bigger the space, the more useful the method suggested. Notice that as children grow, new types of discipline become useful (shaded area).

24. Discipline Strategies for Different Ages

	Under 2 yr.—5 Strategies	2 to 4 yr.—Add 3 New Strategies	4 to 6 yr.—Add 2 New Strategies	
The taller the box, the more useful the strategy.	Childproof: Make the environment as safe as possible.	Childproof.	Childproof.	The taller the box, the more useful the strategy.
			Redirect.	
			Move child, use time-out.*	
			Ignore harmless actions.	
		Redirect (distract).	Set up routines and rules.	
	Redirect (distract): Show children what they can do; trade one thing for another.	Move or hold child, or use time-out.*	Withhold privileges and other natural and logical consequences.***	
		Ignore harmless actions, such as jumping off the sofa.	Offer choices.	
		Set up routines, such as pajamas first, then story.	Talk and plan solutions ahead of time or talk about issues in the moment, if things are calm.	
	Move or hold child.			
		Withhold privileges: "You threw the truck, so I put it away."		
	Ignore harmless actions, such as banging cupboard doors.	Offer choices.**	Use humor.	
	All Ages: Show children what to do and thank them for their help and cooperation.			

* See page 121, chart 25, "Discipline and Children's Sense of Time."
** See page 61, "Offer Wise Choices."
*** See page 119, "What Kind of Discipline…4s and 5s…"

Compiled by Helen F. Neville

25. Discipline and Children's Sense of Time

Question	2 yr.	3 yr.	4 to 6 yr.
How soon does time-out/consequence need to start to be effective?	Right now.	Right now.	Within 1 to 2 hrs.
How long should time-out last?	2 min. (1 min. for each yr.)	**Starting between age 3 and 5:** Until children feel able to control their behavior. "You can come out when you are ready to . . ."	
How long should we take away privileges?	5 min. to 1 hr.	1 hr.	1 hr. to ½ day

Compiled by Helen F. Neville

How Should Children's Sense of Time Affect Our Discipline?

Time moves much more slowly for children than it does for adults. We need to consider their understanding of time in order to make discipline appropriate and effective. If we use time-out, both how long it lasts and how we use it change as the years go by. It helps if *parents* model taking time out: "I'm really angry, so I'm going to take a time-out to calm down." Time-out works with some children and not others.

What Else Might Make It Hard for Children to Cooperate?

Children have many reasons for not being able to cooperate at one time or another. These are some of the more common:

Separation concerns. It is hard for children to cooperate in getting ready for bed or going to preschool when they would rather stay with us. Be kind and firm.

Temperament. Inborn temperament makes a big difference in when children are able to follow rules and other expectations adults may have. Active children need *hours* of exercise each day and can sit still for only a few minutes before 5 years. Cautious children need extra time to get comfortable in new situations. Easily frustrated children find it harder to complete tasks that are difficult or boring. Natural planners (those who need time to adapt) don't like sur-

prises at any age. They are more cooperative when they know *ahead of time* what to expect. Active, intense, curious children need more time than average to control their strong impulses.

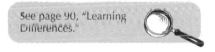

See page 157, "Impulse Control."

Learning style. Many children are more tuned in to information coming in through their eyes and their bodies rather than their ears, so they may not hear us call to them. To get their attention, we may need to *touch* them or move to where they can *see* us. Otherwise we may end up shouting a lot.

See page 90, "Learning Differences."

Adult expectations may be too high. We may be unrealistic about what this child is able to do and how quickly he or she can do it. Children are less able to cooperate when rushed, tired, or ill.

Food. Hunger makes kids (and adults) fussy and resistant. Though some parents are sure that sugar makes children wild, scientific studies haven't clearly supported this. More likely, children are excited by the party where cake and candy are served. A very small number of children do get wild or have trouble sleeping because of reactions to artificial food colors and additives, or to specific foods. This is more likely in children with eczema, asthma, or other allergies, or if someone in the family gets migraine headaches. Pay attention to how your child behaves after eating the same food on different occasions.

> See the Feingold Association's web site at www.Feingold.org.

Why Do Children Follow Our Rules?

Psychologists talk about shame and guilt as the two basic forces that cause children (and adults) to follow social rules. Guilt gets a great deal of bad press: it certainly *can* be overdone. Appropriate guilt, however, is the glue that holds families and societies together. It motivates social responsibility. Without it, most of us would be more self-centered and harder to live with. When children do something wrong, they usually feel either shame or guilt. Which one they feel depends on their age, level of understanding, what happens, and how we react.

Shame stops us cold. Dad shouts at spirited Shauna for pulling the cat's tail *again*. Shauna suddenly feels rotten to

the core, unlovable, and helpless. At 2, she has no idea how to get back into a loving relationship with Daddy. She closes her eyes, lowers her head, and cries. Afraid she's lost her safety net of love, she wants to hide. She feels shame.

Guilt motivates us to fix mistakes. Evan, 5, bumps into Mom who is pouring frozen peas. Some spill on the floor. Seeing his mistake, Evan says, "Uh-oh." Mom asks, "Can you help pick them up?" Evan does so and smiles proudly. Mom says, "Thanks for helping." Evan knew he put something out of order and guilt motivated him to fix it.

Shame or guilt? People who respond due to guilt believe they are basically *good people* who sometimes make mistakes. They tend to feel hopeful about themselves. Research shows that adults who feel a great deal of shame fear that they are bad people. They often try to hide such painful feelings from themselves. They more often lie or blame others when things go wrong. Their anger gets out of control more often, and they show less concern when others get hurt. Given that children react to mistakes with either shame or guilt, it is better that we steer them toward guilt.

What Do Children Understand and How Do They Feel About Rules?

Under 3 yr. Toddlers rarely follow rules on their own. Rules are just words and don't seem important. Toddlers respond instead to people, emotions, and the visible world. They follow requests most easily when they match self-interest, "Please bring the ball," or "After you sit in your chair, then I will give you lunch."

They don't feel bad when they break a rule. They only feel bad if we get upset or something unpleasant happens to them.

3s. Threes understand simple rules, such as "Use your words. Don't hit." But they can't always stop the impulse to do the wrong thing. We can't count on toddlers or 3s to do the right thing, so we have to protect them, other people, and property.

Elena was cutting paper with scissors. Curious, she tried cutting her sweater. She was surprised by how easily the scissors cut the blue wool. Experiment complete, she returned to cutting paper. Dad, who had been across the room, stepped close and was also surprised by the damage. Startled, he asked, "What happened to your sweater?" Suddenly frightened and ashamed, Elena dropped her head and whispered, "I don't know." It is common that children under 4 aren't bothered by their actions until the results are discovered.

4s. Fours can follow rules more easily if they believe an adult will notice and there will be a consequence. They usually know what they are supposed to do but many still don't have the needed impulse control. Impulse control is especially hard for active, curious, intense children. Most fours can't yet complete a hard or boring task on their own.

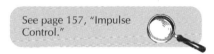

See page 157, "Impulse Control."

Given their all-or-nothing thinking, when fours get in trouble they often feel like total failures for a time. They can't separate out what they do from who they are. They are afraid of losing our love, so they often feel shame. As they learn to hold our rules inside their heads, they begin to feel ashamed even when we don't catch their mistakes.

Shame is very painful. To protect themselves, they may unconsciously cover up their shame with instant anger. We may see a lot of anger this year.

5 to 7 yr. Gradually between 5 and 7, children begin to learn that their core goodness remains even when they do something wrong. They are good people who make mistakes. Thus, they more often feel guilt instead of shame. (Even as adults, of course, we may still feel shame at times.) Feeling guilt instead of shame, they more often feel able to fix their mistakes.

6 yr. General moral standards, such as "Don't lie, cheat, or ignore chores," now begin to stick in children's minds. As a result, they begin to feel guilty about such misdeeds.

Spare the Rod and Spoil the Child?

Many parents with good intentions have learned to use corporal punishment. What are the effects of pain, punishment, and fear on children? Throughout human history,

children have been controlled with pain and fear. In recent years, this topic has been thoroughly studied. We've learned that the greater the pain and fear, the more distant children feel from their parents. The more distant children feel, the more they act out, especially when away from home. They are at higher risk for delinquency and drug abuse. Because of their behavior, children who are strong willed, emotionally intense, or have trouble with impulse control, may be at special risk for repeated, severe punishment.

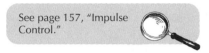

See page 157, "Impulse Control."

People who grew up with severe discipline need a sense of control over the bad memories of their childhood. One way to overcome that sense of helplessness is to *dominate others*—to treat children (or partners) as we were treated. Unfortunately, this keeps the painful cycle going. Fortunately, many parents now choose a better life for their families. They get the help they need to get beyond their painful memories and learn new ways to manage children's behavior.

How Can We Correct Behavior and Also Support Self-Esteem?

Young children think of themselves as all good or all bad in any given moment. How can we correct their behavior and still support their belief in themselves?

Manage our own anger. The more upset we get when they do something wrong, the more children feel frightened, ashamed, and unloved. Then they want to hide. The more we control ourselves, the better able they are to help fix the problem. Spirited Spencer, 4, spills (or curiously pours) honey on the table. Today, Mom is rushed. She gets upset and yells at him. Spencer fears that he has lost her love. He wants to hide and can't learn anything.

It helps to talk kindly about people inside our own heads. Instead of "Why can't I be more patient!" or "My kid is a brat," our motto can be, "Life is tough for 2s and 4s." As with other parenting jobs, it is how we *usually* handle misbehavior that counts. Sometimes our children need to take a time-out so *we* can get a break. If we can't safely shut ourselves in our bedroom or bathroom, we can clearly say, "You have to stay in your room for five minutes because *I* need a break." Ask family and friends for help, and look for other creative ways to get breaks and exercise.

Give much more positive feedback than negative. We need to notice and appreciate their effort and success. "You splashed water *in* the bathtub!" "Thank you for closing the cupboard door." "You asked for the truck instead of grabbing." We can also show support with a pat or back rub. Researcher John Gottman, Ph.D., says in marriages that work well, there are five positive connections for every negative interaction. If we adults need that amount of support, it seems likely that children also do.

Criticize specific actions, not general qualities. Say, "You tore the book" instead of "You are careless." For the moment, little ones will feel badly no matter what we say. But we don't want them to carry labels like "careless" inside their heads for the rest of their lives. (Note that praise is the opposite of criticism. With praise, it helps to point out the behavior *and* the quality behind it. For example, "You're friendly. You played with the new child at school today.")

Help children feel understood. Express understanding and concern when children are upset. "It is hard not to get cookies at bedtime." If, instead, we defend our rule at that moment—cookies are bad for your teeth—while children are still upset, they just get more frustrated. Explain reasons *later*, when children are calm and may be interested.

Help children fix mistakes. Guilt creates the desire to make things right. Given that we all make mistakes, it is a good thing that most of them can be fixed. Starting around 3, we can begin to help children repair their mistakes. Spencer's spilled honey is still on the table. If Mom grits her teeth and cleans it up herself, Spencer doesn't get a chance to help fix his mistake. Mom reminds herself that Spencer is only 4. She calms

---

Definitions

Spoil: To continually give children things they don't need. To do things for them they need to learn to do for themselves. To protect them from the consequences of their mistakes once they are old enough to make better choices. Grandpa always picks up the toys Spencer has scattered everywhere because he doesn't want to hear Spencer complain.

Bribe: To give children things *ahead of time* in hopes they will now behave better. Dad hopes Elena will stop crying in the store, so he gives her the candy she wants. With this success, Elena is sure to cry again next time.

---

down, apologizes, and hugs him. Spencer now feels loved and connected. He now *wants* to help Mom clean up the honey. He *was* a troublemaker and now he is a fixer-upper.

Give hope. "You and Evan can try playing together again in five minutes." "I put the truck away because you threw it. You can try again after lunch." "We'll try again tomorrow." "We left the grocery store because of your meltdown. You can try again next time." Suggest, "I think you'll remember next time."

Reactions to Rules and Control

It is one thing to make children do things our way at times, and another to expect them to *like* it. How they protest depends a great deal on their age as well as their temperament. Over time, children resist less with their bodies and more with words. Some kinds of protest, such as hitting, we need to stop and redirect. However, we can do this more patiently if we aren't surprised that it happened.

Chart 26 shows that children commonly resist or oppose our control in different ways as they grow. In each age column, the bigger the space, the more common the behavior. Notice that as the years go by, children learn to use their bodies and voices in new ways. They gradually use their voices more often (shaded areas) and eventually use them in more positive ways.

See page 62, "How to Manage Anger and Upsets" and page 71, "You're Not the Boss of Me! 4½ Years."

What Makes Discipline Hard?

There are many challenges to discipline. We want to honor our children's individuality and we also want them

26. Ways Children Resist Adults' Control

	Under 2 yr.	Especially at 2½ yr.	Especially at 4½ yr.	5 yr. and up	
Non-Verbal	Ignore us. Walk away.	Ignore us. Run away.	Ignore us, cover their ears.	Ignore us.	**Non-Verbal**
				Dawdle.	
			Dawdle	Tantrum.	
		Dawdle.		Make faces, roll eyes.	
			Tantrum, hit, throw things.	Cry, yell.	**Verbal**
		Tantrum. (Fall to the floor, may hit, etc.) Tantrums are most common at 2H. High energy kids have more tantrums than others.	Make faces.	Whine or argue with attitude.	
			Cry, scream. Shout "No!"		
			Whine or argue with attitude.	Manipulate or lie.**	
		Cry, scream. Say "No!"		Suggest, negotiate, solve problems, discuss.	
Verbal	Cry.		Manipulate* or lie.**		
		Whine. Low energy kids whine more than tantrum. (Whining is most common with 3s.)	Suggest, negotiate, solve problems.		

* May sweet talk, ask questions to distract us, make threats, or play one parent off against the other.

** For more about lying, see page 77, "Communication: Truth, Tact, and Wishful Thinking."

Compiled by Helen F. Neville

to be respectful and responsive to others. Many of today's children have less experience than earlier generations in adjusting to the needs of others. They may spend their days in delightfully child-centered environments. In small families, there is less pressure to adapt to brothers and sisters. In China, with one child per family, parents sometimes talk of the "little emperor syndrome."

Unrealistic expectations. Kids can't perform better than their body, mind, and temperament permit at a certain age. Disneyland will be easier to enjoy with a 5 than a 2½.

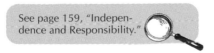

See page 159, "Independence and Responsibility."

Consistency. Try not to change more than one or two rules at a time. When we are tired or under stress, it's all too easy

27. Ping–Pong Parenting

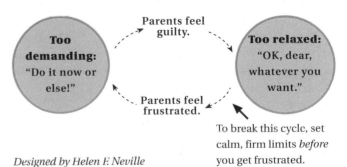

Too demanding: "Do it now or else!"

Parents feel guilty.

Too relaxed: "OK, dear, whatever you want."

Parents feel frustrated.

To break this cycle, set calm, firm limits *before* you get frustrated.

Designed by Helen F. Neville

to bounce back and forth between "Whatever you want, dear" and "Stop that right now!" We need to choose our battles, especially with intense, high energy children. This means hold firm to rules on safety and not hurting others, but ignore the little stuff.

Sometimes we tell ourselves repeatedly, "I will be more patient," only to blow up again. In that case, it may work better to set a firm limit *sooner,* so we don't get pushed over the edge.

Children's disappointment. Because children react so strongly, we may assume that their relatively small disappointments are as significant as the major disappointments we have experienced in life. In fact, children's small setbacks teach them that they are able to survive disappointment. If we protect toddlers and preschoolers from all disappointment, we teach them that they are fragile and give them unrealistic expectations about life.

Guilt about being away so much. At the end of the day, we may feel guilty about our absence and jump to fill children's every wish. However, they need both time with us *and* appropriate limits. To hold back on limits because we are short of time is not a favor. Try to arrange some additional quality time at least once or twice a week to decrease parental guilt.

When to Get Help

Check with your child's doctor or clinic, a family counselor, or a parent hotline if you:

- Are unsure what your child is able to understand or do.
- Often give in and then feel resentful. When children sense frequent resentment, they get confused or feel bad about themselves.
- Often use strong punishment. Difficult behavior may be a sign children have a learning difficulty or other emotional problem. Some children don't seem to learn except from harsh discipline. Nonetheless, strong discipline can make them resentful and even harder to discipline. Sometimes they learn to follow orders at home and then act out their resentment in child care or school.
- Can't bear to see your child upset, or it doesn't bother you when he or she is upset.

Peer pressure. People glare at us when we put an active child in a harness instead of a stroller or let a 5 have a bottle of warm water at bedtime. It is hard to remember that we know our children better than anyone else. Look for supportive friends, including those with children who are similar to our own.

Love creates a warm connection with caregivers so that youngsters want to communicate and cooperate and grow. Love is the base which supports limits on the one hand and independence on the other, as the diagram below shows. Limits protect safety and the needs of others. Independence allows children to gradually have control and responsibility for their own lives as they become able. The loving parent seeks to provide a balance of limits and independence.

Temperament plays a role here too. Some kids dash towards independence; others need gentle encouragement. Some rarely push the limits, while others do so regularly. It's usually clear when typical children need our support and understanding, but very easygoing children may not be so clear. With strong-willed children, we not only spend more time on limits, but also need to give extra time and attention to balance their need for warmth and support.

28. Striving for Balance in Parenting

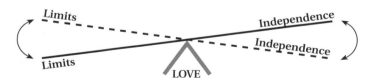

Designed by Helen F. Neville

Diversity: Understanding Differences

"You eat that? That's yucky!" "Why does that man have only one leg?" "How come you have funny hair?" "You talk funny!" Preschoolers notice differences. It is our job to help them understand differences without hurting feelings. It is also our job to help them appreciate diversity.

Without help, young children misunderstand the meaning of differences. Shauna thought the man's leg had simply fallen off; she was afraid the same thing would happen to her. Melody thought Malik's skin was dark because he hadn't taken a bath. Elena thought Evan didn't like her because he said his favorite color is blue and her skin is brown.

Understanding Diversity at Different Ages

3 yr. Threes are just learning to recognize colors. If we ask them to draw a picture of themselves, they are just as likely to color their skin green as brown. Once they learn colors, we might point to a classmate and ask, "What color is she?" They are more likely to tell us the color of their classmate's shirt than her skin color. Threes live in an ever-changing world. They believe skin color, like clothing, can change. They may be a different color tomorrow or when they grow up. At this age, children are color-blind to skin color.

3½ yr. These preschoolers accurately describe their own and other people's skin colors. They may use words such as *chocolate, vanilla,* or *peach* according to Marguerite Wright in *I'm Chocolate, You're Vanilla.* But they do not understand the idea of *race.* A well-tanned Caucasian is "brown," and a light-skinned African American is "white."

4 yr. Without our help, children at this age *guess* why people are different. Maybe Aunt Shelby rides in a wheelchair because she is lazy. Maybe people have different colors of skin because they drink white or brown milk. If 4s have learned insulting words about learning ability, race, or sexual orientation, they will use these words—unless we stop them.

5 to 7 yr. Children learn that skin color doesn't change and that "color" means more than skin color. If asked to sort out pictures of other children, they first separate by boys and girls. If asked to separate pictures by who is African or European or Asian, they sort not just by skin color but also by hair and facial features. They have learned to identify racial differences. When a child's skin color is different from his or her parents', children this age want to understand why.

Fives repeat and act according to stereotypes they have learned at home, on television, or on the playground: "I won't play with her because she's Mexican." "He'll hurt me because he's white." "He's not smart because he's black." One child didn't believe he had just met a Native American because the man was wearing a business suit. Unfortunately, even at this tender age, prejudice can pass from one generation to the next if children hear that certain groups are mean, tell lies, and so on.

How to Help Children Understand Diversity

Focus on the positive. Tell all children good things about themselves. Compliment physical and mental traits; skin tone, hair texture, style of dress, language ability, and knowledge of culture. Read and discuss stories about the accomplishments and successes of a variety of groups of people. Show children role models that vary in race and ability. Protect young children from the terrible facts of history and prejudice. When they are older, they will be less frightened by the past and better able to understand progress.

Talk about differences. If we pretend not to notice differences, children have to figure them out on their own. It is better that we give them accurate information. Look for occasions to mention differences in positive ways. When explaining a word—for example, *disabled* or *gay*—refer, if possible, to people children know and like. This helps children react positively to the word. Point out helpful and successful people of different backgrounds. Arrange for children to spend time with people whose backgrounds and abilities are different from their own family's. Attend multicultural events. Enjoy music and food and games from other cultures.

Always stop teasing or name calling when it is about appearance, race, sexual orientation, culture, or disability. We can say, "We do not use that word," "Those words hurt people's feelings and make them angry," or "Use other words to tell us why you are upset."

Never ignore children's comments. Use their comments as opportunities to teach: "Where did you hear that? Do you think it is true? Fair?" Teach 5s the meaning of *stereotype*: "A stereotype is when we expect everyone in a group of people to act the same way just because they look the same, or come from the same country, or speak the same language. Do *all*

girls act the same way? Do *all* grown-ups act the same way? People are *all* different." "We can't guess what someone will do just because of how they look." "Stereotypes are not fair. They hurt people's feelings and often make them angry."

Listen when children say they want to be different. Encourage children to talk out their fantasies. If they wish to be different, try to find out why. They may be worried about something important. Or they may simply want to match a playmate. We can explain, "People can be friends no matter what color their skin is."

Answer children's questions. Once we have answered their first questions, ask if they have more. This way we can provide more information when children are ready.

29. Children's Curiosity About Differences

Children's Questions	Helpful Answers
◆ *Why does he walk funny?* ◆ *Why is she in a wheelchair?*	◆ *His legs don't work like ours do.* ◆ *One of his legs didn't work right when he was born.* ◆ *Her legs aren't strong enough to walk. The wheelchair helps her go where she wants, like you do.* (When we know people with disabilities, we can ask if they would like to explain their situation to our children.)
◆ *How come Sean looks and talks funny?*	◆ *He was born with Down syndrome. He learns more slowly than you do. Do you have any other questions?*
◆ *How come she doesn't talk like we do?*	◆ *You speak English like your mommy and she speaks Spanish like her mommy. She already speaks one language and is learning ours, too. She will speak English like you after she has more practice. You can help her by talking with her.* ◆ *She speaks Vietnamese and English. She says English with some of the sounds [or order of words] that are in Vietnamese.*
◆ *How come his hair is straight/puffy?* ◆ *How come her eyes are funny?*	◆ *People just look different. Cookies look different, too, but they are all yummy.* ◆ *People look different on the outside, but are much alike on the inside, like M&Ms®.* ◆ *People look different, just like flowers look different. The world is prettier and more interesting because people look different.* ◆ *Her eyes aren't funny. They are different from yours.*
◆ *Why is he different from his mom?* ◆ *How come his skin is so dark/light?*	◆ *Because other people in his family have darker/lighter skin.* ◆ *We all have something in our skin called melanin. If we have more, our skin is darker. If we have less, our skin is lighter.*

Continued on next page

29. Children's Curiosity About Differences *(continued)*

Children's Questions	Helpful Answers
◆ I'm brown. Why does Auntie call me black?	◆ Yes, your skin is brown. But we are part of a big group that is called black even though some of us have very light skin and some very dark. Our ancestors came from Africa, so we often call ourselves African Americans.
◆ Why don't white and black make gray?	◆ They do when we mix paint. But with people you're really mixing very light brown and very dark brown, so that makes brown.
◆ Why aren't his mom and dad the same color?	◆ People can have different skin colors and still be a mommy and a daddy together.
◆ She says she's part Cherokee. Which part is Cherokee?	◆ All of her is part Cherokee—all of her is all mixed together, like lemons, sugar, and water all mix together to make lemonade.
◆ Spencer says I can't be Superman because my skin isn't the right color.	◆ Yes, you can be Superman. You can be whoever you want. We can't choose the color of our skin, but we can choose what we wear and how we act. Let's go together and talk to Spencer about this.
◆ Sean says he's adopted. What does that mean?	◆ Sometimes a family really wants a baby. Before the baby is born, it grows inside one mother (the birth mother) and after it's born, the adoptive family takes care of it.
◆ Why does he have two mommies?	◆ Families are different. Some have just one mommy and some just one daddy. Some have a mommy and a daddy. Some have two mommies and some have two daddies. And some have a grandma or grandpa, or aunt or uncle.
◆ What does gay, lesbian, or homosexual mean?	◆ Usually, a man and a woman fall in love with each other. Some men fall in love with other men: they are gay. Some women fall in love with other women: they are lesbian.

Compiled by Helen F. Neville

Divorce

Divorce and domestic violence are the main reasons for stress in the lives of American children. Both issues cause feelings of helplessness, fear, confusion and grief.

When Separation or Divorce Happens, What Do Children Need?

Children's greatest need is to stay closely connected to their main caregiver. Whenever possible and appropriate, children also benefit from ongoing contact and good quality parenting from the other parent as well. Assuming the child will spend time with both parents, T. Berry Brazelton, M.D., and Stanley Greenspan, M.D., support the recommendations of King County, Washington State, regarding different types of visits at different ages.

Children need to know they will be cared for and loved. Reassure children, for example, "Daddy and I are not living in the same house anymore. And we both love you very much." "You will be here with me most of the time and with Daddy part of the time," or whatever fits the situation.

Children need to know they are not the cause of the divorce. Little ones assume they are the cause of all painful and difficult things. Consequently, they need to be told

30. Divorce—Recommended Visits with the Noncustodial Parent

Age	Recommended Place and Length of Time
Under 3 yr.	◆ Visits at the home of the main caregiver. Separation and new places cause double stress to young children who don't understand how long separations may last. If visits can't take place at the home of the main caregiver, then visits in the child's familiar child care setting may be the next best option.
3 yr.	◆ Outings can include going to the home of the parent who is not the main caregiver, the home of another family member, a park, or a restaurant.
4 to 6 yr.	◆ Overnight stays are now possible, as well as visits of three to four days. (A week or two would be a long time for these children to be away from their main caregiver.) ◆ The more rules and routines are the same in both households, the easier it is for the child to adjust and be comfortable.

From *The Irreducible Needs of Children* by T. Berry Brazelton, M.D., and Stanley I. Greenspan, M.D.

often they are not the cause. These are some suggestions on what to say:

- ◆ "Daddy and I fight too much when we live together. It is not because of anything you did."
- ◆ "Even if you were always good, Mommy and I would not live together."
- ◆ "This is a grown-up decision. It is not because of anything you did or didn't do. It is not something you can change."
- ◆ "We did sometimes fight about things you did, but we separated because of other, bigger problems."

Children need to be protected from excessive fighting between parents and from being caught in the middle. Children naturally feel loyal to *both* parents. As they grow, children know that in part, boys take after their fathers and girls after their mothers. If one parent often complains that the other parent is "mean," "bad," "unfair," etc., then they think, "Maybe I will turn out that way too." This can be a real problem for self-esteem. Or, if the opposite sex parent is "no good," it may be harder to look for a mate someday.

Children need to be able to talk about their feelings and worries. When we are overloaded by the emotions and added work of divorce, it is nearly impossible to give children all the time and support they need. They in turn may get very quiet in order to protect us. Or they may act out to get the attention they so desperately need. We can ask friends, family members, and other regular caregivers to spend extra time with them until life settles down. Play therapy can help children express emotions they don't feel able to talk about at home.

Children need to have as few other changes as possible during this difficult transition. The change will be easier for children if routines, living space, child care, grandparent visits, and friendships can continue as before. If children can no longer attend good quality schools, the economic downturn that often follows divorce may have significant, long-term effects.

Domestic Violence

Domestic violence is usually harder to talk about in public than divorce. In fact, many more children suffer from the effects of watching domestic violence—seeing an adult they love hurt by another adult, time after time. If physical or emotional harm is an issue in your life, get the information and help you need for long-term safety. What children see in their parents' relationships, they commonly expect or fear in their own future relationships. For the good of yourselves and your children, you need to break the cycle. **Get help.** Check with your doctor or look for resources in the telephone book or on the Internet.

Eating: Month After Month

An attraction to sweets is hardwired into the human brain. Breast milk tastes sweet and sweet-loving taste buds helped early humans find calories. This section is about sweets and many other food-related topics.

Lifelong weight management. With healthy foods to choose from, most young children eat the amount of food they need and a balanced diet over time. However, this inner body knowledge can get thrown off by *too much* concentrated sugar and fat from cookies, donuts, chips, etc. (Don't worry about an occasional birthday party. It's what we *usually* eat that has the most effect.) Lifelong weight management will be much easier if little ones don't *expect* most foods and drinks to be sweet or salty. Even diluted juice sets expectations for sweetness. Give juice no more than once a day and avoid sodas (except maybe for special occasions).

Some people crave sweets much more than others. If you have regular battles about sweets, lock them away and give only one per day, or remove them all from the house (and keep your own stash at work if you need to).

Temperament affects body weight. Babies and children who are easily frustrated and low in energy are at risk for excess weight. Because they often fuss, it's tempting to quiet them with things to drink or eat. Being low in energy, they run off very few calories. Unless these little ones are truly hungry, find other ways to soothe them.

Birth to 6 mo.

Weight. Babies aren't very hungry at first, and breast milk isn't in yet, so they usually lose a few ounces during the first days of life and regain it in the next 10 to 14 days. Most babies double their birth weight around 4 months.

Growth spurts. Growth spurts usually come along at 6 to 10 days, 6 weeks, 3 months, and between 4 to 6 months. Babies suddenly get really hungry and want to nurse very often for 24 to 48 hours. Extra nursing causes the breasts to make more milk. Babies then return to their usual schedule, but now they get more milk at each feeding.

Water. Babies don't need water unless the weather is very hot or the baby is ill. All they need is breast milk or formula. (Plus vitamins or iron if doctor/nurse advises so.)

Birth to 12 mo.

Breast milk is recommended as the main milk, if possible. Antibodies in breast milk help keep babies healthy. (If we can't breast-feed, we can still build strong emotional bonds while we bottle-feed.)

No regular cow's milk! Regular cow's milk is for calves. Regular cow's milk has a dangerous amount of protein for human babies. (Because calves grow much faster they need all this protein.) To make formula, water and sugar are added to cow's milk, so it has the right types and amounts of protein and sugar for human babies.

No honey or corn syrup. Before age 12 months these can cause a serious illness called infant botulism.

Weight. Most babies triple their birth weight around their first birthday.

4 to 5 mo.

Nursing problem. Babies may seem to lose interest in nursing. Babies' eyesight suddenly gets better, so many want to see the sights. Nurse in a darker or less interesting place for a few days or wear a bright necklace to hold their attention toward the breast.

4 to 8 mo.

Bowel movements (BMs) start to come less often. The large intestine starts doing its job. It recycles water back into the body. With less water in the intestines, bowel movements are firmer and less frequent. Nothing is wrong if babies skip two or three days as long as BMs are soft like toothpaste, instead of hard like little rabbit pellets (which indicates constipation). Diet changes also play a role.

6 mo. to 1 yr.

Start solid foods after babies can sit up by themselves. They should be able to show their wishes: close lips and turn away, or open mouth for more. Start with vegetables, not fruits, so they don't expect sweet foods.

Prevent allergies. Under 1 year, it is best not to give certain foods because they may cause rashes or diarrhea, especially if allergies run in the family. Babies are more prone to food allergies because whole, undigested proteins are more likely to pass through the delicate walls of their intestines into the blood. Early on, wait 2 to 3 days before each new food. Then if there is a problem, you can tell what caused it. Talk with a doctor or nurse about what foods to avoid.

6 mo. to 3 yr.

Iron needs. Late in pregnancy, full-term babies stored a 4 to 6 months' supply of extra iron. Now they need more than they get from breast milk. Iron-fortified baby cereals and many baby formulas are easy sources. Check with your doctor or clinic.

6 mo. to 3 or 4 yr.

Prevent choking. Babies can't chew, and 2s don't chew carefully. Give foods that get soft when wet, such as crackers. Or give foods that mash easily between your fingers, such as well-cooked carrots. These will also mash easily between baby's gums. Avoid round foods such as grapes, baby meat sticks (unless cut in small strips), or M&Ms®. Avoid peanuts and other nuts, popcorn, or big globs of sticky foods like peanut butter. Cut off the peel from foods like hot dogs and apples.

9 to 12 mo.

Self-help. Many babies now want to join in. Let them have the spoon they grab. Use a second spoon to feed them. They'll want to try finger foods when they can pick up little bits with thumb and index finger. They don't need special baby foods. Offer safe, nutritious table foods. They can hold and drink from a cup. "Sippy cups" with a small opening avoid spills.

Messy eaters. Some baby spoons are bent or twisted. They look funny but make it easier for baby to get food in his or her mouth. These babies also like to drop food from the high chair. Put plastic under the high chair or remove them sooner.

See page 112, "Signs and Sounds."

Standing up. Because of their strong desire to stand up, some refuse to sit in their high chair. Let them stand on the floor instead.

12 mo.

Type of cow's milk. Babies can now make a gradual transition to whole cow's milk. (Until 2, babies need whole milk because the fast-growing brain needs fat.) Limit milk to 16 to 20 ounces a day. (If babies fill up on milk, they're too full to eat high-iron foods and may become anemic.)

Soy milk. If we give babies soy milk, it needs to be fortified with calcium and vitamin D to help their bones grow strong.

Calcium needs. Some babies will now drink only 4 to 12 ounces of milk a day, which is fine if they also eat some yogurt or cheese. If they refuse all dairy products, check with your doctor or clinic.

18 mo.

Self-feeding. Some toddlers now refuse adult help, if they haven't done so earlier. At this age, it is often easier to eat with the fingers than a spoon. Thicken soupy foods with baby cereal so they are easier to eat by hand.

2 yr.

Small appetite. If babies kept gaining weight as fast as they did in the first year, they would weigh 200 pounds by age 3! Instead, they become picky eaters.

Number of meals and portion sizes. At this age, they may eat only one big meal per day and just very small amounts of nutritious food the rest of the day. Think of it this way: because these tots weigh only one-quarter what we do, they only eat one-quarter as much food. Multiply by four to compare the size of their meal with ours. For example, Elena eats a quarter of a piece of toast and drinks two ounces of milk. That's the same as Mom eating a whole piece of toast and eight ounces of milk. That's more reassuring!

Picky eater. Many eat the same food for days and then go on to something else. They may seem to pick the week's favorites by taste, color, or texture. However, if only nutritious food is available, toddlers tend to balance their diet over a few weeks. Eating the same few foods makes their big new world more predictable. Rather than fight about food, give a daily vitamin if needed. Around the world, most families eat the same few foods month after month.

Type of cow's milk. Toddlers can start to drink 1% or nonfat milk. (Check with your clinic or doctor.) Limit milk to 16 to 20 ounces a day from now through the preschool years.

2½ to 4 yr.

Eating and serving utensils. They may start to use a fork in addition to their spoon. Many can now serve their own food and pour from a small pitcher.

4 yr.

More variety. Because of 4-year-old curiosity, many are now willing to try new foods. Throughout the world, most adults prefer the foods they ate when they were young. This is an important time for setting long-term, healthy eating patterns. However, some cautious, sensitive children may still insist on just a few foods.

Table talk. Some talk so much that they forget to eat at family meals. They may do better if they start early and eat before others sit down. Then they can talk with family or leave the table so others can talk. Fours often start talking before they swallow their food. We can remind them to slow down.

Around the world, children can now eat neatly and efficiently, even if chopsticks are the norm. In some cultures, children are not allowed to feed themselves until 4. Where food is scarce, it may be considered sacred and must not be wasted.

4 to 5 yr.

Manners. They learn to chew food with their lips closed.

5 to 6 yr.

Manners. They usually remember to swallow their food before talking. Unlike a year ago, the big talkers are more able to both eat and talk at a family meal.

Weaning

Weaning from the breast or a bottle is strongly affected by children's individual temperament, parent preference, and culture. Before birth control, toddlers were generally weaned around 2 years because that's when the next baby usually arrived. Last babies often nursed longer. The International Lactation Consultant Association and the World Health Organization recommend breast feeding to age 2 or longer.

In terms of development, life is tough for many 2s, so weaning is often easier a little before 2 or after 3. Gradual weaning is easier for most little ones. Cutting the number of feedings slowly also avoids big hormone shifts for Mom, and protects her from a possible cause of depression. Some children suddenly show less interest in breast or bottle and then wean themselves. With most children, Mom decides when it's time.

Family Meetings

Family meetings show that family relationships and family business are important. Most 4s are old enough to join in and contribute. If possible, set a regular weekly meeting when younger children are asleep. Keep meetings short—15 to 30 minutes, depending on age and attention span of youngest child.

Collect and Choose Topics for Discussion

Keep a paper on the refrigerator and add topics as they come up during the week. If there are several things on the list, take turns choosing what to discuss. Bring up things that seem difficult for children: "Mornings seem hard for you. Let's think of some ways to make them easier."

Discuss rules that children want to change. This keeps children interested and involved.

The goal is to help the immediate family work more smoothly. If time allows, then include a child's difficulty with a friend or other outside issues, such as visits to the home of a separated or divorced parent.

Holding a Family Meeting

Express appreciation. Tell how each person was appreciated during the past week. Give concrete examples, such as "I appreciated how quickly you picked up your toys before bed."

Discuss the week's schedule. Go over what's happening: dental appointment on Tuesday, Dad home late on

Wednesday, sitter on Friday evening, etc. Mark or draw the schedule on scratch paper, a chalkboard, or a white board so preschoolers can see it even though they can't read yet.

Plan outings or home activities. For example, "Do we want to go to the beach or build the tree house next weekend?"

Solve problems. Discuss an issue from the list and use the problem-solving process below.

Deal with money matters. Pay weekly allowance. Discuss some charities the family will support.

See page 162, "Money: 'Mommy, Can I Have. . . ?'"

End the meeting with a snack or game. Take turns choosing which game to play.

Keep the tone of the meeting pleasant and positive so that family members look forward to them. Include hugs! Some preschoolers like snuggling on the sofa. Others prefer meeting at the kitchen table with a snack. This isn't an adult board meeting, so expect some silliness and disorganization. Make it a rule to listen with respect and not criticize the feelings and opinions of others. Tell what you *like* about each person's openness and opinions.

Rotate the Meeting Leader

After a few weeks of adult leadership, let children take turns running the meeting. The leader makes sure that everyone gets time to talk if they want to, people stay on the subject, and others don't interrupt. (It may help to have a "talking spoon." When someone has finished talking, he or she passes the spoon to the next speaker.) Once children can write, they too can take turns taking notes. It is important to have a record to avoid later confusion.

With time and practice, family meetings usually run more smoothly. Don't give up because a few are difficult or complicated. Relax and try to figure out what will work better. Over the years, family meetings should be fun and help everyone improve their problem-solving skills. Some parents feel unwilling or unable to join such meetings.

One parent can go ahead alone and report the results. With time, your fun and successes may win your partner over.

Problem-Solving Process

1. **Figure out exactly what the problem is.** "Let's see whether I understand this correctly. Shauna, you feel upset in the mornings because you never know what I'll serve for breakfast."

2. **Brainstorm possible solutions without evaluating or commenting at this point.** "Let's make a list of how we might solve this problem. We can put down all of our ideas, even ones that seem crazy."

3. **Pick one solution from the list to try for a week.** If the family members can't all agree, parents may sometimes need to choose a temporary solution. Write or draw the plan (for non-readers) to be sure that everyone remembers clearly what to do. "Shauna, let's draw a picture on the calendar of what we'll have for breakfast each day. You can check it every night before you go to bed."

4. **Evaluate the plan at the next meeting** and make changes as needed, or choose a different solution from last week's list. Mornings went better when Shauna knew what to expect for breakfast.

Feelings

Emotions are the language we share with all other humans. When do babies first feel these common feelings? How can we tell what they feel before they talk? Emotions may be much easier to recognize once we know what to look for on babies' faces.

One of our goals is to understand our children's feelings. Another is to help them understand their own feelings: what feelings feel like in the body, what they are called, and what they mean. An additional goal is to teach how to *regulate* emotions. This means learning what to do with emotions and how to calm them down.

Several factors can make children's feelings stronger than adults':

Limited control. Children are still learning how to manage emotions, so these are often expressed in strong ways. By 4 or 5 (and even younger), many children have learned to hide or exaggerate the feelings they show us. However, like adults, they more often tone down emotions while they are away from the safety of home.

Time. Young children don't know that feelings will pass. Each mood feels like it will last forever.

Single-mindedness. Children feel only one emotion at a time, so one feeling is not softened by another. As adults we can feel both frightened by an accident *and* relieved that it wasn't worse.

Temperament. Those who have intense emotions and have trouble making changes have a hard time getting *out* of a bad mood. They need more help and support with difficult emotions.

How Do Children Learn About Feelings and How to Handle Them?

Children put feelings into action. Toddlers and many preschoolers can't yet *think* their way out of an upset feeling once they are in one. They have to *do* something. It may help to stomp on the floor, take deep breaths, get a hug, or move away from someone who is bothering them. Low energy children mainly use their voices. Emotionally intense, high energy children use their voices and their bodies. It is our job to help them find socially acceptable things to do with their upset feelings. It may help to remember that even as adults, we sometimes need to take action to work our way out of an emotional corner.

Children learn names for feelings. To talk about *happy, sad,* and *mad* is a good start. However, these three emotions don't cover the richness of children's experiences. When they are old enough to understand the words *refrigerator, elevator, woodpecker,* or *hippopotamus,* they are old enough to understand *disappointed, frustrated, silly,* or *excited.*

If we name emotions *while kids feel them,* they can easily connect the word to the feeling: "You look excited!" For very strong emotions, however, they learn new words more easily after the tantrum or meltdown has subsided: "You were *scared* when that big dog barked," or "You were *disappointed* when your balloon broke." As the months go by, talk about feelings in different situations. When we talk about anger, it is important to name the feelings that came just *before* the anger. We are almost always scared, lonely, hurt, worried, jealous, disappointed, or something else unpleasant before we get angry. Once we know what feeling underlies our anger, we can think of better ways to handle the situation.

Children learn to talk about how emotions feel inside their bodies. Fours may be able to answer questions like these: "Where do you feel energy in your body when you get excited?" "What do your hands and feet want to do when you are angry? "Does your throat tighten when you're disappointed?" "Does your stomach hurt when you're worried?" "Does your heart beat fast when you're scared?" Such awareness of how emotions affect the body will be helpful in the years ahead.

Children watch how we handle our emotions. They especially notice how we react to *their* emotions. Are we usually helpful? When they get angry, do we get angry in return or helplessly give in, or do we stay calm and focused?

The two charts opposite, one describing angry bodies and the other angry voices, show how children commonly express anger at different ages. Notice that children express more anger at 2½ and 4½ than at other ages, as the greater shaded area shows. For effects of temperament, also see the chart on page 23, "Temperament Creates Peaks of Challenging Parenting."

When Do Children Feel Gratitude?

Feeling grateful means we feel happy someone did something nice for us that they didn't have to do. To feel genuinely grateful, we need to understand that others went out of their way for us. The more we understand how far they go out of their way, the deeper our gratitude. It's not until age 7 that children have enough experience with life to start understanding this idea. They will understand more at 9, and each year thereafter. Here is how gratitude develops in children:

2 yr. Because toddlers don't understand our world, they don't understand our effort and don't feel gratitude. Polite words have no real meaning for them. A few adaptable 2s willingly copy our "please" and "thank you." With others it's better to simply model what we want rather than pressure and argue about politeness. Shauna says, "Gi'me cup." Mom says, "Shauna means, 'Please give me the cup.'"

3 yr. Because 3s want to act like adults, more will copy our polite words this year. Or, gentle reminders may do the trick: "What's the magic word?" This is simple rote learning— they still don't understand gratitude.

4 yr. The language of good manners comes more easily at 4 when children understand rules and cause and effect: "When we ask people to do things for us we say 'please,'" Mom tells Shauna, "I don't feel like doing it for you unless you say 'please.'" Or, she ignores requests that don't come with "please."

5 yr. Many children who hear polite words regularly and get intermittent reminders start to use them on their own when they are 5. Because feelings are less intense now than at 4, there is more time to remember polite phrases. Given 5s' general desire to please, there will never be a better time to teach these polite phrases if we haven't done so already. If *please* and *thank you* and *excuse me* aren't already in daily use, now is the time to make it happen with almost all children. Waiting longer won't make it any easier. With time, polite words will come to have much more meaning.

Where to find more help with feelings. Books are a wonderful way to teach children about feelings. Check with your local librarian for stories about feelings and how children manage them. Look for books that relate to your child's age, feelings, and circumstances.

See page 62, "How to Manage Anger and Upsets," page 75, "Help 4s Handle Feelings," and page 85, "Communication and Feelings."

31. Angry Bodies—How and How Often

FREQUENCY	Under 2 yr.	Especially 2½ yr.	3 yr.	Especially 4½ yr.	5 yr.
More		Drop to floor.		Hit, push, throw.	
↕		Hit, push, throw.		Kick sometimes.	Hit, push, throw.
↕			Drop to floor.	Make faces, spit.	Make faces, roll eyes.
Less	Drop to floor, hold breath, bang own head.		Hit, push, throw.	Be alone, hide, leave home.*	Be alone.
		Bite sometimes.	May bite.	Exercise.	Exercise.

* With their new sense of confidence and independence, 4s may try leaving home. See page 71, "You're Not the Boss of Me! 4½ years."

Compiled by Helen F. Neville

32. Angry Voices—How and How Often

FREQUENCY	Under 2 yr.	Especially 2½ yr.	3 yr.	Especially 4½ yr.	5 yr.
More		Scream. Cry.		Cry, scream.	
↕				Whine.	
↕				Say mean things.	
↕			Cry, scream.	Blame others.	Cry, whine, say mean things, blame others.
Less			Whine.	Solve problems.	Solve problems.
	Cry.				

Compiled by Helen F. Neville

33. Feelings and Words Children Can Use

When Feelings May First Appear	Feelings and Words to Use Now and Later	How We Can Notice Children's Feelings
Birth	**Calmness** ◆ Baby/toddler: *calm* ◆ Preschooler: *calm, soft and quiet inside*	◆ Eyes open, body still, pays attention.
	Overload, overstimulation, overwhelmed ◆ Baby/toddler/preschooler: *too much*	◆ Baby: looks away, fusses, arches back, cries. ◆ Toddler or preschooler: has a meltdown.
	Fear ◆ Baby/toddler: *scared* ◆ Preschooler: *scared, afraid*	◆ Mouth open and stiff with corners held back. Eyes wide, wrinkles along forehead. After 12 mo., may also bite lower lip.
	Pain ◆ All ages: *hurt, ouch*	◆ Eyes closed, brows down and in, cheeks lifted. Cries.
5 to 10 wk.	**Happiness** ◆ All ages: *happy*	◆ Smiles (may laugh at 3 to 4 mo. because of a strong, surprising, and good feeling, like being kissed on the tummy).
4 to 6 mo.	**Interest** ◆ Baby/toddler: *new* ◆ Preschooler: *interesting*	◆ Eyes wide, eyebrows raised or lowered slightly.
	Surprise ◆ All ages: *surprised*	◆ Same as "interested," plus mouth open and round.
4 to 14 mo.	**Excitement** ◆ Baby/toddler: *wiggly, lots of energy, or happy-wiggly.* ◆ Preschooler: *excited, happy energy.*	◆ Baby: kicks legs or waves straight legs. ◆ Toddler: shakes arms or bounces. ◆ Preschooler: runs around, jumps for joy.
	Anger (Anger is a general reaction to other, big, bad feelings—overwhelmed, frustrated, sad, etc. It always follows another feeling.) Mellow, easy-to-please babies may not show anger until 14 mo. or even later. ◆ Baby/toddler: *mad* ◆ Preschooler: *mad, angry*	◆ Baby: lips press together or pull back so teeth show. May cry. Eyebrows pull together; may get wrinkles between eyes.
	Frustration (Upset because we want to make something happen but can't.) Frustration can quickly turn to anger. To avoid frustration, children may pay attention to something else. To endure frustration, we have to balance anger at what we don't have with hope, interest, and excitement about what we can get. ◆ Toddler: *stuck, mad because you can't make it work* ◆ Preschooler: *stuck, frustrated*	◆ Appears angry, cries, has a tantrum or meltdown, stops trying.

Continued on next page

33. *Feelings and Words Children Can Use* (continued)

When Feelings May First Appear	Feelings and Words to Use Now and Later	How We Can Notice Children's Feelings
4 to 14 mo.	**Disgust** (When something smells or tastes really bad.) ◆ Baby/toddler: *yucky* ◆ Preschooler: *yucky, don't like, hate*	◆ Corners of mouth down and back. May stick out tongue, as when something tastes bad.
8 to 12 mo.	**Love** ◆ All ages: *love*	◆ Smiles, kisses, hugs.
	Jealousy (Upset because the person we love is paying attention to someone else.) ◆ All ages: *left out, jealous*	◆ 8 mo.: May cry when Mom pays attention to others. ◆ 18 mo.: May try to push baby brother/sister off Mom's lap.
	Sadness ◆ All ages: *sad*	◆ Corners of lips pull down. Lower lip pushes up. May cry. Eyebrows pull together; may get wrinkles between eyes.
	Loneliness (Sad because we feel all alone.) ◆ All ages: *lonely*	◆ Looks sad.
	Shyness (We aren't ready to do something because we feel cautious.) ◆ All ages: *shy, not ready*	◆ Looks down, stays back or behind us when around new people or situations.
	Pride (We tried to make something happen and we succeeded.) ◆ All ages: *proud*	◆ Body straight up, shoulders back, head up, smiles. ◆ Pride appears earlier or later, depending on the culture.
14 mo. to 2½ yr.	**Lack of control** ◆ Toddler: *mad, out of control* ◆ Preschooler: *out of control, too upset to think, has meltdown.*	◆ Has tantrums: cries, screams, hits, kicks, bites, throws things.

Continued on next page

33. *Feelings and Words Children Can Use* (continued)

When Feelings May First Appear	Feelings and Words to Use Now and Later	How We Can Notice Children's Feelings
14 mo. to 2½ yr.	**Empathy, Sympathy** (When we connect with another person's feelings.) Children differ widely in when they first show empathy. Some do so as infants. Others don't show such obvious concern until 4 or 4½ yr. Some sensitive toddlers feel other people's emotions so strongly that their own heart rate goes up. These little ones may cry or go away in order to calm down. By school age, they too are usually able to help others. Whether children show empathy early or late seems to be partly genetic. Children from loving, responsive homes express more empathy. Abused preschoolers tend to get frightened or angry, or even attack other children who are in distress. ♦ All ages: *caring, helpful, a good friend* ♦ Preschooler: *sympathetic*	♦ Some infants cry when they hear another baby crying (but not a recording of their own cry). ♦ Some toddlers offer a hug or a blanket when someone else is upset. ♦ Preschoolers can talk about how others might feel, and look for a way to help them feel better.
	Disappointment/Envy (Disappointed means upset because we hoped for something and didn't get it. Envious means someone else has something we want: a toy, a turn, an opportunity, or a quality, such as strong legs that run fast.) ♦ Toddler: *sad* or for an intense child who becomes instantly angry: *sad-mad* ♦ Preschooler: *disappointed*	♦ Looks sad, cries, screams, grabs or pushes, hits, bites, throws things.
2 to 3½ yr.	**Shame** (Ashamed means afraid that important people don't like the kind of people we are. Therefore, we want to shrink out of sight and hide. We feel small, helpless, and are at a loss for words.) ♦ Toddler: *scared, feel like hiding* ♦ Preschooler: *scared, afraid that no one loves you*	♦ Toddler: looks down, covers face with hands, hangs head, or turns away. ♦ Preschooler: squirms, hunches shoulders, pouts, frowns, or tucks lips between teeth or blushes. May say, "Don't look at me." May blame others when there is trouble.

Continued on next page

33. Feelings and Words Children Can Use (continued)

When Feelings May First Appear	Feelings and Words to Use Now and Later	How We Can Notice Children's Feelings
2½ to 4 yr.	**Guilt/Regret** (With shame, we want to hide. With guilt, we want to make things better.) We feel guilty when we break a rule or standard that is inside our own head. Even if no one else sees, we know we have done the wrong thing. Fours, who understand cause and effect, understand being sorry more than most 2s. If 2s won't apologize after hurting someone, it is rarely worth having a battle about it. ♦ All ages: *sorry, how can we fix this? or make it better?*	♦ Guilt involves a lot of thinking, so it shows up differently on our faces. Toddlers take action to fix some mistakes and preschoolers, like adults, can talk about how to fix mistakes.
4 to 6 yr.	**Nervousness or Anxiety** (Afraid about what will happen or how it will happen.) ♦ All ages: *nervous or anxious*	♦ Afraid may be a strong or subtle expression on the face. Body may tremble or be jittery.
	Worry (When we keep thinking over and over about the same unpleasant thing that might happen.) ♦ All ages: *worried*	♦ Worried may be a strong or subtle expression on the face.
	Discouragement (Sad or worried because it is so hard to make something happen. Then it is hard to keep trying.) ♦ All ages: *discouraged*	♦ Looks sad, may refuse to try again.
	Boredom (Tired of doing the same thing that isn't interesting anymore.) Children sometimes say they are bored when something is too hard or when they are lonely. ♦ All ages: *bored*	♦ Eyes dull. No sign of interest. ♦ May look sad or some children may get angry.
	Embarrassment (Afraid people we care about will see us and laugh at us or put us down.) ♦ All ages: *embarrassed*	♦ Giggle, silly smile, smile while looking away, or touching hair, face, or clothing.
5 yr.	**Ambivalence** (Feeling two different ways about the same thing.) With their all-or-nothing thinking, 4s do not understand this possibility. At 5, children can understand the idea when it is explained to them: Spencer is angry that Mom is late for day care pickup and glad to see her. But it is not until age 8 or 10 that most children, on their own, can sort out two opposite emotions that come at the same time. ♦ All ages: *ambivalent*	♦ First one emotion and then the other is likely to show, whatever those two may be.
7 yr.	**Gratitude** (Feeling glad someone did something nice for us.) See page 136.	♦ Happy, relieved.

Compiled by Helen F. Neville

Common Fears of Childhood

Fear protects us: we all jump with unexpected loud noises in case they signal danger. Depending on their age, children are frightened by different things, and gradually learn that many of these are not dangerous. Temperament also affects fears. Some children are rarely frightened. Those who get frustrated easily (and therefore depend more heavily on parents) are often more upset by separation. Sensitive, intense children are especially prone to fears before they can tell the difference between fantasy and reality.

Fantasy that Frightens

To 2s and especially 3s with their active imaginations, any dark corner of their bedroom can turn into a fearsome monster. Fight fantasy with fantasy. Say with confidence that Teddy Bear will scare off mean creatures. Supply a magic wand, a flashlight, or a spray bottle of magic water that smells "yucky" to monsters and keeps them away.

Up to 8 years, children may confuse fantasy and reality. When they see a scary picture, they have no way to know whether such an event is likely to happen to them. As a re-

34. Fears of Childhood

Age	Common Fears	How to Help
7 to 12 mo.	◆ Separation anxiety and stranger anxiety	◆ Depending on when *separation* anxiety starts, *stranger* anxiety begins about a month later—usually around the time crawling begins. Both these fears tend to be greatest around 15 mo. and taper off between 3 and 3½ yr. See page 41, "Why Does My Baby Cry When I Leave?"
18 mo. to 3 yr.	◆ Animals (bouncy dogs are especially scary) ◆ Noises, especially loud ones: thunder, wind, rain, vacuum cleaners, sirens, water going down a drain	◆ Hold toddlers when they are frightened. Give them time to get acquainted with more peaceful pets. ◆ These fears often fade after several months. If toddlers have sensitive hearing, teach them to hold their hands over their ears. If very sensitive hearing is accompanied by many other behavior issues, check with your doctor or an occupational therapist about "sensory processing." ◆ Vacuum when your child is out of the house.
2 yr.	◆ Falling/getting hurt ◆ Dark ◆ Masks and clowns	◆ 2s are often afraid of falling through the toilet or bathtub drain. Elena's mom finally put a basketball in the toilet and flushed it to prove that big things couldn't go down the drain. ◆ Night lights or company can help. ◆ Avoid these surprises if little ones are frightened. Let them enjoy such things when older.
2 to 7 yr.	◆ Nightmares ◆ Fantasy in books, movies, videos	◆ See page 142–143, "Fantasy that Frightens."
3 yr.	◆ Falling	◆ 3s may be afraid of heights because their vision and coordination are changing rapidly.
3 to 5 yr.	◆ Shadows, dark corners	◆ See page 142–143, "Fantasy that Frightens."
4½ to 6 yr.	◆ Death/safety of parents	◆ See page 143, "Fears About Safety."

Compiled by Helen F. Neville

sult, they can get very frightened by movies and television, even if they are watching a fairy tale. Some very sensitive children (even those older than 8) with strong emotions can become frightened for *weeks* by a scary scene. A few then have trouble eating, sleeping, or being alone in a room, even when their parents are nearby in another room.

Nightmares commonly start around 2½ years. They occasionally bother about 30% of 3s and 50% of 4 to 6s. Preschoolers' scary dreams are often about dogs, monsters, and occasionally ghosts. Nightmares can be harder to manage before little ones can talk about them. At 2½, Melody repeatedly woke at night, crying with fear. Dad invited her to scribble a "picture" of her bad dream. He put it out in the garbage can with a brick on top until the garbage truck came. Melody's bad dreams stopped.

Nightmares are often a code for the fear felt during the day, such as a big dog (or angry parent) that barked. These strong, leftover feelings come back at night dressed in different costumes. Shauna was very angry this afternoon because Mom wouldn't let her eat all the cookies. She wished Mom would go away and never bother her again. Tonight, Shauna dreams that Mom really does go away. She's all alone and frightened. The angry thoughts she had about Mom during the afternoon turn into an angry monster that chases her. Now she is terrified. Mom thinks back to yesterday and makes a wise guess. Mom tells Shauna, "Maybe you wished yesterday that I'd go away and let you eat all the cookies. Maybe you wished I wouldn't come back and bother you. We all have angry thoughts. I'm going to stay here and take care of you even if you get angry."

At 4, Dad asks Spencer to tell his scary dream in the safety of morning light. Then Dad asks, "What would be a *good* ending to this story? Tell me again; I like that ending!" This process helps Spencer feel more in control over his worries and he has had fewer nightmares. Malik slept better after he started asking for "good dreams" during his bedtime prayers.

Fears About Safety

Children at this age need to know that we are okay. The fact that they sometimes get angry at us and wish us harm can fuel their fears. At 4, spirited Spencer often pushed hard against the family rules. At the same time, he started drawing pictures of fires and asking many questions about what would happen if there were a fire.

Some 4s and 5s worry that fires, earthquakes, tornadoes, or other disasters might happen. They are afraid they may be left to manage all on their own. Because 4s and especially 5s can now self-reflect, they realize that they can't get along without their parents. After her aunt died, Shauna was afraid that Mom might die, too. Some children even worry about any change we make. Evan was worried when Mom cut her long hair. Mom told him, "Even with short hair, I still love you and I'll take good care of you."

Helping 4s and 5s Feel More Secure.

Videos and television. Cut down on scary things they see, including fairy tales and the news.

See page 179, "Screen Time: Television, Videos, and Computers."

Take children to visit your workplace. At this age, they'll feel more confident when they know where and how we spend our time when we are away from them.

Talk about safety and emergency plans. Discuss what each family member would do in an emergency: "Let's have a fire drill so we all know just what to do if there is a fire." Discuss how everyone would find each other after the emergency. Talk about other possible emergencies and teach how to call 911 and what to say. This is a good age to begin teaching simple first aid.

See page 176, "Safety: Step by Step."

Talk about other caring adults. Some children ask who would take care of them if something were to happen to their parents. Writing a will and choosing a guardian for children is very important. Then it will be easier to talk to them about the arrangements we've made if they want to know. Some feel better knowing (or meeting) those who would care for them if needed.

Make use of spiritual practices if they fit your beliefs. Children this age often feel reassured to know there is a protective power looking out for them and those they love.

Seek professional help. Get help if kids seem worried for more than 4 weeks, or sooner if they are very upset.

Friends

As adults, our friends bring us joy and support, and sometimes challenge us to grow. Toddlers aren't interested in real friendships. Fours spend months beginning to learn the basics about how to make friends and be a friend.

When Do Children *Need* Playmates?

Toddlers enjoy watching other toddlers. However, 2s and under don't play much with others their age. Their major goal is learning to control their environment. Both toys and adults are much easier to control than other little people. Another goal is to learn language. They hear more words from children over 4 and from adults than they do from other toddlers. They have difficulty sharing, taking turns, and cooperating. There will be some delightful moments, but playing with age mates usually requires almost constant attention from adults.

At 3, children more easily learn the give-and-take of friendship. Threes rarely play with more than one other child at a time. They need adults nearby to help settle disagreements. In order to improve their language, 3s also need to spend a great deal of talking time with adults.

Not until almost 4 do children talk more with age mates than nearby adults. At this age, imaginary and cooperative play with other children becomes very important. Fours rarely actually play with more than two (or occasionally three) other children at a time.

See page 109, "With Whom Do Children Practice Talking?"

Parents may get frustrated to see children playing alone after they have brought two together for a play date. It is perfectly normal for 3s, 4s, and 5s to spend slightly more than half (55-60%) of their time playing near each other rather than directly with each other.

The Introvert or Extrovert Factor

Around 3 or 4, we can begin to see that some children (like adults) are introverts. Even though introverts like to play with others part of the time, they often need time by themselves. Being social is hard work for them; it drains their emotional energy. Being alone recharges their emotional batteries. Over time, introverts tend to have few or even just one good friend. That, however, is enough to learn the give-and-take of friendship.

Most children (and adults) are extroverts—about 60%. For them, being around other people recharges their emotional batteries, so they rarely want to be alone. In the past with large families living close together, there were always other children nearby—an extrovert's paradise. Today, it takes extra work to find the playmates that young extroverts naturally crave.

What Happens When Children Play Together?

18 mo.

Watch and copy other children. They need adults to keep the peace.

2 yr.

Play side by side, independently, not cooperatively.

See page 63, "Help with Friendships" and page 64, "Sharing
Takes Time to Learn."

2½ yr.

Trade. Some children can learn to trade rather than grab toys at this age.

3 yr.

Share. With help, 3s start learning to respect the rights of other children. They can sometimes share, take turns, and cooperate. They still need adults to help them tell other children their wishes and needs.

One at a time. They usually play best with just one other child at a time.

Choose friends. They may begin to prefer playing with some children more than others—usually those with a similar amount of energy.

4 yr.

Talk for themselves. Fours use words to change the actions of other children. For example, they can get others to cooperate ("Let's . . .") and can suggest solutions to social problems ("You can play with it in a minute, okay?"). Now that they understand the difference between "by accident" and "on purpose," they can more easily let it pass when someone bumps them accidentally. Most become better at sharing toys, though some still have trouble taking turns and cooperating.

Prefer kids. Many 4s now become more interested in other children than in adults.

Group play. With their new social skills, they gradually learn to play in small groups of three or occasionally four. (Some are not yet comfortable in groups and may need help building one close friendship.) They can more easily share toys. They enjoy working together toward a goal they've chosen, such as building something or playing imaginary games. As they learn about cause and effect, they gradually learn from experience that "Other kids won't play with me if I always make them do things my way." (Other single-minded 4s find friends who are content to follow orders. They will learn later about sharing leadership.) Fours still need occasional help from adults to get started in a new activity or settle disputes.

New playmate. They often accept a new child if an adult says, "Here's a new friend who wants to play with you." With time, they generally choose friends with similar energy levels and interests. They often become very attached to special friends and may hug and kiss. When their favorite friend plays with someone else, they easily feel jealous and may tell the third child to "Go away!" Children need help learning how to manage and express all these strong feelings in tactful ways.

See page 79, "Foster Friendships"
and page 182, "Differences
Between Boys and Girls."

5 yr.

Less supervision. Most 5s can share and play with others for long periods without adult supervision—unless they are siblings. Some, however, still have trouble cooperating and waiting for turns.

Less active boys. Boys who are physically unsure of themselves may be ignored and left out of free play with other boys, but do fine in supervised games. If boys have trouble measuring up in sports, help them find other activities to shine in. Help them with friendships.

Health and Development

35. Physical Development-Related Health Issues and How to Help

Age	Issues	Why	Things to Do
Birth through first week	◆ Jaundice: yellow skin and maybe yellow eyes	While in the uterus, babies need extra blood cells to collect oxygen. Once babies are breathing air directly, the extra cells break down and cause the yellow color.	◆ Check with your doctor or nurse. May go away on its own, or need home or hospital treatment.
Birth to 6 mo.	◆ Sudden, irregular muscle jerks and twitches	Muscles and nerves aren't yet well connected. Muscles don't yet work smoothly.	◆ If you see a number of repeated muscle jerks, one right after another, check with your doctor.
Birth to 9 mo.	◆ SIDS: sudden infant death	See page 193, "Sleep Location and SIDS."	◆ See page 193, "Practical Tips for SIDS Prevention."
Birth to 3 yr.	◆ Colds or viruses, eight to ten per year	More than 100 viruses cause colds. Adults usually fight them off before any symptoms appear. Children's immune systems are still learning this skill.	◆ Wash hands. ◆ Plan for extra time off work to care for child. ◆ Check with doctor or nurse about treatment.
	◆ Ear infections are among the most common reasons for visits to the doctor.	In babies and small children, bacteria easily pass from the throat and nasal passages into the eustachian tube and from there to the middle ear. Secondhand smoke: tiny hairs line the inner walls of the eustachian tubes and normally sweep bacteria out. Smoke relaxes these tiny hairs so they can't do their job.	◆ In smaller day care situations, children are exposed to fewer viruses. ◆ Don't let babies drink from a bottle while lying flat because milk is more likely to run into the eustachian tubes. ◆ Don't smoke around babies.
1 to 9 mo.	◆ Belly button pushes out and is marble size when a baby cries.	At birth, there is space between the abdominal muscles for the umbilical cord. In most babies, the muscles grow together by about 9 mo., which holds the belly button in.	◆ No reason to worry as long as you can gently push the belly button back in when the baby is relaxed and it is gradually getting smaller, not larger, over time.
6 wk. to 6 yr.	◆ Fever	Young brains don't regulate fever as closely as adult brains do. Fevers of 102–104°F are common and don't cause harm. Fear of high fever dates from the time when they were often caused by measles and meningitis. These *infections themselves*, not the fevers, caused brain damage.	◆ Fever helps the body fight off infection so illness doesn't last as long. Don't give medicine for fever unless advised by your doctor. Ask your doctor or clinic when your baby should be seen for illness with fever.

Continued on next page

35. *Physical Development-Related Health Issues and How to Help* (continued)

Age	Issues	Why	Things to Do
6 wk. and up	◆ Infectious diseases	Before we had vaccines, common diseases disabled or killed millions every year.	◆ Check with your doctor or clinic for current recommendations.
9 to 18 mo.	◆ Soft spot on top of head (fontanel) closes.	Soft spots allow head to fit more easily through the birth canal. (Small soft spot at the back of head closes around 4 mo.)	◆ Be gentle with the soft spots.
3 to 5 yr.	◆ Colds or viruses, six to seven per year.	Children who start day care now may get more colds than children who have already been in day care. The new children haven't yet developed as much immunity.	◆ Plan for extra time off work. ◆ Check with doctor or clinic about treatment.

Compiled by Helen F. Neville

Illness and child care. Children should not be with others in child care if they have diarrhea, are vomiting, have an unknown rash, or are tired or fussy due to illness. Children with mild or moderate fever, who don't act sick, do not need to stay home. About the third or fourth day of a cold, nose drainage often turns green. This is good! This green drainage is the millions of immune cells that did their job and then died—they are not contagious in an active, healthy child.

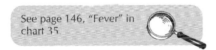

See page 146, "Fever" in chart 35

The University of California Medical Center in San Francisco has clear information on when to keep children out of child care: www.UCSFchildcarehealth.org. Click on "Publications," then "Illness Sheets." Choose the illness of interest, then look for "When Should People Be Excluded." For more information about fever and other illness, see the Mayo Clinic at www.mayoclinic.com.

36. *Teething*

```
              6  8 mo.
                        8–11 mo.
        3  2  1  1  2         16–20 mo.
     4                  3
                           4    10–16 mo.
   5        Upper Jaw        5   20–30 mo.
───────────────────────────────────
20–30 mo.→ 5                  5
10–16 mo.→  4        Lower Jaw    4
16–20 mo.→   3  2  1  1  2  3
 7–10 mo.
              5–7 mo.
```

Designed by Helen F. Neville.

When Do Baby Teeth Usually Come In?

Sometimes teeth just show up. For other kids, teething comes with extra chewing and fussing. Drooling is generally *not* related to teething. More often

Around the World

Teeth come in at different ages depending on a child's race. Children of **African** descent tend to get teeth earlier than children of **European** descent.

it means that the salivary glands now make more saliva and baby hasn't yet learned to swallow it all. The diagram above shows the average age when teeth come in for most children.

37. *Taking Care of Teeth*

Questions	Answers
Will sucking a thumb or pacifier harm my child's teeth?	Before the 3rd birthday, sucking thumb or pacifier doesn't harm children's teeth. See page 181, "Self-Soothing and Security Objects."
What about brushing?	Ideally, start when the first teeth come in. If little ones dislike the feeling of a toothbrush, wipe their teeth with a washcloth while they are in the bathtub. At 3, children can spit out toothpaste. At 3½ to 4, they can brush teeth up and down and back and forth.
How often should we brush?	Ideally twice a day. When that isn't possible, evening brushing is more important.
What about flossing?	Begin flossing once teeth are too close together to reach in between with a brush. Usually this is about 3. Floss two to three times per week at this age. Children can floss their own teeth at 5½ to 6.
When should the first dental checkup be?	At 3, unless there are concerns before then.

Compiled by Helen F. Neville

Help—Is My Child Okay?

All children develop at their own pace. When we watch a group of children who are the same age we see many different levels of skill. Most of these differences are normal. So how do we know whether to wait and watch, or get help, if our child progresses more slowly than others? Because the next step in development usually depends on the one before it, we now know that it is often better *to get help sooner rather than later.*

In general, the following charts show when approximately 75 to 85% of children can do each activity. If, at this age, a child can't do something yet, it *doesn't* mean there is definitely a problem. This skill may soon arrive all on its own. However, if a child is this much later in learning new activities, consider this a "red flag" which simply means it is a good time to check with professionals. Individual evaluation is the only way to decide whether it is better to wait or to get extra help.

There are now many ways professionals can help our little ones directly or *teach us* how to help them. In addition to pediatric nurses and doctors, there are specialists in vision, hearing, social relations, and inborn temperament, as well as speech and language. If kids have trouble with muscle skills or how their body senses the environment, physical and occupational therapists can help. If we sense that our child still needs help, we can keep asking questions.

Every state in the United States has an early intervention program. Federal law requires these intervention programs to test children from birth to 3 years if doctors or *parents* are concerned about development. Children between 3 and 5 can also be tested if they are clearly behind their age mates. School districts or other agencies may run these programs. To find an early intervention program, check with your doctor, nurse, clinic, hospital, or local school district. Even though the states *test* young children, they may only *treat* those with the most difficulty. Children who score above the state cutoff may still benefit from extra professional help. Health insurance may pay these costs or parents may need to pay on their own.

Using these development charts. There are many different reasons why children may be late in learning new skills. If babies were born early, measure their development from the *expected* due date, not the actual birth date. Get more information if little ones are not yet able to do things *at the times listed below,* or if they *lose* skills they had earlier. For example, children with autism are usually diagnosed before age 3. These children may not be learning new skills when expected; or between 12 and 24 months, they may *lose* their earlier ability to make social contact. The guidelines below suggest when to ask professionals for more information.

38. One Month to 12 Months: Concerns About Development and When to Get More Information

See	Hear, Communicate	Relate to Others	Muscles
1 mo. Eyes usually cross. **1 mo.** One or both eyes don't yet move in all directions. **2 mo.** Don't yet move their eyes and head to follow a nearby toy from one side to the other. **3 mo.** Don't yet seem to notice their hands.	**1 mo.** Don't notice loud sounds when awake. **2 mo.** Don't yet make sounds like "ooo" or "aaahhhh."	**1 mo.** Don't like to be touched. **6 wk.** Don't yet smile back at familiar faces or voices. **2 or 3 mo.** Seem very frightened by faces or surroundings. **2 or 3 mo.** Don't yet pay attention to new faces.	**3 mo.** Don't yet hold head up briefly when adult holds baby in a sitting position. **3 mo.** Don't yet bring their hands together.
4 mo. Eyes seem very sensitive to normal daylight: babies continue to fuss, cry, turn their heads, or close their eyes because their eyes don't quickly adjust to brighter light.	**4 mo.** Don't yet turn their heads to a familiar voice or an unusual sound.	**4 mo.** Don't like to cuddle or be touched. **4 mo.** Don't yet seem to enjoy being around people.	**4 mo.** Arms or legs are tight, or limp like a rag doll's. **4 mo.** Don't yet push feet down to hold some weight when held in a standing position. **5 mo.** Don't yet roll from front to back. (All babies need "tummy time" when awake to practice rolling.) **5 mo.** Don't yet reach toward toys.
6 to 7 mo. Don't yet move eyes and head to follow a person or toy that is 6 feet or more away. **7 mo.** Often close one eye or hold head in an odd position when looking at things.	**6 mo.** Always turn the same ear to listen. **6 mo.** Don't yet try to copy sounds we make. **8 mo.** Don't yet "babble," or make sounds like "ba-ba-ba." (Some late talkers don't babble for another few months, but check with your doctor/clinic now.) **8 mo.** Stop babbling a month or so after starting. (Babies who can't hear sounds lose interest in making them.)	**6 mo.** Are still very hard to soothe or comfort. **6 mo.** When we smile, or make faces or sounds, they don't spend several minutes taking turns back and forth with us. **7 mo.** Don't yet try to get our attention with smiles or sounds. **8 mo.** Don't yet play peek-a-boo. **8 mo.** Don't yet actively try to hold our attention with eye contact, sounds, or making faces.	**6 mo.** Don't yet bring a toy to their mouth. **6 mo.** Don't yet shake or bang toys. **6 mo.** Don't yet push head forward to help when we slowly pull them from lying on back to sitting. **6 mo.** Don't regularly use left and right hands to reach for things. (One hand may not be as strong as the other.) **7 mo.** Don't yet stay sitting without support. **10 mo.** Always bounce when held in a standing position and seem uncomfortable with weight on their legs and feet. **11 to 12 mo.** Still drag one side of body after one month of practice crawling. (Some children skip crawling entirely.)

Compiled by Helen F. Neville. Information in charts 38–43 is based primarily on the following sources: Denver Developmental II. California Department of Education: Early Warning Signs. National Easter Seal Society: Are You Listening to What Your Child May Not Be Saying? Alta Bates Medical Center, Berkeley, Calif.: When to Refer a Child for an Occupational Therapy Evaluation. VORT Corp.: HELP Checklist for Early Learning and HELP Checklist for Preschool. Shelov, Steven P., M.D.: Caring for Your Baby and Young Child: Birth to Age 5.

39. Twelve Months to 24 Months: Concerns About Development and When to Get More Information

See, Hear, and Communicate	Pay Attention, Think, Feel, and Relate to Others	Big and Small Muscles
12 mo. Don't yet follow our eyes to see what we are interested in when, for example, we say, "I see a ball over there!" **12 mo.** Don't yet see and pick up small objects from the floor. **12 mo.** Don't yet react when we call their name. **12 mo.** Don't yet understand common words, such as bottle, milk, ball, or doll. **12 mo.** Don't yet use gestures, such as waving "bye-bye," pointing to things, or shaking their head "yes" or "no." **12 mo.** Don't say words such as "Mama" or "Dada."	**12 mo.** Don't yet look for a toy they watched us hide.	**12 mo.** Don't yet clap hands or bang objects together. **12 mo.** Still eat only pureed foods. **12 mo.** Don't yet drop things on purpose, pass things from hand to hand, and pick up things with thumb and finger.
15 mo. Don't yet hand a toy back to an adult. **16 mo.** Don't yet say words for a purpose, such as "up," "bye," "gone," or "me." **18 mo.** Don't yet say 10 to 15 words.	**15 mo.** Don't yet copy what we do with common things, such as a telephone, spoon, brush, etc. **18 to 21 mo.** Don't yet fit easy shapes into a shape board.	**15 mo.** Don't yet walk. Or, after several months of walking, they still walk on their toes, or toes still point way out to the side after 1 mo. of practice. **15 to 18 mo.** Don't yet use a spoon or cup. **18 mo.** Don't yet feed themselves with their fingers. **18 mo.** Don't yet turn thick pages in a book.

Compiled by Helen F. Neville

40. Two Years: Concerns About Development and When to Get More Information

See, Hear, and Communicate	Pay Attention, Think, Feel, and Relate to Others	Muscles
2 yr. Don't see and turn to movement that is off to the side. **2 yr.** Never answer when we call them from a different room. **2 yr.**. Don't yet follow single, easy directions, such as "Get the ball." **2 yr.** Don't yet point to things they want or point to answer a question, such as "Where's the ball?" or "Where's Daddy?" **2 yr.** Don't yet use any two-word phrases, such as "Mommy, up!"	**2 yr.** Don't yet recognize themselves in a mirror. **2 yr.** Don't yet enjoy some activities or toys for two or three minutes. Or go from one thing to the next without interest in any of them. **2 yr.** Bang their heads on floor or wall when angry. **2 to 6 yr.** Often stare into space, rock body, or avoid eye contact.*	**2 yr.** Don't yet sit on and push a wheeled toy with their feet. **2 yr.** Fall often or can't yet walk up and down curbs and stairs easily. (Most children still put both feet on each stair.) **2 yr.** Still drool a lot. **2 yr.** Don't yet build a tower of 4 blocks.
2½ yr. Don't yet point to five or six body parts as we name them. **2½ yr.** Don't yet talk clearly enough that we can understand some words.	**2½ yr.** Don't yet seem interested in other children. **2½ to 3 yr.** Don't yet pretend, as in "driving" a toy car along the floor or "feeding" a doll.	**2½ yr.** Still hold a crayon or marker with whole hand instead of just fingers.

*In some cultures children are taught not to make eye contact as a sign of respect to elders.

Compiled by Helen F. Neville

41. Three Years: Concerns About Development and When to Get More Information

See and Hear	Understand, Think, and Talk	Feel and Relate to Others	Muscles
3 yr. Don't yet see things that are a block away.	**3 yr.** Don't yet understand "more" and "less." **3 yr.** Don't yet understand simple stories we read. **3 yr.** Don't yet speak clearly enough that we can understand most (about 80%) of what they say. **3 yr.** Don't yet use "me" and "you" correctly. **3 yr.** Don't yet use three-word sentences, such as "Go away, kitty."	**3 yr.** Refuse to talk or play with familiar children or adults outside the immediate family. **3 yr.** Don't show interest in playing with other children. (Many preschoolers have just one friend, which is fine.)	**3 yr.** Don't yet balance on each foot for one second. **3 yr.** Don't yet pedal a tricycle and jump up and down in place. **3 yr.** Don't yet pull up pants or unbutton large buttons, even when given plenty of time.* **3 yr.** Don't yet use one hand (left or right) more than the other. **3 yr.** Don't yet cut paper with scissors, build a tower of 8 blocks, and do a puzzle where each piece fits in its own space. **3 yr.** Don't yet copy a circle after watching an adult draw one. (Doesn't have to be a good circle, just one that closes pretty well.)
	3½ yr. Don't yet follow two-part directions, such as "Open the drawer and take out a spoon."	**3½ to 4 yr.** Don't yet know how to join other children in play, so they push and hit to get started.	**3½ yr.** Don't yet close fingers and wiggle just their thumbs. **3½ yr.** Still hold a crayon or marker with whole hand instead of just fingers.

* In some cultures parents regularly dress preschoolers, so they can't yet dress themselves.

Compiled by Helen F. Neville

42. Four Years: Concerns About Development and When to Get More Information

Hear	Understand, Think, and Talk	Feel and Relate to Others	Muscles
4 yr. Still usually talk in a very loud or soft voice.	**4 yr.** Don't yet talk clearly enough that strangers can understand most of what they say. **4 yr.** Don't yet ask lots of questions. **4 yr.** Don't yet answer easy questions, such as "What do you do when you are hungry?" **4 yr.** Don't yet talk about things they like, or play make-believe games, such as "house" or "firefighter." **4½ yr.** Don't yet name four colors.	**4 to 4½ yr.** Still hurt friends (or caregivers) by hitting, pinching, or pushing. Or repeatedly break things or hurt animals on purpose. Such actions are especially concerning if children don't feel sorry afterward. **4 to 4½ yr.** Don't yet play games with other children, such as hide-and-seek. **4 to 4½ yr.** Often seem angry, stubborn, and hard to discipline. **4 to 4½ yr.** Get very frustrated when trying to do simple tasks that most others their age can do. **4 to 5 yr.** Are so shy that it really limits what they can do. **4 to 6 yr.** Don't often try to please parents or caregivers, or don't enjoy getting praise. **4 to 6 yr.** Often stare into space, rock body, or avoid eye contact. **4½ to 5 yr.** Are very impulsive and not aware of dangers, such as traffic.	**4 yr.** Still put both feet on each stair. **4 yr.** Don't yet cut along a thick line with scissors. **4 yr.** Don't yet do a five- or six-piece interlocking puzzle. **4 to 4½ yr.** Don't yet copy a "+" by themselves. **4½ yr.** Can't yet hop on one foot.

Compiled by Helen F. Neville

43. Five Years: Concerns About Development and When to Get More Information

Understand, Think, and Talk	Feel and Relate to Others	Muscles
5 yr. Don't yet talk to age mates while playing together. **5 yr.** Don't yet say their own age. **5 yr.** Don't yet understand "today," "tomorrow," and "yesterday."	**5 to 5½ yr.** Don't yet share and take turns, even for short periods. **5 to 5½ yr.** Don't yet show concern for others who are sad or hurt. **5 to 5½ yr.** Often hurt playmates' feelings by saying mean things. **5 to 6 yr.** Don't act proud and show off at times.	**5 yr.** Don't yet catch a large ball that is bounced and pump themselves on a swing. **5 yr.** Don't yet balance on each foot for five seconds. **5 yr.** Don't yet copy a square after watching an adult draw one. **5¾ yr.** Don't yet copy a square all by themselves.

Compiled by Helen F. Neville.

Humor: What Makes Children Laugh?

When we laugh, we suddenly release emotional and physical tension that has been building inside us. Laughing lifts our mood and relaxes our body. Humor is a great lifetime companion. Not surprisingly, what we find funny changes with age.

2 yr. From 18 months through 3 years, toddlers think it is funny when we, and later they, fall down or bump into things on purpose, or "accidentally" spill things. Around 2½ toddlers light up when things are different than expected, as when we pretend to eat a shoe or drive a toy car into their ear. They love silly sounds and funny questions, such as "Are you going to eat a train for breakfast?"

3 yr. These preschoolers enjoy moving and falling in funny ways. They love it when we put a jacket on inside out or

Troublesome Tickling

Most little ones delight in being tickled. The "tickle feeling" is carried by two sets of nerves at the same time: both light touch and pain. Pain nerves connect to centers in the brain for danger and fear. Because of this wiring, tickling can be great fun one moment and very upsetting the next. If little ones aren't having fun, back off!

make wrong guesses: "Is that a cat barking?" "Is the rain falling up yet?" "Is that a nose on the end of your foot?" They enjoy funny sound effects: "The rain goes plop, plop."

4 yr. Fours love silly sounds, rhymes, and made-up words. Some of their humor seems rather grim to us as they make up stories and laugh about people falling, getting hurt, or becoming trapped. Fours often work hard to restrain their aggressive impulses. Humor lets them talk about being aggressive without actually hurting anyone.

5 yr. Fives are generally more serious than 4s and less likely to think other people are funny. Even so, they may enjoy fooling us and watching for the funny, unexpected things that happen in daily life.

Imagination Blooms

Using our imagination is just plain fun most of the time. Children also use it to practice activities of daily life, including how to manage feelings. They also try out adult roles: Elena talks to her dolly in the same way Mom talks to Elena. Children pretend to be store clerks, astronauts, and more. Imagination improves language, creativity, and the ability to solve problems. All children go through the same steps in learning to use their imagination, but some move along faster than others. This timetable shows how most children progress. It is especially important for us to join in and encourage imaginary play if children haven't started on their own by 2 or 2½.

What Children Pretend at Different Ages

18 mo. to 2 yr.
- They pretend to be themselves doing something different. For example, they may pretend to eat or sleep.
- They pretend a single scene with realistic toys, such as eating from a toy dish or talking on a toy telephone.

2 yr.
- They talk to stuffed animals, trains, and dolls.
- They act out daily events, such as going to the store.

- In particular, they act out difficult events, like saying "bye-bye" to Mommy or Daddy or getting a shot at the doctor's office.
- They begin to tell stories that flow from the toys at hand. For example, with a train and cow: "Cow rides the train. Cow falls off."
- Both boys and girls this age commonly imagine falling, crashing, and getting hurt because these are common experiences for toddlers.

3 yr.

- They begin to pretend that one thing is something else.
- A stick becomes a spoon, a row of blocks becomes a fence, or a pat of mud becomes a pie.
- They can imagine things that are entirely in their heads without props or without ever having done them before: "We're in the spaceship." "I'm a firefighter."
- They begin to talk to toys, based on what they imagine the toy is doing: "No, Bear, you can't get up. It's bedtime. You have to stay in bed."
- Play becomes less self-centered. When younger, they always played one of the parts. Now, Teddy Bear takes Debbie Doll to the store.
- They imagine a set of connected events: "They go to the store and get milk and bananas. Then they go home and make a banana milkshake."

4 yr.

- Imagination is now triggered from the inside. The 2-year-old played "train" because the toy train was there. At 4 he thinks, "I want to fly an airplane. I'll go get the blocks and build one."
- Children often work with each other to play out a set of events which might occur at school, in an office or hospital, or whatever. Their minds are flexible, so they may start with one scene and then easily blend it into another.
- Boys most often make up stories about boys, while girls most often make up stories about mothers and girls.

- 4s' stories are often violent. This was the case long before television. Dishes break and cars crash. People fall and get eaten up or otherwise killed. Such stories may reflect how often children this age accidentally drop, break, and spoil things. They may also suggest how hard they try (and how often they fail) to keep their actions and feelings in control. At 4, girls' stories are more violent than at any other age.

5 to 7 yr.

- Sometime during these years, they figure out who the real tooth fairy is.

How to Encourage Imagination

We can encourage imagination by joining in our child's make-believe play.

With toddlers. Make "vvrroom vvrrroomm" noises as you move a toy car across the floor. Pretend to be a cat—crawl, "meow," and rub noses.

With preschoolers. Invite them to continue their stories. Evan said, "The cow falls off the train," and had nothing more to say, so Dad asked, "Then what does the cow do?"

Invite children to process emotions. Use an animal or doll to ask a question, then wait for the child to answer. "Mommy, do I have to get a shot today?" "When will you come get me from child care?" "How does Bear feel when Mom is away on a trip?"

Invite children to solve imaginary (and real) problems. "What could we do if our car didn't work? How would we get some food to eat?"

Imaginary Friends

Between 3½ and 4½ children often have invisible or imaginary friends. There's no reason to worry unless children often prefer to be with these companions *instead* of regular ones. Be friendly. Ask, "How is Aurora?" or "What did Aurora tell you about today?" (If children repeatedly blame an imaginary friend when something gets spilled or broken, read these additional sections: page 77, "Why Do 4s Stretch the Truth?" and page 122, "Why Do Children Follow Our Rules?")

Impulse Control

■■■

An impulse is a sudden wish to throw a spoon, pull someone's hair, run in the street, or give Mom a hug. Unfortunately, the part of the brain that *stops* unwanted impulses matures later than the part that *has* impulses. Therefore, **most 2s** can't control their impulses. It is vital to childproof our homes and watch our children carefully so they don't hurt themselves or others. **At 3,** most quiet, mellow, and adaptable children have fairly good impulse control.

At 4, about one out of ten preschoolers still can't control their strongest impulses. They *know* they should not throw their toys, scream, hit people, or grab the pretty vase at Grandma's house. They *know* they should stay near Mom in the store. However, they don't yet have brakes strong enough to stop themselves every time. The brakes for impulse control are in the frontal lobes of the brain, just under our foreheads. This part of the brain doesn't fully mature until the early twenties. Not surprisingly, these children often feel bad about themselves because they know what they are supposed to do (or not do), but they can't do the right thing. Their self-esteem can get badly bruised. They need a few clear rules, as well

44. Temperament and Impulse Control

Traits That Make Impulse Control Harder	How to Help
Activity: High Energy	**All ages:** Make sure children get plenty of exercise, sleep, and snacks. **2 yr. and up:** Show them what they can do with their angry energy—bite a rubber bracelet on their arm, stomp their feet, hit pillows, etc. **5 yr.:** Teach ways to wiggle without disturbing others—wiggle tongue inside mouth or toes inside shoes; rub the underside of the wrist with the thumb; or squeeze a ball inside a pocket.
Curiosity: Very Curious	**All ages:** Some kids are attracted to new things like bees to flowers. Encourage them to ask before exploring. Try to teach them how to explore gently, carefully, and safely.
Intensity: Strong Emotions	**2 to 5 yr.:** "Let's pretend we're angry. What can we do?" (A good answer: Stomp our feet!) **4 to 6 yr.:** Help them practice appropriate words.
Frustration: Easily Frustrated	**All ages:** Offer rewards for waiting: "We can walk to the end of the block and back now. Or, if you wait till I finish putting away the laundry, we can walk all the way around the block." **3 yr. and up:** Help them to break difficult tasks into smaller, easier parts.
Sensitivity: Not Very Sensitive	**3 to 5 yr.:** Some children look impulsive as they race and whirl around, crash into friends, and break things. Unlike other children, their bodies may not tell them exactly where they are in space or how fast they are moving. They don't understand that what doesn't hurt them does hurt others. **For more information,** see *The Out-of-Sync Child* by Carol Kranowitz, or talk to an occupational therapist about "sensory processing."
Sensitivity: Very Sensitive	**3 yr. and up:** Help these children find a quiet place away from others where they can take a break when they feel overloaded by a busy environment or hemmed in by people coming too close. **4 to 6 yr.:** Help them find plain, quiet places where they can concentrate more easily. **For more information,** see *The Out-of-Sync Child* by Carol Kranowitz.

Compiled by Helen F. Neville

45. Games to Encourage Impulse Control

Age	Games
18 mo. and up	◆ Set something interesting on a low table. Say, "Wait for me. I'll hold it and then you can touch it." Over time, gradually wait a few seconds longer. Praise child's success.
2 yr. and up	◆ Take turns: Parent or child walks until the other says, "Stop." Gradually try it with other activities, such as squeezing a finger, clapping, running in circles, jumping, etc. Praise child's success.
3 yr. and up	◆ Take turns talking: One person sings or talks until the other says, "Stop." ◆ Set out something interesting. Say, "Sit on your hands and tell me about it. What do you think it would feel like?"
4 yr. and up	◆ Play children's games, such as "Red Light, Green Light" and "Simon Says." ◆ Put a piece of popcorn on the child's shoulder and say, "Stand still so it doesn't fall off. Now turn your head slowly, stick out your tongue, and catch the piece of popcorn." Praise child's success.

Compiled by Helen F. Neville

as reminders, support, forgiveness, emotional outlets, and opportunities to try again.

By 6 or 7, most children usually have good impulse control. Some usually don't. There are several possible reasons, but one is that their brains work differently due to ADHD (Attention Deficit Hyperactive Disorder). Both trouble paying attention and trouble controlling impulses are common symptoms of ADHD. Most of us rely on a small part of the brain to automatically keep us out of trouble: "I'd like to . . . , but it's *not* a good idea!" Imagine your life if those brain cells were often napping. It would be like driving a car with brakes that rarely work. Without auto-

matic impulse control, it's constant hard work to do the right thing. To understand the difference between automatic and voluntary actions, imagine people complaining every time you blink—and imagine how hard it would be to remember all day, everyday, not to blink.

See page 104, "Attention Deficit Disorder."

Games to Practice Impulse Control

We usually want children to control their impulses "right now" while emotions still run high. However, we all learn better with relaxed practice. Games are an enjoyable way to practice impulse control. Play those in chart 45 above and use your imagination to make up more.

Independence and Responsibility

Realistically, how much can young kids take care of themselves and help around the house? With our strong cultural belief in independence, we often want them to take care of themselves, their rooms, and their toys *by themselves*. However, helping *others* gives kids a greater sense of pride and importance. (They don't yet understand that taking care of their own things helps us.)

Because most children under 6 or 8 generally work better as part of a team, doing household chores together is likely to go more smoothly—we

Around the World

In cultures which emphasize *interdependence*, such as **Japan and China,** parents often dress children long after they are able to dress themselves.

help with their things and they help us with some family chores. By the way, studies suggest that "helpfulness" is in part genetic—some children naturally pitch in. Others need more encouragement to do their share.

Children (like adults) are more capable when they are relaxed. When we rush them, they need more help. Try to keep mornings relaxed. If weekdays are really hectic, help them dress if needed. Encourage them to dress themselves on weekends. Praise them as they succeed.

46. Self-Care—What Can Most Children Do?

Age	Task
2 yr.	◆ Can pull pants off. (If skin is sensitive, may resist having clothes put on. Find soft, comfortable ones.)
2½ yr.	◆ Can pull shoes off, unbutton large buttons, unzip zippers and Velcro.™
3 to 3½ yr.	◆ Can undress if clothes are easy and pull pants on. ◆ Know where to find own clothes and toys. ◆ Can hang jacket on a low hook and put dirty clothes in an easy-to-open, low hamper.
3½ to 4 yr.	◆ Can wash and dry hands. ◆ Can hang up a towel.
4 yr.	◆ Can get dressed in easy clothes when not rushed. (Use large buttons and easy zippers. Put dots on shoes to show how the "big toes kiss" and put dots inside waistbands that "kiss the bellybutton.") ◆ Can blow own nose, wash own hands, and manage own hair if it is easy.
5 yr.	◆ Can find fronts and backs of clothes. ◆ Can bathe, dress, and go to the bathroom alone, though may occasionally need help.
5½ to 6 yr.	◆ Can remember to cover mouth or nose with elbow when coughs or sneezes. (Coughing onto hands spreads germs more easily.) ◆ Can dress and undress without being reminded. ◆ Can hang a jacket on a clothes hanger. ◆ Can think ahead about clothes that will be appropriate for the day's weather.

Compiled by Helen F. Neville

47. Around the House—How Can Most Children Help?

Age	Task
2 yr.	**Kitchen:** Rinse fruits and vegetables, rip lettuce for salad, rinse or "wash" plastic dishes, and help clear dishwasher by handing things to parents. **Laundry:** Put family clothes in hamper. **Other:** Dust with a feather duster; collect snails in the garden.
3 yr.	**Kitchen:** Fill and level a measuring cup, stir batter, hand grate from a big piece of soft cheese, use hand eggbeater, butter toast, sweep table crumbs into a bowl, help load dishwasher, put away silverware, and sort recycling. **Laundry:** Help load washing machine. **Other:** Hold the dustpan, sweep hallway or steps with a small broom, collect household litter into wastebasket, wipe dirty woodwork, collect and sort toys, water indoor and outdoor plants, help plant seeds and plants, and clear the lawn of toys before mowing.
4 to 6 yr.	**Kitchen:** Plan a simple meal, make simple snacks, use vegetable peeler and can opener, use toaster and microwave, cut soft fruit with close supervision, set the table (mark place setting on inexpensive place mats), help clear table (a bread pan on sink counter holds silverware), put away groceries, rinse dishes, and clean kitchen sink. **Laundry/Bath:** Sort clothes by color, match socks, fold towels and pillowcases. Rinse out tub after bath, wash sink, clean toilet bowl, change pillowcases, fold T-shirts, and put away laundry. **Other:** Polish furniture, clean windows and mirrors, vacuum easy areas, help make beds, sort and stack magazines, turn off lights, put stamps on the bills and family cards, feed pets, wash pet dishes, empty trash and recycling, carry in firewood, wash car, pull weeds, rake leaves, clip off dead flowers, stomp out bad bugs, fix things with screwdriver and lightweight hammer, load the grocery cart, and run an errand to a next-door neighbor.
5 yr.	May be ready to cross a quiet street for an errand to a neighbor's or the corner store.

Compiled by Helen F. Neville

How Do We Get Children to Help Around the House?

Children can build pride and self-confidence from helping at home. On the other hand, they often resist our control. How do we work with these two facts? Chart 48 shows realistic expectations and how to encourage effort. These techniques can be used to help children learn and do the tasks in chart 47 above.

48. How to Encourage Cooperation

Age	What Are Realistic Expectations?	How to Say It
2 yr.	Expect nothing! The load is entirely on us to take care of children, their belongings, and our home. We'll only be disappointed and frustrated if we expect them to help. On the other hand, we can invite them to help. Toddlers like to copy us, so they sometimes help a little bit. When they offer, it is wise to welcome and appreciate their "help" even if it slows us down and makes our life more difficult at the moment.	◆ *Would you like to put away this block or the doll?* (Accept "No" if that is the answer.) ◆ *I have to pick up the toys before I can read you a story. Thank you for helping!*
3 yr.	3s sometimes enjoy being helpful for a minute or two and sometimes they don't. Make household chores a regular part of your routine so children see the *how* and *when* of housework: clothes go in hamper before bath, toys get picked up before story, bed is made before going out of the house, etc.	◆ *I need to collect all the trash before I read a story. Could you bring the wastebasket from the bathroom? I'd really appreciate your help!* ◆ *Maybe you'll help me next time.*
4 yr.	Because 4s are good at so many things, it is easy to expect too much of them. They don't have the self-discipline to work on things that are hard, long, or boring, especially when they are alone. They quickly get discouraged. Even getting dressed from start to finish is hard for some. They can't remember when chores need to be done, unless these are part of the daily routine. They work better as part of a team—especially a team that's fun to be on. The team will be fun if we make the job easy and interesting. A few are able to work alone and prefer to do so. 4s are still self-centered, so they need to see the personal benefit of helping. They are just learning about cause and effect. They are impressed when they can see that their effort makes a difference.	◆ *The laundry needs to be sorted before we go out [or before we eat, watch the video, etc.] Some help would be really nice. Can you find all the washcloths? Put pairs of socks together?* ◆ *If you help with the toys, we'll be ready sooner.* (Dad works slowly when Spencer just watches and faster when Spencer helps.) ◆ *Thank you for helping me. Now we're ready sooner!* ◆ Reminders often work better in the form of questions: *What needs to get done before we go out?* or *What comes before bedtime stories?*
5 yr.	If we want children to help around the house before they move out, it will never get any easier than now. Fives are eager to be trusted with responsibility and are strongly connected to home. They have the physical skills to be genuinely helpful. Discuss needed jobs, how to rotate them and whether kids prefer to work alone or together. Helping the family feels more important than just taking care of their own things. At 5, Malik plans and cooks easy Sunday dinners with Mom as his assistant—he'd started with Sunday lunches at 4.	◆ *Thank you for....* ◆ *You're a terrific helper when you....* ◆ *Life is easier in this family with your help!*

Compiled by Helen F. Neville

Money: "Mommy, Can I Have...?"

We can begin to teach the basics about money at 4 and 5.

It takes money to buy things. Let children pass money to the store clerk. They can play store at home with food, toys, and some real coins.

Money doesn't grow on trees. At the bank machine explain: "The bank keeps money for people so they won't lose it. It gives us back our own money." Show them when we deposit money, and say, "When we get money from work, we put it in the bank to keep it safe." When using a credit card explain: "It is sometimes easier to use this plastic card than to carry money. But later we have to pay real money for what we bought with the card."

Family living is about cooperation, not dollars. In general, avoid paying children for regular household chores. If it is just about money, kids sometimes refuse to help, saying, "I don't want to buy anything." Furthermore, as the years go by, we'll resent paying more each year for them to do their part.

There are ways to save money. In the store, point out that things cost more or less depending on the brand and package size. Children can help look for sale signs on items we use regularly.

What does an allowance teach? A regular weekly allowance is the most effective way to teach that money is limited, and we have to make choices when we spend it. Many children are ready to start around 5 when they can count ten dimes. Instead of listening to "I want" and "Buy me a . . . ", we can say, "I don't want to spend *my* money on that, but you are welcome to spend *yours*." Children learn faster when *they* make the choices.

How Much Allowance Should Young Children Get?

When planning an allowance, realize that in the beginning children may spend it all on candy and cheap toys. Fig- ure out about how much you already spend on such items. Or ask yourself, "How much am I willing to see 'wasted' each week while my child learns important lessons about money?" Either amount of money can be used as a baseline. Children gradually learn what lasts and has more value. If candy is still a problem after several months, some families say that only a certain amount of money (or none) may be spent on candy.

Because Melody, 5, loves art, her parents adjusted her allowance so she could buy her own crayons, markers, and paint. At 5, Elena's parents started her allowance with coins, a purse, and two bottles. Each week Elena decides how many coins to put in her purse for immediate spending, how many to save in one bottle for bigger items, and how much to put in her charity bottle. This way she can see the amounts grow. Dad found charities that interested her. Elena chose to give her charity money to the baby elephant fund at the zoo. In Malik's family, 10% of his money goes into a long-term savings account. Whatever Spencer puts in his savings account, his parents *match*— they put in the same amount to encourage saving.

Before going to the store, Evan's dad asks, "Do you want to take your wallet or leave it at home?" Without his wallet, Evan has no money to spend. Because some children are apt to lose money, parents may pay at the store and settle accounts back home. Raise allowances just once a year on birthdays to avoid constant discussion.

What to Do When Children Can't Afford Something They Want

We have many options to help show children ways they can afford things.

Draw a chart so they can see when they will have enough allowance to buy the item they want.

Offer special jobs to earn extra money—such as sort drawers or sweep the garage.

Go to a secondhand store where they can find something similar for less.

Put it on layaway. Store it in our closet until it is paid for. (Dad avoided this approach with spirited Shauna because he knew there would be no peace while the doll was in his closet.)

Have a wish list on the refrigerator for future birthday or holiday presents. Let children add and cross things off as their interests change. (Evan's final birthday list was shorter after Mom made a new family rule: "For each new toy that comes into the house, we need to make space. We give away an old toy to children who don't have many.")

Split fifty-fifty. Some parents, if they believe something is especially worthwhile, offer to pay half. This works well in some families, but in others it causes endless discussion.

Offer sympathy. Tell about a time when we had a similar disappointment of not being able to have what we wanted.

Muscles in Motion

There is no way to drive quickly across a city before the expressways are built. Similarly, there is no way to quickly coordinate our muscles before "superhighways" are built between control centers in the brain and our muscles. In our bodies, turning streets into freeways means building the layer of myelin insulation around the nerves. Just as cities build expressways in one area before another, young brains improve some areas before others. For this reason, milestones in normal physical development vary tremendously. For example, some babies sit before they crawl and others crawl before they sit. Some concentrate on walking first, others on talking first—one big job at a time.

In general, the more complicated the task, the greater the age difference when children learn it. Imagine we observe a large group of *typical* kids for five years. They all learn to sit without support over 1½ months and say "oooh" and "aah" over 3 months. During 6 months they all say their first few words. They all learn to copy a square during a 16-month time frame, and all balance on one foot for a few seconds over the course of 20 months.

Temperament and gender also affect muscle skills. Higher energy children more often practice large muscle activities. Lower energy ones more often practice small muscle skills. For this reason, a particular child is often farther ahead in one area than the other. Because boys begin to develop larger muscles around 4, they can usually jump farther. And because the lower part of their arm is longer, most can also throw farther. On the other hand, most girls do better with balance and fancy footwork, such as hopping and skipping.

Tummy time. Start tummy time in the first few weeks of life, when babies are awake and alert. Place them tummy down for a few minutes several times a day on a firm mattress or on your chest or lap if they are more comfortable. Some babies resist a lot if you start later. Tummy time develops the neck strength needed for head control. It encourages babies to exercise their arms and prevents the back of the head from getting flat. Low energy babies who move less may need extra tummy time to build neck strength. Because babies now spend much more time on their backs to prevent SIDS, many learn to roll over later than they used to. A few even roll from back to front before they roll from front to back.

Swimming. Because babies and toddlers are prone to ear infections, putting their heads under water is not recommended. Sometime between 3 and 6 years most children become comfortable in the water. Gradually they put their faces in, float, dog-paddle, and swim. Children who have trouble learning to swim may do better in warm water where they can relax more easily.

Left-handed or right-handed? About 5% of children are left-handed. Some identical twins are mirror images of each other, so their fingerprints, handedness, and hair whorls are opposite. Left-handedness is more common in boys. Left-handedness is more common in babies whose mother's labor was difficult. Lefties are more likely to be ambidextrous—use both hands equally—or use different hands for different skills. (Regular scissors are harder to use left-handed than right-handed.) Left-handers are slightly more likely to have physical, learning, or behavioral problems. They are also slightly more likely to have exceptional talent in language or math. Most children have settled on being either right-handed or left-handed by 30 months of age.

See page 174, "Learning Is Harder."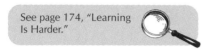

On Average, What Might Happen, and When?

The following chart looks at averages for new skills—the point at which **about half of children, or 50%, have al-**ready learned the skill and about half are still working on it. Many normal, healthy children will learn these skills *months* after the times noted here. These charts simply show the obvious: over time children become amazingly more capable.

As their parents, it is *not* our job to push. Most young children perform worse under pressure. Our job is to offer timely opportunities and enjoy the process along the way. The best way for children to learn is by *having fun at their own pace.* If you are worried that your child may not be developing normally, talk with you doctor or clinic.

See page 149, "Help—Is My Child Okay?"

49. What Can Muscles Do at Different Ages?

Average Age	Large Muscle Skills (Gross Motor Skills)	Small Muscle Skills (Fine Motor Skills)
2½ mo.	◆ Lift head while awake and lying on tummy for "tummy time."	
3 mo.	◆ Hold head up when adult holds body in a sitting position.	◆ Bring hands together.
3½ mo.	◆ Roll from tummy to back. This will be later if babies don't get much "tummy time." Caution! Some young athletes roll off beds when just a few days old.	◆ Hold a toy.
5 mo.		◆ Reach and grab a toy.
5½ mo.	◆ When held in a standing position, support most of their own weight.	
6 mo.	◆ Sit without support and use hands for play.	◆ Bang a toy on the table. ◆ Pass a toy from one hand to the other.
6½ mo.	◆ Roll from back to tummy.	
8 mo.	◆ Stand while holding on.	
9 mo.		◆ Pick up little things with thumb and index finger. ◆ Hold a block in each hand and bang them together.
9½ mo.	◆ Sit down, while holding onto furniture.	
10 mo.	◆ Crawl on hands and knees	◆ Open hand on purpose to drop things.
13 mo.	◆ Walk easily without support.* (About 15% walk without ever crawling.)	

* When toddlers begin to walk, their toes normally point outwards toward the side. This gives them better balance. After several months of practice, toes gradually point more toward the front.

Continued on next page

49. *What Can Muscles Do at Different Ages?* (continued)

Average Age	Large Muscle Skills (Gross Motor Skills)	Small Muscle Skills (Fine Motor Skills)
14 mo.	◆ Walk a few steps backwards.	◆ Point with an index finger.
15 mo.		◆ Build a tower of two small blocks.
16½ mo.	◆ Throw a ball underhand.	
17 mo.		◆ Use one hand to hold a toy and the other to poke or tug at it.
18 mo.		◆ Put six round pegs in a pegboard.
20 mo.	◆ Kick a large, still ball.	◆ Build a tower of four small blocks.
21 mo.	◆ Ride a riding toy that doesn't have pedals.	
24 mo.		◆ Hold a crayon against the palm of the hand, as we hold a broom. See picture on page 173. ◆ String three one-inch beads.
25 mo.	◆ Walk upstairs alone, putting both feet on each step. ◆ Catch a soft 12-inch diameter ball that is tossed or bounced.	
26 mo.	◆ Jump up and down on both feet.	
26½ mo.	◆ Walk downstairs alone, putting both feet on each step.	
27 mo.	◆ Ride a tricycle.**	◆ Fold a piece of paper once.
30 mo.	◆ Jump on a trampoline while holding an adult hand.	◆ Generally prefer to use either the left or right hand. ◆ Build a tower of eight blocks. ◆ Put six square pegs in a pegboard.
32 mo.	◆ Walk upstairs alternating feet without holding railing. (Walking down comes later.)	◆ Cut along a thick line with scissors.
33 mo.	◆ Walk easily on tiptoes. ◆ Jump over a string a few inches high.	◆ Copy a circle that is seen on a page. This may not be a very exact circle.
3 yr.	◆ Run on toes.	◆ Hold a pencil with thumb and fingers, more like an adult—except pointer finger's last joint bends inward instead of out. See picture on page 173.
3 yr., 3 mo.		◆ Build a bridge with three blocks.
3 yr., 4 mo.	◆ Jump off a 12-inch-high step. ◆ Bounce and catch a large ball.	

** Before 7, most children need training wheels on a two-wheel bicycle.

Continued on next page

49. *What Can Muscles Do at Different Ages?* (continued)

Average Age	Large Muscle Skills (Gross Motor Skills)	Small Muscle Skills (Fine Motor Skills)
3 yr., 6 mo.	◆ Hop on one foot.	◆ Cut with scissors along an easy curve.
3 yr., 8 mo.	◆ Jump with two feet together.	
4 yr.	◆ Copy a model: string beads or put blocks in the same easy pattern as one they see.	
4 yr., 2 mo.	◆ Pump self on a swing.	
4 yr., 4 mo.		◆ Put paste on one side of a paper, turn it over and place it in the desired spot.
4 yr., 5 mo.	◆ Forward roll or somersault. ◆ Balance on each foot for five seconds.	
4 yr., 8 mo.	◆ Kick a large ball that rolls toward them.	
4 yr., 10 mo.	◆ Walk along a 4-inch-wide beam.	◆ Trace around own hand.
4 yr., 11 mo.	◆ Throw a ball ten feet, overhand.	
5 yr.	◆ Hang from an overhead bar.	
5 yr., 3 mo.		◆ Copy a square without any help.
5 yr., 9 mo.	◆ Skip forward.	

Compiled by Helen F. Neville

Music for Minors

Newborns recognize music they heard often before birth, especially what Mom sang to them. They pay more attention when we sing or play a tune they already know. Babies recognize pitch, tune, and rhythm, the basic components of music. Five-month-olds notice when we change a note in a familiar tune. Their surprise shows up as a change in heart rate.

With relaxed practice, some 6- to 9-month-olds can match the pitch of a single sound, as when we sing "ooo" higher or lower. First, match the pitch the baby makes, then try it the other way around. Threes and 4s may sing a single line in tune, such as the first line of "Twinkle, Twinkle, Little Star." At this age, they tend to lose pitch when they start the next line. Many 5s sing a number of short familiar songs entirely in tune.

It is much easier to learn to sing in tune with just one or two other people, so children can hear and adjust their pitch as they sing. When singing in a group, they can't hear whether or not they are in tune. Some children sing on pitch more easily after they turn 6. This can be a good time for gentle practice to learn this skill, if they haven't already done so. For some, it is easier to learn songs that include hand or body motions.

Bedtime, at the dinner table, and in the car can be especially good times to sing to and with little ones. If you're not comfortable leading, play a CD and sing along.

People who have *absolute* pitch can always start a song on the exact same note, no matter where they are. It is as if they have a piano inside their head so they can "play" and sing the same note every time. This was long thought to be a rare, genetic ability. However, musical training in Japan suggests that about half of all children can learn this skill if they get practice between 3 and 6 years.

Babies as young as 9 months to 1 year begin to make up little songs—a pattern of several notes that they repeat. Twos and 3s add words to their songs. We can encourage these young composers if we enjoy their songs and sing them back.

Motion and rhythm go together. Most babies and young children love it when we hold and rock them or dance. Toddlers and 2s enjoy making music with drums, maracas, cymbals, xylophones, and clapping. Find instruments that have a pleasant tone. Once they are securely able to stand, toddlers love to sway or wiggle their bodies to music in their first dances. Threes enjoy the two-beat rhythm of marching. With 4s, take turns leading and copying different rhythm patterns of two, three, or four beats. Music, sometimes mistaken as a track all on its own, also supports and improves other kinds of learning.

See "The American Music Conference" at www.amc-music.org for more information.

Numbers and Sense of Time

Numbers and time are a basic part of modern life. We sometimes forget that numbers don't yet mean very much to our little ones. Even *saying* numbers is not the same as *understanding* them. (See chart 50.)

Parents often wonder how far ahead to tell children about upcoming events. For many children, especially those who are "natural planners" (slow to adapt), knowing about things ahead of time is very important. However, giving more warning than children can understand just confuses them. Chart 50 suggests how far ahead to tell children about day-to-day events such as a visit down the street to Grandmother's house or a doctor's appointment.

For big events, such as a vacation, family move, or new baby, children know far ahead of time that something important is coming up, but they don't understand *when*. Mom told 2-year-old Spencer that she would go to the hospital when his brother was born. Spencer was upset and clingy, day after day. Then Mom marked her due date on the calendar. Every morning for the next two months, they crossed off one day. With this daily reminder that "today is not the day," Spencer became much calmer.

See page 121, "Discipline and Children's Sense of Time" chart.

50. Numbers—What Do Children Understand?

Age	What Most Children Understand
2 yr.	◆ Can say "1, 2, 3 . . ." but only understand the idea of "one." (A few may use "2" to mean all numbers larger than 1.)
3 yr.	◆ Can say and understand "3," as in 3 crackers. ◆ Understand the meaning of *more* and *less*.
4 yr.	◆ Can say numbers 1 through 10. ◆ Understand and count on fingers to 3 or 4.
5 yr.	◆ Understand and count 10 to 12 things as in 12 crackers.

Compiled by Helen F. Neville

51. Time—What Do Children Understand?

Age	What Most Children Understand	When to Tell Children About Coming Events
2 yr.	◆ "Now." ◆ "In a minute." ◆ "After lunch." ◆ "After dinner." ◆ "When the timer rings." ◆ "After the video."	Five minutes to an hour ahead.
2½ to 3 yr.	◆ "Tomorrow." ◆ "Someday" means any day after tomorrow. ◆ "Yesterday" means all days before today.	One hour to one day ahead.
3 yr.	◆ The difference between a point in time (right after dinner) and a period of time (tonight). ◆ A month and a year are equally far away.	One day ahead.
4 yr.	◆ "A minute" is different from "5 minutes." ◆ "Next week." ◆ "Next month" means a long time. ◆ "Next year" means a very long time.	One day to several weeks ahead.
5 yr.	◆ Days of the week, months, and seasons.	One day to several months ahead.

Compiled by Helen F. Neville

Pets

It takes a patient pooch to put up with a 2 who pokes eyes and pulls tails. Not surprisingly, most pets keep their distance from small children. Starting around 3, however, it can be a joy to watch a preschooler snuggle with a purring cat or romp with the family dog. Pets can bring fun and a deep, loving connection. They also remind our children to consider the needs of another.

Realistically, *we* will be the primary caregivers of any pet in our home. Though they are willing helpers, most 5s can't remember to feed pets regularly. Cleaning guinea pig cages or fish tanks may be exciting the first few times, but few 5s will carry through with the task unless it is a family project.

If *we're* not ready to commit to a long-living cat or dog (10 or more years), then a fish, rat, guinea pig, rabbit, or parakeet (2 to 8 years) may be a better choice. Or the short-term enthusiasm of a 4 may be best suited to a caterpillar or beetle that visits in a jar for a few days and is then released. Some communities have pet lending libraries. These libraries are wonderful resources that allow families to borrow a rabbit or guinea pig for a few weeks—which may be as long as a preschooler is interested. If there is a family history of allergies, get more information before choosing a pet.

Praise: The Art of Support

Up to 6, youngsters take pride in themselves only if we take pride in them. We are literally building their self-esteem every time we offer support and praise. In addition to frequent praise, there are many ways we can help them along in this process. There are several different types of praise.

Celebrate Success

Most parents have a few standard phrases that are easy to pull out at any moment: Bravo, Cool, Wow, Terrific, Excellent, Wonderful, Good Job, Three Cheers, Beautiful, I love it.

A hug or pat on the back adds strength to any compliment. We show our appreciation when we hang children's artwork and use the things they make for us. Positive words carry even more weight when children overhear us praising them to someone else. Dad reported to the neighbor, while Elena was nearby, "Elena was a big help in the garden today. She helped me pull lots of weeds."

Encourage Effort

Young children fail again and again at many things they try. Fortunately, children under 6 tend to measure their success by how positive our reactions are, not by whether the ball hits the target. This focus on us, rather than the outcome, allows them to keep trying despite all their inevitable failures and mistakes. Because we want them to keep trying, it is important that we appreciate their effort, whether or not things turn out ideally. Some families regularly include praise and appreciation as part of their dinnertime ritual or family meeting.

Praise that Pressures

"You're the best!" "You're the smartest." "Perfect!" Extreme praise sets up extreme standards. Some children will take up such challenges, but many will become discouraged and resentful because they can't measure up. For long-term stress management, it is better when perfectionism is not an automatic habit, but a decision we make consciously when perfection is important to the task at hand.

What to say:

- "Way to go. You can do it. You're on the right track"
- "Keep trying—you'll get it. You're getting better."
- "You've been practicing."
- "You tried again and got it."
- "Nothing can stop you now."
- "I'm proud of you. You worked hard."
- "That was a good try, don't worry about the mistake."
- "You tried. It doesn't need to be perfect."

Point Out Positive Qualities

Praise that helps children become aware of their positive qualities is even more powerful than celebrating accomplishments and encouraging effort. In his book *Learned Optimism*, Martin Seligman, Ph.D., reports that optimistic people commonly believe that good things happen, in large part, because of their own positive qualities. They also tend to believe that bad things happen because of temporary difficulties. (Pessimists tend to believe the opposite, that bad things happen because of their personal shortcomings and good things happen by accident.) Helping children see their positive traits gives them confidence that they can cope effectively with the future.

Both children and adults learn more quickly with specific praise. We don't know what other people value when we hear, "You're a good employee" or "You're a good boy!" We can combine the power of qualities with the importance of specifics by giving both: "Melody, you were kind to hug your friend when she was upset." Appreciating qualities also tells children that we value *who they are,* not just what they do. (Note that how we give praise is the opposite of how we give corrections. With correction, we do *not* name a quality. We say, "You spilled your milk" rather than "You are clumsy.")

Chart 52 gives samples of some positive qualities along with specific examples. What are other good qualities you see in your child?

Tell Children How Important They Are to Us

Because 5s are so dependent on us, they are especially pleased and relieved to know that they are important to us, too. (A note of caution: If children see and hear that they are the *only* important thing in our lives, they can become frightened by how much responsibility they have for our happiness.) Children love to be told any or all of the following:

- ◆ "I love you. You're important to me."
- ◆ "It's great to know you. It's great to work with you!"
- ◆ "You're a joy. This wouldn't be fun without you."
- ◆ "I'm proud of you. You brighten my day/light up my life."

Prepare for the Future

While children are 5 is a good time for us to get ready to make a basic shift regarding praise. Around 6, most children start to evaluate their own actions. Around 7, they pay more attention to *what happened* than to *our reaction*. Also around 7, they begin to grow beyond their all-or-nothing thinking. They more easily see themselves as more capable in some areas than others.

Honesty. Once children look at both what actually happened and at our reaction, they will be distressed by fake or dishonest praise. If things didn't go well, it is better that we acknowledge their concern and support their ideas for improvement. If, at this age, we choose to positively evaluate the *quality* of their work ("You haven't missed a thing." "You do beautiful work!"), it is important that we are genuinely pleased.

52. Encouraging Children's Strengths

Name the Quality "You Are…"	Then Give an Example
Careful	◆ *You watched where you climbed.* ◆ *You didn't spill any milk.*
Creative/ Imaginative	◆ *That was a really interesting story!* ◆ *You made a colorful painting.*
Funny/Pleasure to Be With	◆ *You tell good jokes. You make me laugh.* ◆ *I have fun when I run in the rain with you.*
Good-looking, Pretty, Handsome	◆ *You have beautiful hair, eyes, etc.*
Helpful/Cooperative	◆ *I really appreciate your help with …* ◆ *You helped me … [make a salad, pick up toys, etc.]*
Honest	◆ *You told me the truth about …*
Kind	◆ *You shared your …* ◆ *You showed the new child around your school.*
Persistent/ Good Worker	◆ *You kept trying … until you got it.*
Problem Solver	◆ *You figured out how to …* ◆ *You followed the directions/figured it out.* ◆ *You asked for help when you needed it.*
Smart	◆ *You remembered …* ◆ *You learned the song quickly.*
Talented/Skillful	◆ *You ran really fast.* ◆ *You drew that picture with an artist's eye.*
Unique/ One of a Kind	◆ *Nobody else does things the way you do.*

Compiled by Helen F. Neville

53. Praise/Encouragement— *What to Do at Different Ages*

	Birth to 6 yr.	6 yr. and Up	
The taller the box, the more useful the strategy	Encourage effort.	Invite children to identify their own good qualities and evaluate their own progress and success. Ask: *How did it go?* *How did you make it happen?* *How did you feel about it?*	The taller the box, the more useful the strategy
	Name children's positive qualities with specific examples.		
	Celebrate their successes.	Encourage effort.	
		Name qualities with examples.	
		Celebrate success.	
	Tell them they are important to us.	Tell them they are important to us.	

Compiled by Helen F. Neville

Self-evaluation. As children gradually become able to self-evaluate, we could continue to shower them with praise and act as though *our* opinion is the only one that matters. Doing so, however, risks turning them into praise junkies who always look to others for evaluation. Alternatively, as they approach 6 and 7, we can begin to ask *their* opinion: "How did that go for you?" "How did you feel about it?" "Did you have a good time doing that?" "Did you like how it turned out?" In this way, we place value on their growing ability to evaluate their own actions. Their honest self-evaluation will help them find their way in life.

Over time, it's still important to celebrate success, point out their positive qualities, and so forth. However, our occasional, heartfelt praise serves them better than frequent, offhand praise. The new goal will be to honor how children feel about themselves and support their honest self-evaluation.

Chart 53 shows that helpful praise changes as children grow. In each column, the bigger the space, the more important the method of praise.

Reading and Writing

Reading and writing are essential skills in our modern world, and they are extremely complicated to learn. Many different parts of the brain need to work together in order to take sounds apart, put them together, turn wiggly ink marks into sounds, and turn all the tiny parts into meaning.

The Debate. There is disagreement about how children best accomplish this challenging goal. Two general types of preschool and kindergarten have evolved in the process. On one side are expert school educators and curriculum planners. They believe that with enough repetition, children learn many skills including reading and writing, and that the sooner they learn to read and write the better. Such *academic* programs are teacher-directed, with emphasis on repetition and drill for skill-building. To feel successful in such programs, children need to be able to sit still, handle repetition, and be *able* to meet teachers' academic expectations.

On the other side are experts in child development and in how young children learn. They believe that as with using the toilet, one can avoid much fuss and frustration by waiting until body and mind are ready. *Developmental* programs accept that healthy children's brains and muscles are on widely different schedules of growth. Children learn best when they are relaxed and having fun. They feel successful when creative activities, based on individual levels of development, lead to further learning.

In fact, we put children at risk when we start the process too late, or push certain skills too early, or ignore individual differences. How children pay attention is also an important part of the picture.

See page 88, "Age and Classroom Readiness" chart, page 102, "Attention Span: How It Grows" and page 110, "Types of Child Care and Preschool Programs."

When Do Most Children Learn to Read?

Whether children learn to read at 3 or 7 makes *no* difference in their final ability to read, their IQ, or their later success in school. Half of all girls start reading by 5½, and half of all boys by 6. For centuries, reading has been taught at 7. That's when most children naturally become interested all on their own, and 80% learn easily at that age. Several countries in Europe and the American Waldorf schools still wait until age 7 to begin formal reading and writing. Montessori schools let each child decide when he or she is ready. Other public and private schools vary widely.

Natural early readers. Evan, 3, handed Mom a scrap of paper and said, "Here's your Macy's tag." Amazed, she asked, "How do you know that?" Evan pointed to the tiny print and reported, "It says 'Macy's.'" After that he started reading street signs. A few unusual preschoolers figure out how to read long before anyone teaches them. These are more often boys than girls.

Natural late readers. Spencer's cousin couldn't read at all until well into second grade, when he was almost 8. Before then, the more he watched his classmates make sense of those meaningless marks, the worse he felt. Then suddenly, reading became easy. He went on to be an excellent student in high school and a college professor.

Steps in Learning to Read

Here are important stepping stones along the path to reading:

Build a positive attitude. The first step is a warm feeling about books. We create this positive attitude when we snuggle with our little ones and share books with them. When babies are between 6 and 12 months, we point to pictures and name what we see. Before long we take turns; they ask us to name things by pointing to pictures. Toddlers often want us to return to the same book again and again. With 3s, we can talk about the stories and imagine changes: "If this were your truck, would it be red or green?" With 4s and 5s, we can discuss the pictures, the stories, *and* the ideas: "If you were the bunny, what would you do next? Why?" To build a positive attitude, it's also important that children see that we read. If parents have trouble reading, we can still sit with our children, look at pictures, make up our own stories, and talk about them.

Hear separate sounds. Beginning around 3, most children begin to notice and like hearing words that rhyme—words that end with the same sound such as "sit" and "fit." Many children's songs, stories, and nursery rhymes use lots of rhymes. These repeating sounds gradually help children learn that words are made up of smaller parts. Most 4s enjoy saying rhymes. They can also hear that some words are made from two shorter words, such as horseback, wheelchair, or rainbow. Most 5s can hear the syllables (the separate *sounds* inside words), such as *bas*-ket or *ta*-ble. It is not until 6 that some children can hear the very short sounds that make up words: *bat* is made up of b-a-t. *Hearing the many short sounds inside words is basic to reading.*

Link letters with sounds. Many 4s can say the *names* of alphabet letters. The next step is to say the *sounds* of the alphabet letters. Then young readers have to connect sounds they know with letters on the page. After that, they can

sound out short, easy words, such as m + a + t for *mat*. At some point, they learn to recognize a few common words by sight, such as *my* and *the*. All these different steps don't turn into reading until all the needed brain cells connect. For a few, this happens at 4, while for many other smart, normal children it doesn't happen until 6 or even 7. Expecting children to read before the needed brain cells connect is like expecting the lights to turn on before the electricity is connected. Unfortunately, some enthusiastic educators forget the wide variation in normal development. As mentioned at the beginning of "Muscles in Motion," the more complicated the task, the wider the time span over which different children learn it.

Steps in Learning to Print

A positive attitude toward writing is important, just as it is toward reading. When we post a note on the refrigerator, or say, "I'll write that down to remember it," or write down what children tell us, we show them that writing has a purpose.

Sometime between 4½ and 6, most children develop the necessary control of tiny finger muscles needed to print letters. To understand what it is like before finger muscles are ready, hold a kitchen broom upside down and "print" while holding the broom in different hand positions.

Active, high energy preschoolers are much more interested in running and jumping than in drawing and printing.

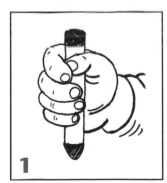 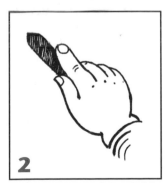 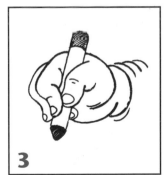 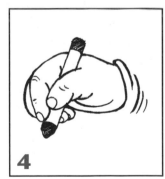

Note: We are likely to see hand position 2 only if the child is writing on an easel or blackboard.

They generally learn to write later rather than sooner. One sign that children are ready to print is that they comfortably hold a pencil between their thumb and first two fingers with a relaxed grip (with the joints bent out, not in). If they hold a pencil in other ways, their small finger muscles aren't yet strong enough to write easily. Drawing with large crayons and markers helps finger muscles get ready to hold a pencil.

Until 7, many children can't easily remember the proper order and direction of the strokes to print each letter. Often practicing the *wrong* order of strokes makes it much more difficult to learn *correct* printing. Easily writing the correct order of strokes will be especially important when the time comes for children to learn cursive writing. A few children will always have difficulty writing easily and clearly. For them, a computer keyboard will be a lifesaver.

Here are further steps in learning to print, from easier to harder:

- Control a crayon or pencil easily, being able to fill in a circle, for example.
- Draw a person with a head, a body, and arms.
- Trace simple shapes and then trace letters.
- Copy letters.
- Print letters from memory with strokes in the correct order.
- Print name and gradually other words.
- Print words according to how they sound.
- Print words with correct spelling.

> See page 149, "Help—Is My Child Okay?" Look at 4 years and 5 years in the "Concerns About Development" charts, if you are concerned about your child's progress toward printing.

Problems with Pushing Too Soon

Just because you can heat hot chocolate in the microwave doesn't mean you can fix a fancy meal. Similarly, just because children can say the alphabet doesn't mean they can read. Here are possible risks to pressuring children to read before they are ready:

Learning is harder. When adults read English, our eyes automatically move from left to right. Young readers may look at letters from either direction. Depending on the direction the eyes move, *b* and *d* can look the same—a line followed by a circle. For many children, it is not until second grade that they have a clear sense in their body of left and right. Until then, reading and writing can be very confusing. This is especially the case for children who are ambidextrous—who use both hands well. One such mother remembers that she finally learned that *left* was the steering-wheel side of the car.

Many young children learn to recognize a few words by their general shape, such as "it" or "dog." However, if they try to remember *many* words by shape alone, (it, at, dog, dug) before they can sound out letters, reading gets harder and harder.

Children may get discouraged. Just as we can't make children walk before they are ready, we can't make them read before they are ready. The earlier we expect *all* children to read and write, the more children will be labeled and will feel like failures. Pushing children to read and write before all the necessary brain cells connect causes unnecessary frustration. With too much academic pressure, even young children may decide that they don't like learning or school. They may get silly and disrupt the classroom, or they may become discouraged or even depressed. Children who have to repeat grades, even as early as 2nd or 3rd, often don't try the next time through. Instead, they assume, "I couldn't learn this before, so I can't learn it now."

Problems with Starting Too Late

Most children, because they hear sounds remarkably quickly and clearly (and get some help along the way with nursery rhymes, etc.), can easily hear the sounds that they later learn to read. In normal speech, the brain has only 1/100th of a second to hear the different sounds of "b" and "d" as in "bid" and "did."

For about 20% of the population, telling one quick sound from another doesn't come easily. These preschoolers benefit from extra help to get more practice in hearing the sounds that make later reading possible. Many adults live with lifelong reading disabilities because they didn't get the extra help when they needed it. The "sound map" in the brain, which makes it possible to tell one similar sound from another, gradually becomes less flexible after age 8. Most of those who learn to read at 9 or later continue to find reading difficult throughout their lives. Once children can hear sounds easily, any further extra help they need with reading is most effective if started before third grade.

Reading difficulty sometimes runs in families. In this case, it is especially important to get extra help in the preschool years. Delays in learning to talk are sometimes a sign of the same hearing difficulty that could later make reading difficult. (Late talkers may not say any real words before 12 months, or at 24 months, may not yet put two words together, as in "Mommy, up.")

In *Overcoming Dyslexia*, Sally Shaywitz, M.D., tells how to recognize if children have trouble hearing the quick sounds they will later need for reading. If they do, it is better to get help sooner rather than later. (When with a child they don't know, caregivers and teachers need to ask, "Does this child have trouble hearing?" or "Does the child just need some time to learn this new activity?")

Here are red flags for different ages:

15 mo. to 2 yr. There are many reasons why some children talk later than others. Children who talk later than expected because they can't hear sounds clearly are more likely to have difficulty learning to read when the time comes. Check with health care providers for the following: At **15 mo.** toddlers don't yet say any words. At **24 mo.** children don't yet say several dozen words and use two-word phrases, such as "go bye-bye." At **2½ yr.** adults who know child well still can't understand most words the child says. Children don't join simple activities or enjoy looking at books with us.

3 yr. They don't yet notice or enjoy hearing rhymes. They may not enjoy listening to stories.

Around the World

Traditionally, **Chinese children** start writing at 3. Unlike English letters, however, simple Chinese characters stand for the meaning of the word, rather than the several sounds that make up the word. For example, the character for "person"

gives no clue about how to pronounce it. Writing these easy characters is rather like drawing. Children start with a large brush that they can control with the large muscles of the arm rather than the small muscles of the fingers. Young children brush in characters that are already drawn for them rather than paint characters themselves.

4 yr. They can't yet hear two words inside a longer word, for example *cow* and *boy* in *cowboy*. They don't yet say easy rhymes. They still use baby talk. Children who have trouble *hearing* sounds are likely to leave off the first sounds of words—"lephant" for *elephant*—or put sounds in the wrong order—"am-i-nal" instead of "an-i-mal." These mistakes suggest difficulty hearing short sounds. Until they are 5 or 6, many children don't yet say the more difficult sounds of English, such as "r" or "zh" as in *measure*. This is because of muscle development in the mouth; it is not a hearing problem.

See page 111, "Children's Communication" chart.

5 yr. They can't yet separate words they hear into syllables, for example, *today* into "to" and "day." They can't tell whether two words rhyme: "Does *kind* rhyme with *mind*? Does *kind* rhyme with *kiss*?" They can't think of a word that rhymes with another word.

6 yr. They can't say whether two words start with the same sound. They can't separate easy words into sounds, for example, *feet* into f + ee + t. They make wild guesses about words; for example, they look at the word *red* and guess *sit*. They complain that reading is too hard.

The eyes, of course, also affect reading. The usual vision test at a doctor's office only checks *distance vision* because that is where most children have trouble. However, without good close-up vision, a child can't tell the difference between E and F. To see well, the brain has to take two slightly different views (one from the left eye and one from the right eye) and put them together exactly. Otherwise, one might see "ond eog" instead of "one dog." If your child has trouble reading in early elementary school, it may be important to get his or her eyes tested by a pediatric vision specialist.

Safety: Step-by-Step

One of our most basic jobs as parents is to protect our little ones from harm. As they grow, we gradually need to teach them to become safety conscious. The ages listed below are *general guidelines.* The more active and curious the child, the sooner he or she can get into danger. Children's age, temperament, and understanding affect when they are ready to take more responsibility for their own safety.

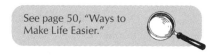

See page 50, "Ways to Make Life Easier."

Specific Safety Concerns for Young Children

Adult anger that is dangerous. We can feel totally helpless around crying babies and stubborn toddlers or preschoolers. Then we may become angry. Because we are so much bigger and stronger, we can easily cause much more harm than we intend if we handle little ones roughly while we are upset.

Sadly, upset and overloaded parents are the most common cause of injury to babies. *Never shake a baby or child.* Of babies who get shaken, one out of four dies. If the baby lives, there may be brain damage. If we're often frustrated or sometimes dangerously angry with our children, it is extremely important that we get the help we need. Ninety percent of child homicides (under 12 years) are caused by an angry family member or acquaintance, not a stranger. Call family, friends, a doctor or therapist, or a parent stress hot line to get help.

Animals. Children of all ages need to learn to follow the directions from animals' owners. It is best to approach animals slowly, calmly, and gently. Let the animal first sniff a child's hand and keep the child's face away from the dog's muzzle. Show the child how to pet dogs without petting or pulling their tails. Do not allow a child to hug dogs because weight around a dog's neck may feel like a demand for it to submit and it may resist by biting the child.

Babysitters. The general recommendation is that babysitters be age 13 or older. Check references carefully and ask prospective babysitters about their experience.

Burns and fire safety.
All ages. Have smoke alarms and check labels on fire extinguishers for information on maintaining them in working order. Keep water heaters at 120°F or lower. Hotter water causes serious burns more quickly. Cover electrical outlets. Avoid dangling electrical cords and keep appliances out of reach. Protect children from the fireplace, space heaters, and low heater vents. Keep matches out of reach—locked up, if necessary. Turn pot handles inward on the stove. Stir and test foods from microwave before drinking or eating or offering to a child. Do not heat baby bottles in the microwave.
Crawling to 3 yr. Avoid using tablecloths because children can pull them off the table along with cups of hot coffee and platters of hot food.
Teach: Only Mom or Dad turns on water faucets in the tub. (Remove toddler if necessary.)
Teach: Let child touch a cup of hot water and one of cold to learn the meaning of "HOT!"
3 yr. Your child may be safer if you let him or her use some appliances *with supervision,* such as the toaster.
Teach: Only touch this if Mom or Dad is right here.
4 and 5 yr. Take children to visit a fire station where they can see firefighters' masks and fire suits so they won't get frightened and hide in an emergency.
Teach: If clothes catch fire, stop, drop, and roll. Crawl under smoke. Leave a burning home and don't go back. Go to the neighbor's and ask an adult to call 911.

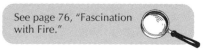

See page 76, "Fascination with Fire."

Car safety.
All ages. *For car seats and booster seats.* Check with medical professionals or the police department for latest standards and requirements in safety equipment. Ask your car dealer or County Health Department for

help with installation or to check it—many seats get installed incorrectly and are therefore less safe. *Lock your car and take your keys (even in your own garage or driveway).* There are hazards ranging from your child climbing in and taking the brake off to someone stealing the car with your child in it. *Don't leave children alone in the car.* In some states it is illegal to leave a child under 6 years alone. *Avoid overheating (hyperthermia).* Cars trap heat when sitting in the sun. Even at 60°F, they can get dangerously hot for small children, especially with the windows closed.

Toddling to 4 yr. While walking, if your child is inclined to head for the street, use a stroller or a safety harness or wrist leash.

Teach: In parking lots, child must keep both hands on the car while waiting and hold parent's hand or clothing or the shopping cart while walking.

4 and 5 yr. *Teach:* Invite children to check the streets you cross together. Ask, "Is it safe for us to cross the street now?" Careful, reliable 5s may be ready to cross quiet streets alone.

Choking/Suffocating.

All ages. Check with your local hospital to learn how to treat choking in infants and young children. Do not leave long strings, ropes, cords, or drawstrings on shirts or jackets where children can get at them. Keep drapery cords up high. Throw away broken balloons. Do not use or store plastic bags (grocery, dry cleaners, trash) where children can get to them.

Infants. See page 193, "Sleep Location and SIDS."

Babies to 3 yr. Cut long strings off Mom's nightgowns. Use short strings (3 to 5 inches) on pacifiers. Keep crib mobile out of reach above crib. Use only pierced earrings that screw or lock on. Do not put necklaces on babies or young children. If objects are small enough to fit through a toilet paper roll, keep them away from babies and toddlers.

Teach: "Sit (or stand still) when you eat." "Walk (not run) with gum in your mouth."

4 and 5 yr.

Teach: "Never put cords or rope around your neck."

Cuts. Keep knives, scissors, and other sharp things out of reach. Not only can young children hurt themselves, but much damage can be done to things around the house.

4 and 5 yr.

Teach: How to carry and use knives and scissors safely; what is okay to cut and what isn't.

Drowning.

All ages. Never leave a young child alone in or near a swimming pool, lake, etc. If you have a swimming pool, make sure it has a fence that children can't climb and a locked gate. Next to car accidents, drowning is the most common cause of children's accidental deaths.

Infancy to 4 yr. Do not leave them alone in the bathtub or in or near a wading pool.

Toddlers. Don't leave them alone near containers or buckets of water or in the bathroom—unless you have a "toilet lid lock." Children can drown in as little as 2 inches of water.

4 and 5 yr. Be within hearing range when child is in wading pool or bathtub. Be sure child can climb out of tub safely.

Teach: Always swim with grown-ups. Give swimming lessons between 4 and 7 years.

Emergencies. *Teach:* Teach children **3 to 5 years** old to call 911 in case the adult in the house is too sick to talk (unconscious, injured) and for other emergencies. A quick-dial button labeled in red makes this very easy.

Falls.

    All ages. Have solid handrails on stairs. Wipe up spills right away. Use nonslip mat or decals in bathtub.

    Infants. Do not leave them alone on a bed or other high surface. Some scoot or roll when just a few days old.

    Crawling to 4 yr. In the early weeks of crawling, babies do not have depth perception and are likely to fall off things. Little ones forget to pay attention, are unsteady on their feet, and don't understand danger. Block stairs, keep chairs and stools away from counters, and put safety guards on doors and windows—most fatal falls are from a second story window or higher.

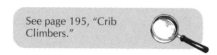

See page 195, "Crib Climbers."

Teach: No crawling on tables or counters.

    4 and 5 yr. Oversized bikes are the most common cause of children's bike accidents.

Teach: Always wear a bike helmet when on a bike.

Guns.

    All ages. In the United States, people are most often shot by accident or by upset family members. Therefore, the best protection is to get rid of guns. If that is not possible, be sure that guns have trigger safety locks and that bullets are locked away separately.

    4 and 5 yr. and older. Do not let children play with realistic toy guns. They can't tell the difference between play and real guns.

Teach: "If you find a gun, leave it alone. Go immediately to get help from an adult."

Kidnapping (abduction). Almost all children are abducted by relatives who want them, not by strangers who will harm them. Get help with difficult relationships. Keep your eyes open for suspicious behavior, but remember that almost all children who disappear just wandered off and will soon be found.

    2 to 4 yr. *Teach:* "Opening the front door is a grown-up job," or "Always wait until I'm here to open the front door," or "Come tell me first if you hear someone at the door." (Install an interior door lock high out of reach.)

    4 and 5 yr. Protect 4s and 5s, rather than make them afraid of strangers. Children are likely to become needlessly afraid if they hear too much before 6 or 7.

Teach: "Strangers (people we don't know) smile and say hello and that's okay. Sometimes strangers offer children presents or candy or to take them for car rides, or ask for help. These things are not okay. If a stranger asks you for help, like to find a lost puppy or to get directions to a place, get Mommy or Daddy or another safe adult. If you got into someone else's car, I'd be very worried because I wouldn't know where you were."

Lost. Watch children closely. It is far more common for them to get lost than kidnapped.

    Toddler to 4 yr. Use a harness or wrist leash with active, curious, or impulsive toddlers, so they can exercise safely when you are out together.

    4 and 5 yr. *Teach:* Home telephone number and address; who to ask for help (a mom with kids or a store clerk, for example).

Poisoning.

    All ages. Keep medicines in childproof bottles and high out of reach. (Note: A bottle of children's vitamins has a dangerous amount of iron.) Never call medicine "candy."

Teach: "Always be with Mommy or Daddy when you take medicine."

Keep the National Poison Control number by your phone: 1-800-222-1222. (If someone is not breathing, is unconscious, or is having a seizure due to poisoning, call 911.)

    Crawling through 3 yr. Lock up all medicines, cleaning supplies, and flammable products. Remove poisonous plants from home and yard. Keep cigarettes out of reach (some children eat them). Check to be sure poisons (and medicines) aren't within reach when you visit other homes.

    4 and 5 yr. Continue to keep dangerous things locked up if children are impulsive.

Sexual abuse. See page 185, "Protecting Children from Sexual Abuse."

Screen Time: Television, Videos, and Computers

The challenge with screen time, whether television, video, or computers, is to sort out the pros from the cons. As with so many other topics, age is an important factor, and moderation is an important concept.

How Screens Are Helpful

Screen time can provide parents with needed breaks. Children today have fewer brothers, sisters, neighbors, and grandparents to keep them busy, so they rely more on our time.

Quality children's programs can broaden a preschooler's view of the world. Good programs teach about social relations, diversity, and problem solving. Young viewers can see other children in their towns and cities. In the long run, computers will become as important to our children's lives and learning as they are to ours.

Concerns about Television, Videos, and Video Games

Children miss learning opportunities and exercise. Young children learn best from back and forth interaction with other people and from touching and moving things in their environment. Most young children need *a great deal* of physical activity. Lack of exercise is a major factor in the nation-wide weight gain among children. When children exercise, they build strength and skill in large and small muscles as they climb, chase, crawl, build, draw, and help us around the house. *All this exercise and most of this learning stops when children sit in front of a screen.*

Children experience unnecessary fear. Up to 8, children still confuse fantasy and reality. When they see something scary, they have no way of knowing whether it is likely to happen to them. Heavy television viewers spend more hours each week with their stress hormones running high. They see the world (including their own neighborhood) as more scary and dangerous than others who watch less television. Watching the nightly news makes children anxious about both their own safety and their parents' safety.

Children can get very frightened by videos and television, even if they are watching fairy tales. Some very sensitive children with strong emotions can become frightened for weeks by a single scary scene. They may then have trouble eating, sleeping, or being alone in their own room.

Children's play is more aggressive. Research compared preschoolers in two different towns in Canada. One town had television while the other (at the bottom of a deep valley) did not. With television, children in preschool were more aggressive.

Children's cartoons have more violence than any other media—as much as thirty violent acts per hour. Young children see the immediate payoff: someone gets what he wants right now. However, the children don't catch on that the "bad guy" may lose out at the *end* of the show.

Screen time encourages short attention span. Much TV and video programming holds our attention by quickly shifting from one thing to another. Children need practice growing their attention span, not cutting it short or chopping it into small pieces.

Children's minds are flooded with advertising. By 6, children begin to connect brand names to status and being liked by others. Much of the food advertised on television and in other media is not good for children (or adults).

Children show less creativity. Those who watch a great deal of television participate less in imaginary play. Televi-

Learning to Talk

Television and videos are poor language teachers. Young children learn language as they trade words with responsive human beings. They need practice *saying* new words. They learn as they talk about things, people, and events as these happen in their moment-to-moment lives.

sion and videos are fast paced. Children do more creative play after hearing easy-to-follow story lines with slow-paced action.

Programs present a narrow viewpoint. Many children's programs show little cultural or ethnic diversity. They also tend to show men and women in stereotyped roles.

Younger is not better for keyboarding. Children who frequently "hunt and peck" on computer keys may have less motivation and therefore find it harder to learn correct fingering. (Correct fingering is faster in the long run.) To learn this new skill easily, children need large enough hands and long enough attention spans—usually around 2nd or 3rd grade.

The tube and temperament. Some high energy children quietly sit and watch the screen but afterward get a rebound surge of very high energy that is hard to manage. Some highly sensitive or emotionally intense children are easily overstimulated by the color, pace, and content of media. Af-

> **Around the World**
>
> Current viewing patterns in the typical home in the **United States** show that the television is on almost fifty hours per week. On average, young children watch two to three hours per day. As of this writing, 68% of American children have televisions in their rooms.

terward, their mood can range from fussy to intensely difficult. They may have trouble calming down, and may be uncooperative or aggressive.

Television, videos, and computers are especially attractive to children who are easily frustrated. It is easy to succeed at watching television. Children who play video games can choose a comfortable level of difficulty, which makes these games very enticing. However, time in most of these artificial worlds won't help children find real-life ways to feel successful.

What Parents Can Do

Turn the television off except during a few chosen programs for children or adults. If we like background sound, use music or the radio. Get news from radio, newspaper, or computer or watch the news when kids aren't around.

> If children have trouble getting to sleep at night, see page 197, "Other Things That May Affect Sleep: Light."

Do not have a television in children's rooms! They don't have the willpower to leave it off and cannot make good decisions about how much or what to watch. If a television's mere presence in the living room is a problem, put it in an entertainment center and shut the door or cover it with a neutral-colored, uninteresting piece of cloth.

Select suitable programs or videos for children. Consider their interests, emotions, and abilities. Fours may begin to request certain types of programs. Consider their requests and decide whether or not the programs are appropriate. Sometimes watch television and videos *with* children and talk about what you see.

Try not to use videos or television as a reward. Instead make viewing part of the daily or weekly routine. Whatever we regularly use as rewards, children want more of—regardless of what it is.

Have a screen-free day once a week, so everyone knows

54. How Much Screen Time Is Okay?

Age	Hours of Television/Videos	Hours on Computers
Birth to 2 yr.	None	None
2 yr.	Ideally none, but no more than ½ hour per day.	None
3 yr.	No more than ½ hour per day.	None is fine, but no more than ½ hour per day shared with an adult.
4 to 6 yr.	Television, videos, and computers combined: No more than 1 hour/day on weekdays and 2 hours/day on weekend days.	

From The Irreducible Needs of Children *by T. Berry Brazelton, M.D., and Stanley I. Greenspan, M.D.*

that life can still go on. If screen time is ruling the home, remove the television or video to an isolated area, turn it to the wall, and leave it unplugged. Bring it out on rare occasions for special viewing dates. Once it is out of sight for a few days, most children hardly miss it and spend their time in imaginative play, building with blocks, playing with friends, or looking at books. Their behavior also tends to improve.

Self-Soothing and Security Objects

Sucking is naturally soothing to babies and is a life-sustaining instinct. Before modern medicine found alternative ways to feed babies, ill ones died if they couldn't suck. Some babies suck their thumbs before they are born, and many continue as toddlers and some as preschoolers. Sucking exercises nerve and muscle networks on both sides of the body, setting the stage for coordination of arms and legs.

Some babies need much more self-soothing and exercise than others. Because they can't yet jog or read a novel to relax, they suck. Babies on bottles can overfeed if they get milk every time they want to suck for exercise or soothing. Breasts don't overfeed, but their owners can feel worn out! In these situations, a pacifier can come to the rescue. Because pacifiers have now been found to protect against SIDS, they are likely to become much more common.

See pages 192 and 193 for ways to protect against SIDS.

It is not until about 3 months that most babies can catch their own thumbs when they need them. An advantage of thumbs is that they don't get lost in the dark. Little ones, who are put to bed *before* they are asleep are more likely to suck thumb or pacifier.

After the early months, we may want little ones to sleep separately, put themselves back to sleep during the night, and sleep easily at day care when we aren't around. Pacifiers, thumbs, or a favorite blanket can be a big help. We can encourage kids to connect to a security object. Such items work because they are a reminder of *us*. We can put the same blanket or bear in our babies' hands whenever we feed and snuggle with them. Mom's old tee shirt that still has her comforting smell often works well. For months, Melody stroked Mom's silky hair as she nursed. When Mom was ready for a change, she bought Melody a piece of silky cloth to stroke instead. To make life easier, we may want to use several items, in which case they all need to *feel* and *smell* the same. Use cloth diapers, washcloths, or cut the old blanket into several pieces.

Some little ones choose a bottle as their security object. This can complicate life because many professionals now recommend that babies not use bottles after their first birthday. Dentists are concerned about teeth. Teeth are prone to cavities if milk dribbles over them hour after hour. Pediatricians are concerned about ear infections. If babies drink milk *while lying down*, milk may run into the tubes (eustachian tubes) that go from the back of the throat to the middle ear and cause ear infections. To protect teeth, we can remove the bottle (or breast) as soon as the baby is asleep, or gradually put more water and less milk in bottles, until they contain only water. (Some babies are very prone to ear infections, because the "doorways" from the throat into the eustachian tubes don't close tightly. For these babies, even a bottle of water or pacifier while lying down can cause more frequent ear infections.)

Let tots under 12 months suck on pacifier or thumb quite freely if they wish. After that, spending all day with a pacifier can slow down language practice. Some experts therefore suggest tossing out the pacifier at 1 year. (Thumbs automatically come out of the mouth for play, so they less often affect talking.) For some toddlers and especially 2s, sucking is still a really important way to self-soothe. For these little

Around the World

In **India,** as in most cultures, little ones calm down with familiar *people* rather than blankets, teddy bears, pacifiers, and other store-bought things. This is possible because they are rarely left alone and are usually with the same few caretakers throughout both day and night.

ones, and their caregivers, it is often a relief to have a pacifier (or thumb) available during the "trying 2s." At some point, between 1 and 3 years, parents may tie pacifiers to the bed (and the car seat) with short elastic or string so they are available for tired, upset kids, but not in the child's possession all day long. At Elena's daycare, children can use their pacifiers at nap time. At Malik's, children can use their pacifiers any time they want, but only on the "rest mat," so they usually prefer to be up and about without one.

Most children lose interest in their security objects by kindergarten, although an occasional well-worn bear has shown up in a college dorm. Just before Spencer turned 5, he ate the last shreds of his well-worn blanket.

Dentists say that sucking a thumb or a pacifier is not a problem before children turn 3. Even if the shape of the jaw changes slightly due to very long, strong sucking, the jaw returns to normal if preschoolers suck less after age 3. If your child is 3 and you are concerned, check with your dentist to see whether your child's continued sucking is a problem.

Sex and Gender

Do boys and girls act differently because of genes or early training? Researchers are still figuring out the details, but it seems to be some of both. In the meantime, young children are figuring out where babies come from and how to tell boys from girls.

Differences Between Boys and Girls

There are wide differences in behavior among boys and among girls, as well as much overlap in how they act. What we'll look at here, for the most part, is how typical boys are different from typical girls. Though many differences between boys and girls are due to nature, some are due to nurture. A study in 1993 found that American adults tend to put more pressure on preschool-age boys to hide fear and sadness and on girls to hide anger.

Boys and girls may begin to choose different activities and toys as early as 18 months. Boys generally prefer trucks, balls, and stuffed animals, while girls more often pick dolls and dishes. We can encourage less stereotyped play, but we aren't always successful. When Dad gave Melody a truck, she put it to bed with a blanket.

In general, girls walk, talk, feed themselves, toilet train, and dress themselves earlier than boys. The *typical* girl is less active and noisy but talks more. She is more interested in people and more willing to do what others want. The *typical* boy is more interested in things. Because boys often speak fewer words between 18 months and 2½ years, they are likely to feel and show more frustration.

As early as 2, very active boys may begin to play separately from most girls. However, most boys and girls are similarly strong and enjoy playing together at 3. By 4, most boys have larger muscles than most girls. Most but not all 4-year-old boys play in more active and vigorous ways than most girls. With their bigger muscles they have more powerful meltdowns. In most mammal species, young males are more active and aggressive. They, too, tend to play in separate male or female groups. Average 4s spend three times as many hours playing with children of the same gender. Average 6s spend eleven times as many hours in all boy or all girl groups.

Around 4, brains are developing differently. In most boys, the right side of the brain matures more quickly at this age. In most girls, the left side develops more quickly. Boys, with their more active right brains, learn to measure space. Boys move themselves through space as they climb, ride, and chase. They drive cars and trains, build towers, dig holes, kick balls, and throw whatever comes to hand. They measure space with sticks, swords, and the imaginary bullets they shoot across rooms and yards. These aren't the only activities that interest boys, but they spend more time here than elsewhere. Michael Gurian, in *The Wonder of Boys*, explains it this way: Boys' brains are hardwired to "move objects through space." Throughout time, we have depended on these skills for hunting, home building, and transportation.

Young girls, with their more active left brains, focus on language. The typical girl spends more time talking. She talks in more detail to dolls, playmates, and parents. Girls

55. Learning About Gender

Age	What Children Do or Think	Things We Can Say or Do to Help
7 to 12 mo.	◆ Notice their own genitals.	◆ Name body parts—penis, vulva (or other accurate words we're comfortable with).
1 yr.	◆ Start to masturbate—enjoy the special pleasure of touching their genitals.	◆ *It feels good to touch there, doesn't it?*
15 to 20 mo.	◆ Become interested in parents' genitals.	◆ Casually go about our daily activities.
16 mo. to 3 yr.	◆ Begin to compare their own bodies with those of other children.	◆ Give them words for what they notice: ◆ *Yes, you can see his penis and you can't see your clitoris.*
2 yr.	◆ Like to show off their naked bodies.	◆ Be calm and clear about when and where nudity is acceptable.
	◆ May masturbate in public.	◆ *We touch our private parts when we are in private places.* ◆ *That's something you do in your own room; that's where big people do it.*
	◆ Girls may demand to stand up to pee.	◆ Sympathize that this works better for boys. ◆ Point out some other activity she succeeds at easily.
3 yr.	◆ Many boys still connect closely to their mothers, so they often dress up in feminine clothes.	◆ Enjoy how cute they look.
	◆ Try to figure out who else is like them, male or female.	◆ Help them when they are confused.
	◆ Believe that people may change between male or female, depending on what they wear or do.	◆ *Boys and girls are different because their bodies are different. Boys are boys and girls are girls no matter what they wear or do.* (They may not believe us until 4, but we can give them the data.)
	◆ May use gender stereotypes to help keep straight who is a boy and who is a girl: "Elena, you can't be a truck driver!" or "Boys don't play with dolls!"	◆ *Boys and girls (men and women) can do whatever they want to do.* ◆ To counteract stereotypes, we can also make sure we mix masculine and feminine tasks with our partners. Point out other adults who cross the typical gender roles.
4 yr.	◆ Most boys start to dress up in boyish outfits: superhero, monster, cowboy, etc. ◆ Low energy boys may continue to play more often with girls.	◆ Neither energy level nor interests at this age clearly predict whether children will grow up to be straight or gay. Although the biology of sexual orientation may be in place well before birth, it is too soon to know how things will turn out.

Continued on next page.

55. *Learning About Gender* (continued)

Age	What Children Do or Think	Things We Can Say or Do to Help
4 yr.	◆ Boys often have contests to see who can pee the farthest.	◆ Whenever possible, ignore it. It will pass.
	◆ Now understand that sex doesn't change.	
	◆ May talk romantically to parent of the opposite sex: *I want to marry you.*	◆ *I love you, too. People marry people their own age. Someday you'll find someone your own age to marry.*
4 to 6 yr.	◆ Are very interested in how their bodies are similar to and different from others. Girls and boys may hang out in the nursery school bathroom or play "doctor" or "Mommy and Daddy" to check out body differences.	◆ If both children are of similar age and comfortable, ignore these games. After a few minutes, calmly distract them into other activities. Later ask whether they have any questions about how or why bodies are different. Check library for books for this age level.

Compiled by Helen F. Neville

also spend more time practicing small muscle skills used in drawing or making an imaginary meal for friends. They study relationships at home and at school and build social networks with their friends. Of course, girls also run and climb, but few keep up with the most active boys. Ultimately, more nerve fibers connect the left and right sides of girls' brains. Due to this, girls may find it somewhat easier than boys to talk about what goes on inside their heads.

Brain development varies. Between preschool and junior high, most boys and girls gradually come to use both sides of their brains more equally. Researchers are still studying how male and female brains work, both similarly and differently, in adulthood. In the meantime, intelligence tests deal with differences in young brains by including questions that are easier for many boys, as well as questions that are easier for many girls. Thus, total IQ scores suggest that boys and girls are the same, even though they tend to be skilled in different ways.

Our Bodies at Home

We humans are sexual beings. One mother, during a routine bath with her 3-year-old son, didn't know whether to laugh or cry when she realized he was thrusting his erect penis into her belly button. She calmly ended their last bath together. Life had moved on to a new phase. Four-year-old Melody snuggled seductively into Dad's lap and purred, "I love you, Daddy." He answered, "I love you, too," and then set her *beside* him and reached for their storybook. When we sense a sexual tone between our children and ourselves, it is *our* job to set quiet limits.

Sometime between 5 and 9, most children become more modest about their bodies. They may start to close the bathroom door, or may be uncomfortable using the bathroom around the parent of the opposite sex or bathing with opposite sex siblings. Again, it is our job to respond. As a general guideline, we should not show them more of our body than they are comfortable showing us. The goal is for them to feel at ease. In the United States, where people are clothed most of the time, a parent's naked body is likely to be more unsettling than in a culture where most people are almost nude most of the time.

Male erections are normal and natural during routine dreaming. (We all have dreams every night, whether or not we remember them.) Because of this, there can be both conscious and unconscious tugs of sexual response between parents and children. Experts, therefore, recommend that families not sleep nude in the same bed once children are 3 or 4. Between 4 and 6 is considered to be a good time to end full-time co-sleeping if children haven't already moved out on their own. There is, however, much cultural variation on this topic.

When parents don't set limits on their children's natural sexual responsiveness toward parents, children may sense both pleasant excitement and possible danger. A significant sense of exciting danger can later make it more difficult for some grown-up children to form sexual bonds with others. If any issues concerning children's sexuality are troublesome, consult with a family therapist.

Figuring Out Sex and Gender

To divide the world into men and women (boys and girls) is not an easy task. Sex—male or female—depends on our bodies. Gender—masculine or feminine—depends on roles in a particular culture. Chart 55 opposite shows steps children take to figure it all out.

The Mystery of Babies

We may learn a great deal about how children think if we start with "Do you have a guess? Then I'll tell you what I think." Don't get ahead of children with many details.

Chart 56, page 186, lists things children commonly wonder at different ages. If we give simple, direct answers, they will come back with the next question when they are ready. On the other hand, some children don't ask questions about babies. If they haven't asked by 5 or so, we can raise the topic: "Malik is going to have a baby brother soon. Where do you think that baby is now?"

Amazingly, it is not until well into elementary school that children really understand that two non-babies (a sperm and an ovum, or egg) combine together to make a baby. Even though they have seen pictures, children usually think of sperm or ovum as tiny, fully formed babies. If we say egg, they think of a chicken's egg because that is what they are familiar with. Consequently, young children are likely to be confused for a while.

More Hard Questions About Sex

Kids' questions about intimate and delicate topics can catch us off guard. Short answers are usually best. How we answer depends on the child's age and our level of comfort. When we are taken by surprise, we can gain planning time with "Let me think about that. Let's talk at lunch." Chart 57, page 187, offers suggestions.

Protecting Children from Sexual Abuse

Most children are sexually abused by people they know and like. At 4 or 5 we can teach two concepts:

- "Some touch feels good, and some doesn't feel right. If touch doesn't feel right, say 'No!'"
- "A secret about how someone might get hurt or that something bad might happen is a dangerous secret. Always tell another adult."

See the bibliography, page 207, and www.ParentingPress.com for books on sexual abuse prevention.

56. *Where Do Babies Come From?*

Age	What Children Believe	What They Want to Know	Ways Parents May Answer
2 to 5 yr.	Unless told otherwise, children often believe the baby comes out of the belly button.	*How does the baby get out of the mommy?*	◆ *The mom's uterus is like a balloon. It closes at the end like a plastic bag tied closed and holds the baby in until the baby is ready to come out. Then it opens and the mommy pushes the baby out. The baby comes out between the mommy's legs—near, but different from where pee and poop come out.*
3 to 5 yr.	Babies just are. They are alive somewhere before they are inside Mom.	*Where was the baby before it was in your tummy?*	◆ *We don't know where it was. But we're glad it is here now. (Or, see below.)*
4 yr.	Based on the what they hear, American children commonly believe that babies are bought ready-made at the store or that the eggs or seeds we eat may turn into babies.	*How do babies happen?*	◆ *When a man and woman want a baby in their family, they make one grow inside the mommy.* ◆ *God makes babies and brings them to families.* ◆ *All mommies have tiny baby eggs inside them. (Put your two thumbs and first fingers together to make a tiny speck of light.) The daddy puts sperm on the mommy's egg so it can grow.* *
		Where does the mommy keep her baby seeds?	◆ *Right near the uterus, where the baby will grow.*
		Where are the daddy's sperm?	◆ *They are in his testicles, beside his penis.*
		Can I make a baby?	◆ *Yes, when you are a grown-up, you can.*
5 to 7 yr.		*How does a baby get into the mommy?*	◆ *When grown-ups love each other and want a baby, they lie close to each other. The man puts his penis inside the woman's vagina. The sperm goes from his testicles, through his penis, into the woman.* **

* If because of artificial insemination or other reasons we're not ready to deal with the "daddy" part, we can say, "A woman has tiny baby eggs inside her. When she is ready, the doctor puts sperm on them so one of her eggs can grow."

** In times past, children watched cats, dogs, and farm animals demonstrate the act of sex. Most of those examples are gone, but children's natural interest remains.

Compiled by Helen F. Neville

57. Questions and Answers About Sex

Children's Questions	How We Might Answer, Depending on Our Comfort Level
Why are boys and girls different?	◆ So they can make babies together when they grow up.
What are "private parts"?	◆ They are special parts of our bodies that we cover with clothes so most people can't see them. ◆ They are the parts of our bodies that people use to make babies.
Mommy, can I see your vulva/clitoris?	◆ No. Grown-ups don't show their private parts to children. But we can get a book that shows how bodies are different. (For girls: We can get a mirror so you can see what yours looks like.)
Daddy, can I touch your penis?	◆ No. Children don't touch grown-ups' private parts. And grown-ups don't touch children's private parts—except sometimes the doctor does to be sure they are healthy.
What are you doing, Mommy and Daddy?	◆ Private things. ◆ Having special time together. We like to hug and hold each other because we love each other and it feels good. ◆ Making love. We want to be alone. We'll be out soon. (Some parents lock their door to avoid such interruptions.)
What was that noise you were making?	◆ We were exercising. ◆ We were making love.
What does "make love" mean?	◆ When two grown-ups love each other, they both want to touch each other's private parts because it feels good to both of them.
What's this? [menstrual blood]	◆ Short answer: *Food for a baby. There was no baby in my uterus, so the food came out.* (Reminder for adults: The blood-rich wall of the uterus nourishes the embryo.) ◆ Longer answer: *Once every month, a woman's body gets ready to grow another baby. The inside of her uterus gets thick and wet to make a nest for the baby. If there's no baby, the water and blood come out. It is called having a period/menstruation.*
What are these? [tampons, pads]	◆ Things women use. ◆ They catch the water and blood that come out during a woman's period.
What are these? [condoms, birth control pills]	◆ We use those so we won't have another baby now.
Why does my penis/clitoris get hard?	◆ It's made that way. When you touch it and it feels good, extra blood goes into it and fills it up. It's like a balloon that gets hard when it fills up with air.
Why can't I pee when my penis is hard?	◆ Your penis puffs up on the outside and the inside, so the tube for peeing gets squished and the pee can't come out.
How did Aunt/Uncle Chris get AIDS?	◆ I'll explain that when you get older. The important thing to know now is that you and I won't catch it from her/him.

Compiled by Helen F. Neville

Sisters and Brothers

■■

When we think of a family with more than one child, we imagine brothers and sisters who will love and support each other long into the future. Though some siblings get along easily from the beginning, we often have to work to bring out the best from both sides.

How Temperament Affects Brothers and Sisters

Mellow, easy-going brothers and sisters usually get along well together. Children who quickly make changes and adapt find it easier to cooperate with us and their siblings. On the other hand, those who are intense and have trouble making changes will have a harder time. Very sensitive children may be bothered by the noise their siblings make. Kids who get easily frustrated are less patient and have more trouble entertaining themselves. They may pick fights with siblings so that Mom or Dad will step in and help them figure out what to do next. Those who are slow to adapt or easily frustrated are often exhausted by late afternoon and, therefore, arguments are more common later in the day. For these intense children, plan easy activities and keep life simple, especially during late afternoons and evenings.

Brothers and sisters affect each other's development. Children don't usually respond to siblings' wishes as quickly as adults do. Therefore, children who grow up with siblings often learn more quickly than only children that other

58. Helping Older Siblings Get Along with Younger Siblings

Age of Older Child	Things to Think About
18 mo. to 3 yr.	◆ Toddlers don't understand that their size and strength can easily hurt a baby. When feeling jealous, they may hit and hurt. We need to watch them closely and separate them when needed. Teach: "If your fingernails change color, you're touching the baby too hard." ◆ Do things together—read while nursing. ◆ Encourage toddlers to ask for attention, rather than hit the baby: "Come pat my hand when you want my attention." ◆ Arrange time alone with toddlers. ◆ Explain that babies can't eat or get things for themselves—and how glad we are that their sibling is the "big" one and can help. ◆ Offer a "baby day" when siblings can play "baby." ◆ Have 2s hold a bottle, give talking lessons, fetch diapers, and entertain, such as make funny faces, roll balls, etc.
3 yr.	◆ Children around 3½ may be very jealous of attention to other family members. Give lots of hugs. Talk about feelings. "You and I can talk while I feed the baby." ◆ Suggest games with baby: peek-a-boo, hide-and-seek, and crawl-and-chase.
4 yr.	◆ Older child may be bossy and may say mean things when upset. (If this child is high energy and intense, hitting may still be an issue.) Encourage taking turns and problem solving, rather than hitting and name calling. ◆ Listen to this child's concerns at family meetings. Then problem solve and set up helpful rules.
5 yr.	◆ Child can often think ahead and help plan how to prevent problems.

Compiled by Helen F. Neville

59. Helping Younger Siblings Get Along with Older Siblings

Age of Younger Child	Things to Think About	
Birth to crawling	◆ With a high need or ill new baby, the older children are much more likely to feel ignored. We can leave babies with other people at times so older children get some undivided attention.	**It is generally not safe to leave these little ones alone with older children.**
Crawling to 18 mo.	◆ Crawling babies can now get into and upset older children's activities. Set up space where older children can play without being interrupted. (If space is limited, this might be in the parent's bedroom.) ◆ Younger children more easily accept a sitter when older siblings are also there.	
18 mo. to 3 yr.	◆ Even adults find it hard to manage 2s. Understandably, this phase is very hard on older children, too. Set up a private space for the older child. ◆ Younger children's urge to copy often annoys older ones. ◆ Younger ones want whatever the older ones are holding. Support older children's rights and suggest a peace offering to younger children. Explain that little ones copy in order to learn from people they like. Make up games where older children try to get the younger ones to copy. ◆ Encourage older ones to ask for help when bothered by the younger ones. Separate them when necessary.	
3 yr.	◆ Now that younger and older children can talk, our role in their arguments should change from judge to reporter. Start with friendly eye contact with each child. Report what each child wants, and ask each for ideas about solutions. ◆ 3½s may be especially jealous of attention to other family members. Remind them that they are loved and that everyone gets turns.	
4 yr.	◆ Some younger children talk so much that the older ones have little emotional space. At the dinner table, use a "talking spoon"—no one can interrupt while someone else has the spoon. Limit turns with a timer if necessary. ◆ All-or-nothing thinking at this age makes it especially painful to be teased by older siblings. Listen separately to each child's concerns about the other. Then try brainstorming solutions.	
5 yr.	◆ Once younger siblings are 5, they can often help plan how to avoid problems.	

Compiled by Helen F. Neville

people are different and want different things.

Order of birth in the family affects emotional development. Oldest children start out comparing themselves only to other adults. They tend to have high standards, be determined, and expect much of themselves as they grow up. Because they often tell a younger brother or sister what to do, they tend to be bossy. They may sometimes need reminders to relax and back off—from their own high standards and from bossing others.

Younger children compare themselves not just to parents but also to another child. They tend to be more realis-

tic about what they expect of themselves. However, some try *very* hard to keep up with an older brother or sister. To help, Dad tells Malik what his big brother could and couldn't do when he was the same age as Malik is now. Most younger children are smaller, so they can't use physical strength to get their way. Instead, they use social skills such as charm and tact, and sometimes they get sneaky.

If there are three children in the family, the middle one tends to be more adaptable. However, this one can also get discouraged because both the older child and the younger child have privileges this middle one does not. For the middle child, spending time with parents is especially important. The youngest of three children tends to feel less confident, be more passive, let others take responsibility, and ask for help by complaining. Protect these children from put-downs and help them stand up and care for themselves.

After a careful review of the research, Judith Rich Harris reports in *The Nurture Assumption* that birth order differences are family roles, not personality traits. Birth order has no significant effect on how children and adults act with their age mates outside the family.

Equal Treatment for All?

We want to treat our children equally. However, a child who is ill, has a disability, or has a very challenging temperament demands more time and emotional space within the family. Around 4, if not sooner, try to get some time alone with the "low-maintenance" child at least once a week. Occasionally ask, "What is hard about living with your brother/sister?" and "When do you most miss my attention?" Then ask, "What do you think might help?"

Sleep: Theirs and Ours

This section begins with important basic information about sleep and how it works. Then we'll look at how sleep patterns change over time, as little ones grow. Finally, we'll look at a number of other topics that relate to sleep.

How Sleep Works

Understanding the basics of sleep helps us manage sleep more easily.

Sleeping. A baby's sleep cycle includes a period of restless "active sleep" and a period of deep, still "quiet sleep." During active sleep, babies twitch, wiggle, and wake easily. Breathing is not regular and they dream a lot. While babies—and adults—dream, we can see their eyes move under their closed eyelids. (This is called rapid eye movement or REM sleep.) During quiet sleep, babies relax, lie still, breathe regularly, and are harder to wake up.

Adults normally start the night by dropping fairly quickly into a very deep level of quiet sleep, the deepest and most restful cycle of the night. Babies under 4 months usually start with about 20 minutes of active sleep, during which they easily wake.

Adult sleep cycles average about 1½ hours. Infant sleep cycles average 50 to 60 minutes. Babies, more often than adults, wake up between their sleep cycles. Researchers have watched babies with low-light video cameras. Most wake up five to eight times per night. Some easily settle themselves back to sleep; others cry for help.

60. How Many Parents Get a Full Night's Sleep?

Child's Age	% of Households in Which Parents Sleep Through the Night
Early weeks	Only 5%
3 mo.	Only 30%
8 to 10 mo.	Only 40%
1 to 3 yr.	60–70% (10–12% of toddlers wake parents once per night and 10–12% wake parents more than once per night. The remaining 10–12% wake parents only once or twice per week.)
3 yr.	Most parents sleep most nights without interruption. (25% of 3s wake parents 3 times per week.)
4 yr.	Almost all parents sleep most nights without interruption. (A few 4s wake parents occasionally because of nightmares.)

Note: Infant sleep studies measure different things at different ages, and different parents need different amounts of sleep, so it is extremely difficult to get accurate information. These numbers give a *very general* picture

Compiled by Helen F. Neville

Waking in the morning. Most animals and even insects have a biological alarm clock—Mother Nature announces when it is time to wake up. With our electric lights we adults may try to ignore our biological clocks, but this may be harder for children. Most people sleep better (and are easier to get along with) when their lives are in sync with their biological clocks.

Most children awake with a power surge of energy about the same time each morning *no matter when they went to sleep.* So if they stay up late, they still wake up at their normal time, even though they didn't get all the sleep they need. The good news is that if we put them to bed somewhat earlier, many will still wake up at their usual time and, therefore, get more sleep. (Do you wonder why you didn't notice *your* morning power surge? Either your electric alarm went off first, or like many Americans, you were too sleep deprived to notice!)

Getting tired. A simple clock in our brain counts how long we've been up. The more hours we are awake, the more tired we get.

Staying awake. Adults get a second power surge of wake up energy around 4 or 5 p.m. Without it, most human beings would be asleep at 8 p.m. The late afternoon power surge is stronger than the one we got in the morning because it needs to keep us going even though we haven't slept for hours. Without a second power surge yet, little ones usually become fussy or droopy around 4 or 5 p.m. *unless they have an afternoon nap.* Once this natural energy surge develops sometime between 2 and 6, they are ready to give up afternoon naps. See below, page 196, "Other Things That May Affect Sleep."

Is It Daytime or Nighttime?

Day and night were all the same in the dark space before birth. Babies wake up because of a call from the "action centers" in the brain. According to Marc Weissbluth, M.D., in *Healthy Sleep Habits, Happy Child,* even if babies are on constant intravenous (IV) feedings due to illness, they still wake and sleep like other babies. For this reason, we know hunger isn't the cause of waking. In the early weeks, most babies sleep for just two to five hours at a time. Their longest period of sleep may be during the day *or* night. Un-

fortunately, there is little we can do right now to make them sleep differently. So *we* have to adjust and get our own sleep whenever we can.

Around 6 weeks full-term babies start to make melatonin—a brain hormone that connects waking up with daylight. Some babies now begin to sleep more at night than during the day. By 4 months, almost all babies make a full supply of melatonin. Patterns of body temperature and other hormones help them settle into a day-and-night schedule. Their longest sleep is during the night and they wake at a more regular hour in the morning. If little ones are still confused about day and night, we can take them outside for a walk each morning—the earlier, the better—once the sun is up. Or have them spend some time each morning in a bright, sunny room whenever possible. Afternoon light is also good, but it may work better to keep lights low during the evening and at night.

How Much Sleep Do Children Need?

Some children need a great deal more sleep than others. How much sleep each person needs is probably genetically based and unlikely to change. Shauna is awake four more hours every day than Evan. That means her parents are on duty 28 more hours per week! Life is especially hard when parents need a great deal of sleep and children need little. Fortunately, many children who are "short-sleepers" have similar parents.

61. Sleep Patterns as Children Grow

Age	Hours of Total Sleep Needed in 24 hours
Birth	11–18
4 to 12 mo.	11–16
1 yr.	11½–15½
2 yr.	11–14
3 yr.	10½–14
4 yr.	10½–13½
5 yr.	10-12½

From Healthy Sleep Habits, Happy Child
by Marc Weissbluth, M.D.

Schedule conflicts with the biological clock. Because of our genetic evolution, some people tend to be "night owls" and others, "morning larks." Such differing biological clocks may have evolved for safety; someone in the human group was always awake and on the alert for danger.

When parents work outside the home, we need time to commute, fix dinner, and perform the evening routine. That puts bedtime between 8 and 10 p.m. in many American homes. For many children this works just fine.

On the other hand, late bedtimes may not work for everyone. *If we have to wake children in the morning, they haven't yet had all the sleep they need.* If they are tired all day, they may run on adrenaline, which will make it difficult for them to get to sleep at bedtime. Research suggests that the biological clock for many babies runs something like this:

Wake up: 6-7 a.m.
Morning nap: 9 a.m.
Afternoon nap: Start between 1-3 p.m.
Bedtime: 6-8 p.m.

Around the World

SIDS deaths in third world countries are less noticeable because many more babies die of infectious diseases. In warm climates, babies sleep without covers or blankets, so they don't run the risk of suffocation. Worldwide, SIDS incidence is getting lower, on the one hand, as more babies sleep on their backs, and higher, on the other, as more parents smoke.

As for traditional sleep location, much of the world is like the countryside in **Mexico and Central America**. Mother and baby sleep together for about 2 years until the next baby arrives. Toddlers then move to the outer edge of the sleeping mat, or sleep with siblings or other relatives. Preschoolers continue to sleep with others.

If children are often grouchy, their schedule may not fit their biological clock. Think creatively about priorities and options for the family schedule.

Jet lag in the nursery? When we keep kids up for an extra few hours on the weekend, they often react as if they had flown across the United States and changed time zones. It may take them several days to catch up on their sleep and return to a better mood.

What are the effects of too little sleep? Lack of sleep affects both children and adults, though adults may cope better with the symptoms.
Mood. People become grumpy, short-tempered, less adaptable, and less able to handle frustration.
Body. People become less coordinated and may have headaches or stomachaches. When tired, we produce higher levels of stress hormones.
Learning. Attention spans become shorter. It is harder to learn and remember things. We have less motivation.

62. *Protecting Babies from SIDS and Suffocation*

Things You Can Do	Do NOT Sleep with a Baby if:
◆ Put babies on their backs, not on their sides or stomachs: "Back to Sleep." ◆ Always provide a firm sleeping surface and be sure baby can't get trapped between the mattress and the wall. ◆ Keep pillows, blankets, soft toys away from baby's face. ◆ Use strings or ribbons no longer than a few inches. ◆ Sleep in the same room as your baby for the first 4–6 months. ◆ Offer a pacifier* for sleep after 1 month or after breast feeding is going well. ◆ Don't dress babies too warmly. See page 194, "How Warm Is Warm Enough?"	◆ You are a smoker (now or during pregnancy) or are under the influence of alcohol or other drugs. ◆ You are obese. ◆ You are on a couch, sofa, or easy chair. ◆ You are exhausted.** ◆ Other children are in the same bed.

  * Researchers don't yet know why pacifiers protect against SIDS.
** Adults normally sleep most deeply when they first go to bed, so later in the night may be a safer time for bed sharing.
  More research is needed.

Compiled by Helen F. Neville

Sleep Location and SIDS

Where babies sleep, especially during the early months of irregular sleep and frequent feedings deserves careful thought. There is an important question of infant safety. SIDS or Sudden Infant Death Syndrome can occur between 2 weeks and 9 months, but most cases occur between 1 and 4 months of age. SIDS babies look healthy, then die of unknown cause while asleep. Researchers are trying to figure out what underlying factors may combine to cause these shocking deaths. Other than prematurity and birth defects, SIDS is the most common reason American babies die. Sleep position is important. Since the "Back to Sleep Campaign," begun in the 1990s, the incidence of SIDS has dropped almost 50%.

SIDS used to be called "crib death" because babies were found dead in their cribs. So it may seem surprising that some experts now recommend babies sleep in cribs for safety, rather than in their parents' bed. After nursing in bed, babies should be returned to their crib, bassinet, or "co-sleeper"—also called a "side sleeper." What is going on?

Over the last 10 to 20 years, more American families have taken to the family bed. More babies now suffocate in family beds that earlier, and some studies show that the risk of SIDS is higher in the parental bed than outside it, especially between 1 and 4 months of age. (Of every 10,000 babies, 5 die of SIDS, and one of suffocation.) Other studies report that sleeping with parents is especially dangerous if parents smoke. SIDS risk is known to be higher in babies born early or underweight and for babies of young mothers. For unknown reasons, SIDS is more common in low-income families. Using a pacifier may

Practical Tips for SIDS Prevention

Keep blankets away from the face: Dress babies in "sleep suits" and skip the blanket. Or, position them so their feet touch one end of the crib. Adjust the blankets and tuck them in.

If you do not have a crib, it is safer to use a drawer pulled from a dresser or a cardboard box for the baby to sleep nearby, rather than a sofa or an unsafe parent bed.

Babies who hate the "exposed feeling" on their backs may do better when swaddled—wrapped firmly in a sheet or receiving blanket.

Babies who refuse a pacifier: Feed them first. Try a different size or shape of pacifier. If they absolutely refuse, take care to protect them in other ways.

When they first learn to roll from back to front, some babies are at extra risk. This risk may be higher for babies who learn to roll early—we don't yet know. "Back sleepers" have raised sides which make it harder for babies to roll, though their effectiveness is not yet known.

help protect babies, though we don't yet know why.

To be as safe as possible, some experts say babies and toddlers should not sleep in their parents' beds at all. Other experts say that by following important safety precautions, risks of both SIDS and suffocation can be cut dramatically and that co-sleeping has important advantages. (Co-sleeping can build closeness with babies and make breast feeding easier.) While we wait for careful, more detailed studies about risk factors for SIDS and its exact causes, parents will have to decide whether or not to sleep separately, especially during the high risk period of 1 to 4 months. For current information about risk factors, research, and safe sleeping practices, see the Mayo Clinic website at www.mayoclinic.com and search for "SIDS." For more information about safe sleeping, see www.askdrsears.com.

Sleep as Time Goes By

Early months. *Most high need babies* need to be rocked, held, and carried in order to calm down and to sleep during the early months. After 4 months, some sleep more deeply on a still, firm surface.

6 to 8 mo. By this age many *parents* are ready to sleep through the night. Many babies are ready as well, but others are not. Careful studies show that starting solid food doesn't make babies sleep better or longer. Some parents happen to start solids just when babies are *ready* to sleep through the night. And so the old wives' tale persists. Some babies are still very hungry during the night and have trouble returning to sleep once they are wide awake. It helps to feed these little ones *before* they wake completely.

Other babies are now ready to load up twenty-four hours' worth of calories during the daytime. Some tired moms encourage this. They gradually nurse for shorter times during the night or give smaller bottles at night. Babies then adjust by taking in more food during the day.

There is no single time or way for the big step to another room, though many parents make it after night nursings have stopped. Some parents are in no hurry to move little ones to their own rooms. They enjoy the connection of nearby sleeping, or may not have another room. Other parents want a break from all-day child care or look forward to a more spontaneous and enthusiastic nightlife of their own. Some parents, especially light sleepers, leave before the kids do, to get an occasional good night's sleep *alone* on the sofa.

Researchers in animal behavior point out two different patterns of family life. Many animal babies grow up in dens or nests. For these animals, the *place* is home—where they can relax into sleep. But animals that don't have dens or nests rely on nearby *family* in order to relax into sleep. We are more like the second group, so these researchers suggest that early on, young humans rely on familiar people to feel safe enough to sleep. With time, our little ones learn to feel safe in a familiar place as well. When we want them to sleep in a separate room, it will often go more easily if we spend enough relaxed, pleasant time in *their room*. Then they connect us with their sleeping place.

How Warm Is Warm Enough?

Most babies need about the same number of layers as we do to keep warm. Feel their backs or thighs for warmth. Expect their hands and feet to be cool on cool days.

Young babies usually fall asleep while we feed or hold them. If we want them to fall back to sleep on their own during the night, it helps to practice at bedtime. When babies are between 6 and 12 months can be a good time to make this shift. Set them gently into bed while they are drowsy but *still awake*.

If left to themselves during the night between 6 and 12 months, some babies fuss or cry for two to ten minutes for a night or two and then are miraculously silent *all night long*. Other babies fuss or cry somewhat longer but are reassured by a pat or soothing voice every ten minutes or so. Over a week or two, with a little more distance and less attention each night, these little ones also learn to sleep on their own. There is no evidence that several nights with some on-and-off fussing and even some hard crying cause psychological damage to a baby who is well cared for. Some cautious, sensitive babies adjust more easily if a parent sleeps with them in their new room until it becomes familiar. A night light helps them see that they are in their usual safe place.

Unlike other babies, spirited Spencer's cries turned to screams whenever Mom came to soothe him but did not pick him up. Some babies who are very sensitive, emotionally intense, or easily frustrated will scream for an hour or more. Some children would continue to be just as miserable, night after night, if left alone. They are clearly not ready to manage on their own. Go back to the drawing board and make another plan.

8 mo. About half the lucky parents who have enjoyed sleeping through the night now wake to the cry of an unhappy baby. Some little ones awaken and pull themselves up to a standing position in their cribs and then they can't get back down on their own. Help them practice the new skill of sitting down during the day. Some babies have just started going to bed earlier, so they need a snack to get through the longer night. Sleep is also more difficult because the fear centers of the brain have grown more effective. Now separation anxiety becomes common.

10 to 12 mo. Many babies this age need five to fifteen minutes, or a little longer, to relax into sleep. This time may pass

as they lie quietly, suck, rock, or listen to lullabies. Some need to fuss regularly for five to ten minutes before they fall asleep. It is as though nothing else can release the day's tension. Others only fuss when overtired.

Almost all babies can now get through the night without food. Nursing at night is now about comfort, not calories. If you would like other comfort options, see page 181, "Self-Soothing and Security Objects." As mentioned earlier, we can gradually nurse for shorter periods or give smaller bottles, cutting down to none. Then we know our babies are not awake at night due to hunger. Some babies make this transition more easily than others.

Studies also show that most parents who soothe their 12-month-olds back to sleep during the night are still doing the same at age 2. Some parents are in no hurry. Others long for sleep without nightly interruption, especially if they work away from home. This is a good time to check out how little ones manage on their own, if we haven't done so earlier. If we are afraid to let them fuss a little, we will miss this window of opportunity.

Toddlers. Many toddlers resist bedtime separation from their parents—not an issue for those with a family bed. At 2, Melody falls asleep quickly and easily with her family in the living room. Dad carries her to bed for the rest of the night. Some parents snuggle with toddlers until they fall asleep. Others parents read to themselves or do their yoga by the child's bedside. Some toddlers quickly settle in with limits: "I'll come back once for a kiss or another sip of water, but not more," or "If you stay in your bed, I'll leave the bedroom door open. Otherwise, I'll have to close it." Spencer starts every night where his parents want him to end up someday—in his own room. During the night, he sometimes sleeps on a sleeping mat beside their bed. He sleeps like a wrestler in the ring, so he's not an easy bed mate. Also, because he makes changes slowly, it would be hard for him to sleep with them on some nights and by himself on others.

Twos often sleep better in an older brother or sister's room than alone. This phase won't last forever. Many sleep difficulties disappear at 3.

Crib Climbers

Once kids stand 35 inches tall some will try to climb out of their cribs and fall. At this point, they are safer sleeping on a low bed, especially if they are active climbers. Childproof their rooms and protect them with baby gates.

Preschoolers. Most preschoolers sleep well in their own rooms. Most need ten to thirty minutes to relax into sleep once they are in bed. Read relaxing stories *after* they climb into bed. Ask about the hard and happy events of their day. Enjoy snuggle time or give a back rub. Help 3s or 4s find calm, soothing things to do or think about. Soothing, familiar music may help. Encourage active preschoolers to blow out slow, deep breaths or take slow-motion stretches, such as alternately stretching a hand or toe toward each corner of the bed.

A few preschoolers climb regularly into their parents' bed during the night. Threes and 4s may need help with nightmares.

See page 142, "Fantasy That Frightens" and page 184, "Our Bodies at Home."

In the morning, 3s usually call or come fetch us when they wake. However, we might snatch a little extra sleep if they find something interesting to play with in their room—or find a morning snack. Most 4s can entertain themselves in the morning.

Naps

Children's need for naps changes over time. Here are the general patterns:

Birth to 5 mo. Some babies nap anywhere. Others need a quiet, dark room. Some sensitive infants need to nap once they've been awake for just two hours or less; otherwise they get overtired and fussy. These babies fall asleep more easily *before* they look tired or get grouchy. Until 5 months or so, sensitive infants do best with three naps: morning, early afternoon, and late afternoon.

If naps are still hard to predict at 4 months, we can write down all the times our babies sleep for a week. Then we may be able to see *some* pattern and encourage it. If we can get mornings to be regular, afternoons and evenings often follow suit.

8 mo. Sensitive babies may now be able to be awake for three hours between naps without getting overtired and fussy.

9 mo. to 1 yr. Babies who used to need three naps a day now do better with two naps and an earlier bedtime. Some babies, who just catnapped in the early months, now start longer naps—though some still won't for another year.

12 to 21 mo. After they drop their morning nap, some toddlers need an earlier bedtime. However, others now need less sleep, so their evening bedtime remains the same.

2 to 6 yr. Once children develop their late-afternoon power surge they no longer need naps. Now they can go through the late afternoon and early evening without getting fussy. If they continue to nap anyway, they will likely be up late into the evening. This schedule works fine for many and is common in many parts of the world, especially where it is hot and everyone takes an afternoon rest. However, other children do better if they now skip their afternoon nap and go to bed earlier.

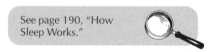

See page 190, "How Sleep Works."

63. Naps—Who Needs Them?

Age	Naps
Birth to 5 mo.	Some babies do better with 3 (or more) naps per day.
Birth to 12 mo.	Most babies need 2 naps per day.
12 to 21 mo.	Most toddlers drop morning naps.
3 yr.	90% still need afternoon naps.
4 yr.	50% still need afternoon naps.
5 yr.	25% still need afternoon naps.
6 yr.	Most do not nap in the afternoon unless it is the custom of the whole family.

From Healthy Sleep Habits, Happy Child *by Marc Weissbluth, M.D.*

Other Things That May Affect Sleep

An amazing variety of things may affect children's sleep. Here is an alphabetical listing of the most common reasons:

Bedwetting. At 4, 40% of children wet the bed at night. By 6, 10% of children still wet the bed. Almost all girls are dry by 5 or 6, and boys by 7 or 8. Just as some children need more time to start walking, some need more time to stay dry at night. Genetics plays a role. If one or both parents learned to stay dry later, their children are likely to do the same. On rare occasions, allergies may be a factor. While we wait for the bladder to grow bigger, we can limit liquids before bedtime, or wake kids and take them to the bathroom before we go to bed.

Tell 5s and 6s that light and deep sleep follow each other during the night. Suggest that an almost full bladder will wake them up to pee *before* the next cycle of deep sleep, during which they have no control. It may help to have a potty right beside their bed. Once kids are dry some nights, rewards may help them become more consistent. Fives and 6s can help change wet sheets. Alarm systems that vibrate when a child starts to wet the bed are not useful until 6 or 7. Check with a doctor if 6-year-old girls or 8-year-old boys don't consistently stay dry at night.

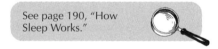

See page 190, "How Sleep Works."

To increase awareness of how the bladder works, preschoolers may enjoy using a plastic measuring cup to see how much their bladder can hold. (A child's age plus two is about the number of ounces the bladder can hold, so 5s can hold about 7 ounces.)

Body position. Even when we close our eyes, we know whether we are standing or lying down. "Position sensors" in our body clue us in. For some people, the position sensors don't work well. When they close their eyes they may feel like they are falling. These individuals gradually find very specific positions that give them reassurance—such as always on the same side or with their head pressed against the top of the bed, or their back against a wall. If preschoolers still have trouble going to sleep, we can ask, "How do you feel when you close your eyes?"

Exercise. Children need plenty of exercise during the day. However, exercise within an hour or two of bedtime makes it hard for some children to fall asleep. Notice how much quiet time your child needs before bedtime.

Family stress. Little ones sense when we are upset, and our anxiety can upset their sleep. For example, we may argue with our partner about how to manage sleep or struggle to get the new baby to sleep. Many other sources of stress, such as finances, family illness, marital problems, work, and problems of other children in the family can affect how calmly we go about the bedtime routine in the evening. Sometimes, leaving children alone at night reminds us of difficult separations from our own past. Sources of help include doctors, family counselors, and social service agencies.

Illness. Earaches, itchy skin, and fever can disturb sleep. A few medicines make sleep more difficult, depending on type, dose, and when they are given. Check with your doctor or clinic.

Light. Most homes around the world are dimly lit compared to ours, which makes it easier for tired children to go to sleep. During the evening, bright room lights and video screens can unsettle the biological clock. Some children may be more sensitive to this effect than others. Pay attention to the effects of light (including even short bursts of bright light) upon your child.

Night terrors are different from nightmares. During night terrors, children's eyes are wide open, but they don't recognize us. Night terrors usually occur 1 to 3 hours after going to sleep. They are most common after long periods of being awake and thus when children have just given up afternoon naps. They are also more common with stress. Stay nearby and don't try to wake the child. If night terrors occur several nights in a row, try waking the child just *before* they usually happen. If they continue, check with your doctor.

Nightmares. Evan, 4 yr., had a frightening nightmare. Dad invited him into his bed. The following nights, Evan said he was frightened, but he didn't look frightened. He'd found an excuse to sleep in his parents' bed. So Dad decided to soothe him in his own bed, dream or no dream. After sev-eral nights, Evan no longer disturbed his parents' sleep. See page 142, "Fantasy that Frightens."

Overtired. Tired children are under *physical* stress. Stressed children have trouble falling asleep and naturally cry for our comfort. Well-rested children are more able to fall asleep on their own or with less fussing. Put children to bed *before* they are overtired.

Sleepwalking. Five percent of children sleepwalk regularly and 15% occasionally. It is most common between 3 and 8. Until they outgrow it, protect them as needed with a baby gate at the bedroom door, the kitchen door, or high secure locks on all doors to the outside. Sleepwalking may be more common when children are overly tired or under stress.

Snoring interrupts sleep. Allergies and large tonsils can cause long-term snoring and sleep loss. Check with a doctor or clinic.

Stomach acid. At birth, the muscle at the top of the stomach isn't very strong, so babies routinely spit up. Over the coming months, the muscle learns to tighten and be able to keep milk and stomach acid down where they belong. In a *few* babies, this takes a long time. In the meantime, stomach acid slips past the muscle when they lie down at night. These babies cry because of a burning pain in the tube to the stomach—the esophagus. Acid may even flow high enough to set off a chemical alarm in the throat, near the airway. This may physically startle babies awake, making it difficult for them to fall back to sleep. This problem is more common if a feeding tube was needed for a period of time. Such babies may continue to cry a great deal after 5 to 6 months and are hard to soothe at night. It may help to lift the head end of the crib up a few inches on blocks. Or talk with a doctor or clinic about testing or treatment for *esophageal reflux*.

Temperament. Some children don't seem to have a regular biological clock, so it can be very hard or nearly impossible to settle them into a consistent sleep schedule. Children who are sensitive may wake easily. Those who make transitions slowly need longer to fall asleep. Active kids find it hard to lie around waiting for sleep. Children who are also emotionally intense may be even harder to manage.

Some high energy children create their own power surges. As they get tired, they run around to keep themselves awake. However, as soon as they are cornered and put into bed, they fall asleep.

Some high strung kids seem to will themselves to stay awake, but they pay a very high price. Being tired is stressful, so their bodies put out adrenaline. This natural body chemical, like coffee, causes the jitters and can make sleep impossible. By the time these children *look tired,*

they are already pumping adrenaline. They need to be put down for sleep a little before they start yawning and rubbing their eyes. Think about their biological clock. How many hours have they been awake? How tiring has their day been? Watch for a slight slowing down, a pause in their activity, a calmer moment, or a glazed look. The goal is to put them to bed during the calm before the storm.

See page 122, "Food."

Spiritual Practices

Two topics are addressed here. First, if parents want to pass their spiritual traditions on to children, what are age-appropriate ways to do so? Second, in what ways can spiritual teachings serve the developmental needs of children? We will consider children's needs for security, community, guidelines for living, and understanding of the world.

For a variety of reasons, many parents are not comfortable with spiritual topics or with particular religious traditions. They may nonetheless want to teach positive humanitarian values that are common to many spiritual paths.

Surveys show that about 80% of people in the United States believe in a supreme power that they may call Allah, Brahman, God, Goddess, Great Spirit, Higher Mind, Jehovah, Love, Mother Nature, or something else. Many follow the spiritual paths of Buddha, Jesus, Mohammed, and others. Not surprisingly, families vary widely on whether and how much they teach spiritual practices to children. Surprisingly, studies of twins show that there is also a genetic piece. People are born with somewhat more or less likelihood of religion being important in their lives.

Loss of Security

Fours worry about their own safety, and 5s worry about their loved ones as well. Both ages also have vivid, dramatic imaginations. Avoid frightening stories that can lead to nightmares. For example, stories or threats about the fires of hell can be extremely frightening. A dedicated religious teacher told Melody's 5-year-old cousin that her father would go to hell because of his "wrong" beliefs. Melody's cousin was afraid to leave her father's side for fear of his safety.

Security

Many adults around the world gain a sense of security from knowing God's love, support, and protection. The same is true for children. Children's early sense of divine protection comes from the loving care we surround them with—our warmth, support, and hugs. Parents use music, verses, and prayers to express the calm and safety of divine love. When parents say, "I love you," they may add, "and God loves you, too."

At 3, Shauna was afraid of the dark. Sleep was easier once she began this bedtime prayer: "Please bring me angels in my sleep." (Keep prayers positive. If children pray, "Please keep scary dreams away," their minds make pictures of scary things.) When Malik was 4, his aunt was in the hospital. Malik's mother said, "Let's pray for her. Let's close our eyes and see a candle in her hospital room. It reminds her that everyone loves her. Now let's see her back home and feeling better."

Because 5s are often concerned about the safety of those they love, Elena prays each night, "Keep Mommy and Daddy and Aunt Alicia all safe."

When Melody at 5 worries in bed about something that happened earlier, Dad says, "Let's lie still and imagine breathing the blue sky in and out."

Community

Like adults, children need a sense of connection to others. Brief family rituals can serve this purpose. Evan, 2, usually liked to hold hands briefly before dinner. (On days he didn't want to, his parents held hands without him and invited him to join in the next night.) Melody, 3, likes to blow out the match every Friday evening after Mom lights the candles. Then Mom says, "God asked us to light candles together each Friday evening and remember what He has done for us."

Fours become interested in relating to the larger world beyond their family. At bedtime, Malik likes to hear stories about how people help and take care of each other. Sharing religious occasions, meals, and rituals with a religious community can provide this wider sense of connection. Evan likes to sit beside his parents in church, as long as he has some crayons to color with.

Formal religious services may be too long for most young children. Spencer's parents took him to several services, but were frustrated because he couldn't be still and quiet. So instead, they leave him with friends or they take turns going to church. Now they come home feeling renewed rather than frustrated.

When Melody is 5 her parents emphasize their connection to others by saying: "The air we breathe belongs to everyone in the world. Let's sit for a minute and gently feel the air come in and out."

Guidelines for Living

Just because 4s (and older children) want to behave well doesn't mean it is easy! Because 4s often struggle to do the

An Attitude of Gratitude

Gratitude does not come naturally to young children, especially before age 7. However, we can still encourage 4s and 5s to look outside themselves and notice the good things around them. Before bedtime or during meals, invite them to think about or give thanks for favorite people they were with that day, a food they like on the table, an activity they enjoyed, or a good feeling they had.

Elena's mom regularly suggests this brief meditation: "Let's walk along this path and not talk. Let's listen to the nice sounds of Mother Nature." Spencer's dad points out, "Look at this beautiful flower that God made!"

right thing, they appreciate stories where good finally wins. Read or tell bedtime stories about both ancient and modern people who model positive spiritual qualities and actions. Some families keep books with religious stories on a separate shelf to show their importance.

Mom encourages Malik to do something each day that will please God. Malik reports at bedtime that he patted a puppy or let a friend take the first turn. Elena's dad uses each day of the week to practice a particular spiritual value. "Today is Tuesday. This is the day we practice being kind to others. Give someone a smile or a hug, or help a friend." At dinner they each tell how they practiced kindness that day.

After Elena had an argument with her friend, Dad said, "Let's sit quietly for a minute and ask, 'What would be the loving thing to do next?'" When Elena threw a candy wrapper on the street, Mom said, "We need to pick it up because it is our job to take care of Mother Nature's world." On her birthday, Dad tells her, "You are here for a purpose. As you grow up you will find out what it is."

Understanding the World

Many 4s wonder about significant issues, including life and death. They often want to know what their parents believe, and to understand how the world works. How we answer their questions will be very different, depending on our own personal beliefs. If we don't know how to answer their questions, honesty is often the best policy: "I don't know" or "I wonder about that, too."

In terms of development, it helps to remember that young children think most easily with pictures and their own personal experience. For example, to help Spencer understand the true meaning of Christmas, his family bakes a birthday cake for Jesus.

Because 4s want to understand the world, it may help them to hear specific examples of how parents use spiritual practices in their own lives. "I'm going to pray for you this morning—that you and your friend get along today. I'm going to keep that good picture in my mind." "I was hurried and worried, so I stopped and took a few minutes to breathe in the peaceful air. It helped me feel better." "There goes an ambulance. I'm going to ask God to help those people get home safely."

Because young children are generally self-centered, they often pray to get toys and pets. If they don't get what they pray for, they may be painfully disappointed. To protect Evan, and help him understand, Mom explains her belief this way: "God doesn't give us everything we ask for because we may not really need it or it may not be good for us." She encouraged Evan to end his prayers with, "If, God, you think that's a good idea. Amen."

Sometimes we forget that children may have their own very clear (and different) ideas about how the world is. Rather than answer their questions immediately, we may learn very interesting things by first asking, "What do you think?" Sometimes we misunderstand what children ask. Shauna asked about the bells she heard. When her parents said they were church bells, Shauna wanted to go to church. Her nonreligious parents struggled to find a church where they could feel comfortable. It later turned out that Shauna wanted to *see* the bells.

Common Questions Children Ask

Parents will, of course, give different answers to these questions, depending on their own traditions and beliefs.

A Viewpoint of Their Own

Children sometimes speak with amazing wisdom, foretell future events, have visions, or tell of previous lives. It is difficult to know how common such events are. Children often keep quiet for years about such experiences because they sense that others would be upset.

In *The Secret Spiritual World of Children*, Tobin Hart, Ph.D., tells of an 18-month-old child. She often looked at the empty rocking chair beside her crib, eyes moving back and forth as though watching someone rock. With fingers to her lips she told her mother to "Shhh." Weeks later, looking at the family photo album for the first time, she pointed with excitement to a picture of her great grandmother and said, "Lady!" While many parents would have ignored this unexpected sign of recognition, her mother asked, "Is that who sits in your rocking chair?" The little girl happily replied, "Yupee."

What is a soul/spirit?
It is the part of us that connects us to all other people.
It is the part of us that connects us to God.
It is the part of a person that keeps living after his (her) body dies.

What is God?
God makes everything in the world—everything we see.
God is bigger and stronger than any person.

Where is God?
God is everywhere, just like the air we breathe is everywhere.
God's love is in each of us.
God is in Heaven.

What does God look like?
We can't see God, but when we feel loved or feel loving, that is God's love.
When we see kindness, we see God.
Everything you see is God: you, Mommy, Daddy, your friends, the house, the trees, and everything.
We can't see God, but we can see the place where we visit with God (church, synagogue, temple, mosque, or place of natural beauty).
Here's a picture of God's helpers.
Here's a picture of how the famous artist Michelangelo painted God.
No one knows what God looks like. We don't draw pictures of God.

Where is heaven/paradise?
Some people say it is up in the sky.
I don't know where it is.

What does heaven/paradise look like?
It is the prettiest place you can imagine.
There are many angels in heaven.
I hope there are beautiful trees and an ocean. What do you hope for? (Evan hoped there would be lots of building blocks.)

Stress: Signs and Soothing

Stress is part of life. Divorce and quiet family deaths can be hard enough, while natural disasters and acts of war throw entire communities into an uproar. As adults we have more ways to cope than our children do. Because we are their main support, it is important that we can recognize their signs of stress, help them during difficult times, and when possible, decrease the stress in their lives.

It is normal for children to cry, get angry, suck their thumbs, and so forth. When they are under stress, they do *more* of these ordinary things. Is there now more crying or anger than usual? Do they *prefer* to suck their thumb, masturbate, or talk to an invisible companion instead of play with others?

Common Causes of Stress in Children's Lives

Overstimulation. We know that sights and sounds encourage brain development. On the other hand, too much noise, light, movement, or skin sensation can make children anxious, especially the very sensitive ones. Recent research shows that some children pay attention more easily after time in a quiet park rather than on a busy city street. One mother related how her sensitive, low energy son refused to return to the noisy, bustling big-city street from the dark, quiet interior of a cathedral. The goal is balance between boredom and overstimulation, according to the need of the individual child.

64. Signs of Stress

Ages	Signs of Stress
All Ages	◆ Easily upset: Cry, scream, whine, hit, bite, throw things—more than usual. ◆ Look away, avoid eye contact. ◆ Fear of being left alone: Children may cling, want to be held, be afraid to go to child care or school. Afraid at bedtime or of the dark—difficulty falling asleep, frequent waking, nightmares, night terrors. (Sleep problems are the most common sign of stress after a natural disaster.) Fear of being forgotten, feeling ignored because adults are busy with other issues. May act out to get attention. ◆ Activity changes: May be more active than usual or may withdraw and play/talk less. ◆ Physical signs: More hungry or less hungry. May refuse to eat. ◆ Illness: Diarrhea, constipation, vomiting, more frequent colds, stomachaches, headaches, etc. ◆ Fear of the same stressful event happening again.
Infant	◆ Arch back.
Toddler	◆ Bang head.
2 to 6 yr.	◆ Accident prone: Fall, run into things, or otherwise hurt themselves. ◆ Toilet learning: Accidents or bed-wetting. ◆ Fear of animals: New fears or old ones get worse. ◆ Anger: Hurt others at home or school or intentionally break things.
3 to 6 yr.	◆ Stutters, face twitches, or eyes blink. ◆ Nervous habits such as biting nails, picking nose, or twisting hair. ◆ Being "too good": Children commonly fear that they caused the problem. They may try to be really good so it won't happen again.

Compiled by Helen F. Neville

Illness, even if it is minor, makes children more upset and clingy. Clinics and hospital stays can be especially upsetting.

Separation may be stressful, depending on the amount of time apart and circumstances.

Child care and schools can cause stress if not suited to children's temperaments, learning styles, and abilities.

Inborn temperament affects both what is stressful and how children react to stress. Cautious children may experience significant stress if we push them to act like other children— for example, jumping right onto the merry-go-round or into the swimming pool without time to get ready. Emotionally intense children are more likely to get stomach problems when they are upset.

Minds and bodies that change are stressful. Imagine if you were to suddenly begin bumping your head where you didn't bump it last week. Many new talkers go through a phase of stuttering, and many 3s blink a great deal as their eyes change.

Parent distress is felt by children even if they don't understand the cause. Financial worries, job changes, strain between partners, divorce, and family illness may all affect our children.

Physical, emotional, or sexual abuse is unfortunately experienced by some children.

Soothing Stress

Sort out minor from major stress. Many babies and young children cry for a few minutes when left in child care, and this isn't harmful. On the other hand, those who cry for an hour, won't eat while in child care, or sit looking sad much of the day instead of playing are clearly in emotional and physical distress.

Figure out the cause of stress. Sometimes the cause is obvious, but reactions can also happen weeks, months, and as long as a year after a death or disaster. Sometimes children don't feel better until we adults feel back to normal. Or after a natural disaster, *we* may feel better as soon as we know our loved ones are safe, but children often need more time to feel secure.

Give information because children commonly believe they caused the bad thing to happen: "Mommy and Daddy got mad at each other even before you were born. It is not your fault." "Nobody makes earthquakes happen—the ground moves and we all feel the earthquake." "Things are hard right now. I'm still worried, but we will be okay—you will be okay and *I* will be okay." For 4s and up, plan what to do if the circumstance happens again. Ideally, it is better if we don't talk much about our own fears when children can overhear.

Work through emotions. Give time and hugs. Talk about and act out the events with children. Replay them with stuffed animals, draw pictures, or write down the event as children retell it to us. Ask questions: "How do you feel?" "What are you still worried about?" Then give reassurance.

Sucking: Breast, bottle, pacifier, or thumb. Some children suck their shirtsleeves or the ends of their long hair, while some suck and bite fingernails. Fours and 5s may find it soothing to chew sugarless gum.

Deep breathing: Cry, laugh, or sing; take long, deep sighs; blow real or imaginary bubbles.

Body motion and rhythm: Rock, swing, clap, drum, run, masturbate, sway to soothing music, dance wildly.

Offer privacy: Time without direct eye contact, alone with others nearby, or some time away from other people.

Use imagination: "Let's imagine this is all over." "Let's imagine how we'd like things to be right now." "How will this look when everything turns out okay?"

Problem solve: "What would help you feel better now?" "Here's what we will do now." "So this won't happen again, we will. . . . " "What would help you feel better if this happens again?"

Get professional help if signs of distress are severe, last more than a month, or get worse instead of better. If your doctor suggests that physical symptoms are caused by stress, get emotional help first. Many medical tests themselves cause stress, so it is better to avoid them if they aren't really necessary. Ask your doctor when you should return if symptoms don't improve.

Toilet Learning: Is It Time Yet?

When children are ready to use the toilet depends on development, gender, inborn temperament, and culture. There are many different approaches to this universal issue. Because of our independent mind-set, parents in the United States generally don't consider children "trained" until they can use the toilet on their own. This takes time.

Individual Differences in Toilet Learning

Some kids get control of urine first, and others get control of their bowels first. Occasionally parents are startled by toddlers who, all on their own, step to the potty chair and tug to get their diapers down. Many mellow, adaptable toddlers can be led regularly to the toilet, and they use it successfully. If they also have regular body rhythms so they poop at the same time each day, parents may easily be able to catch it in the potty. (Once children can follow their body signals, it is better not to remind them regularly to pee. Emptying the bladder more often than needed can keep it from stretching and growing so it can hold more urine.)

For others kids, however, body muscles quickly tighten with even minor stress. If we *make* them sit on the potty or rush them to the bathroom when they start to poop, their muscles clamp tight. They can't relax, let go, and use the toilet. Forcing the issue by making them go to the bathroom can cause *serious* constipation. These children do much better when they are older, interested, and *want* to learn.

Temperament differences strongly affect when children

Around the World

In countries where diapers aren't used, *mother training* starts early. With babies tied to their backs, **East African** mothers quickly learn to recognize the tiny body movements that mean their babies are ready to pee or poop. These movements alert a mother that it is time to take her baby off her back. Mothers may also use "conditioning" as part of the process. For example, when mothers take their babies off their backs, they may always hold them in the same squatting position.

In **Vietnam**, training often begins between and 5 and 8 months. Toddlers are held over the potty at times when they are *likely* to go (such as after meals), and parents make a "swish, swish" sound as the child pees. With time, these familiar positions and sounds suggest to little ones that it is time to pee or poop. Until these children are able to manage on their own, parents continue to pay very close attention to body signals so they can prevent accidents.

are able to use the toilet. Less physically sensitive children may not easily notice body signals and often don't mind being wet. They will need more time. Active children, or those who have trouble shifting from one thing to another may find it difficult to leave their play to get to the bathroom in time. They also need more time. Occasional success in the bathroom does not mean a child is ready for full-time responsibility. Some can manage a day at a time: "Do you want to wear diapers or underpants today?" If your child is likely to need more time, pick a preschool that can work with this fact of normal development.

When kids are interested in learning to use the toilet, there are good books to help both parents and children.

See the bibliography on page 207 and your public library.

65. Toilet Learning—Phases in Control

Ages	Phase
Birth to 18 mo.	Between birth and 18 months, the bladder gradually becomes a more effective reservoir. Early on, babies pee up to 20 times a day. With time, the bladder grows to hold larger amounts and babies then stay dry for several hours at a time.
4 to 5 mo.	A careful observer may now notice regular patterns. Some babies poop about the same time each day. Some pee so many minutes after a feeding or when a warm diaper comes off. Or they may squirm, push, grunt, or relax in particular ways, before, during, or after they empty their bladder or bowels. (Also see page 131, "Eating Month After Month, 4–8 Months.")
16 mo. to 2½ yr.	Children begin to notice when they are wetting their diapers—they may pause for a moment in their playing or change their body position. Many children begin to get some conscious control over the muscles that start and stop urine and bowel movements.
2½ to 3 yr.	Most children can tell the difference between the urge to pee or poop. They may stand a particular way or go to a particular place when pooping. Some say, "Don't look at me!"
2½ yr.	They use words to say that they need to use the toilet.
2½ yr.	Half of all girls now notice body cues on their own and get themselves to the toilet in time.
3 yr.	Half of all boys now notice body cues on their own and get themselves to the toilet in time.
4 yr.	4s are usually fascinated by their own and other people's bathrooms as they try to figure out how the world works. Some want privacy in the bathroom.
4½ yr.	Most can go to the bathroom when needed and rarely have accidents.
4½ to 5½ yr.	They can wipe themselves after using the toilet. (Remind them to wash hands afterwards.)
5 yr.	Occasionally may have daytime accidents when under emotional stress. If not yet daytime trained, it may be due to a physical problem or emotional stress.

Compiled by Helen F. Neville

Cloth or Disposable Diapers?

A few babies get diaper rash easily. Some of these babies do better with cloth diapers and others with disposables. Super-absorbent, disposable diapers and disposable training pants can make potty training harder because children can't *feel* the difference between wet and dry. Cloth diapers and training pants allow children to feel wetness more easily, and this can help speed up learning. Some parents use cloth most of the time and disposables when traveling. Disposable diapers end up in landfills, and over the long haul, usually cost more than diaper service.

RESOURCES

Selected Books
Web Sites
Bibliography
Index
Family Notes

Selected Books for Parents and Children from Parenting Press

Discipline and Guidance

Clarke, Jean Illsley. *Time-In: When Time-Out Doesn't Work.* Seattle: Parenting Press, 1999.

Crary, Elizabeth. *Love & Limits.* Seattle: Parenting Press, 1994.

Crary, Elizabeth. *Without Spanking or Spoiling: A Practical Approach to Toddler and Preschool Guidance*, 2nd edition. Seattle: Parenting Press, 1993.

Feelings

Cain, Janan. *The Way I Feel.* Seattle: Parenting Press, 2000.

Crary, Elizabeth. *Dealing With Feelings* series: *I'm Excited; I'm Frustrated; I'm Furious; I'm Mad; I'm Proud; I'm Scared.* Seattle: Parenting Press, 1992 & 1994.

Crary, Elizabeth and Mits Katayama. *Self-Calming Cards.* Seattle: Parenting Press, 2004.

Crary, Elizabeth and Shari Steelsmith. *Feelings for Little Children* series: *When You're Happy and You Know It; When You're Shy and You Know It; When You're Silly and Know It; When You're Mad and You Know It.* Seattle: Parenting Press, 1996.

Gottman, John. *What Am I Feeling?* Seattle: Parenting Press, 2004.

Kennedy-Moore, Eileen. *What About Me? 12 Ways to Get Your Parents' Attention (Without Hitting Your Sister).* Seattle: Parenting Press, 2005.

Grief

Britain, Lory. *My Grandma Died.* Seattle: Parenting Press, 2004.

Kanyer, Laurie. *25 Things to Do When Grandpa Passes Away, Mom and Dad Get Divorced, or the Dog Dies.* Seattle: Parenting Press, 2004.

Temperament

Neville, Helen and Diane Clark Johnson. *Temperament Tools: Working with Your Child's Inborn Traits.* Seattle: Parenting Press, 1998.

Toilet Learning

Faull, Jan and Helen F. Neville. *Mommy! I Have to Go Potty! A Parent's Guide to Toilet Training*, rev. edition. Seattle: Parenting Press, 2008.

Sexual Abuse Prevention

Freeman, Lory. *It's MY Body.* Seattle: Parenting Press, 1983.

Sleep

Huntley, Rebecca. *The Sleep Book for Tired Parents.* Seattle: Parenting Press, 1991.

Web Sites for More Information

Health

Medical information of many sorts: Mayo Clinic at *www.mayoclinic.com.*

SIDS information: National Institutes of Child Health at *www.nichd.nih.gov.* For information on co-sleeping, search for "bed sharing."

Co-sleeping safety at *www.askdrsears.com*

University of California Medical Center, San Francisco at *www.UCSFchildcarehealth.org.* For information on illness in childcare and when to stay home, click "Publications & Resources," then "Illness Sheets." Choose the illness of interest, then look for "When Should People with This Illness Be Excluded."

Learning

Bilingual education: National Association for Bilingual Education at *www.nabe.org*

Language Development: The Hanen Centre at *www.hanen.org*

National Association for the Education of Young Children at *www.naeyc.org*

Temperament

The Preventive Ounce at *www.preventiveoz.org.* Do a free temperament profile on your child.

Bibliography

Behavior

Carey, William B. and Sean McDevitt. *Coping With Children's Temperament.* New York: Basic Books, 1995.

Chess, Stella, M.D. and Alexander Thomas, M.D. *Goodness of Fit: Clinical Applications, from Infancy Through Adult Life.* Philadelphia: Brunner/Mazel, 1999

Crary, Elizabeth, *Pick Up Your Socks! . . . and Other Skills Growing Children Need.* Seattle: Parenting Press, 1990.

Greenspan, Stanley, M.D. *The Challenging Child.* New York: Addison-Wesley, 1995.

Harris, Judith Rich. *The Nurture Assumption: Why Children Turn Out the Way They Do.* New York: The Free Press, 1998.

Kohn, Alfie. *Punished by Rewards.* New York: Houghton Mifflin, 1993.

Kristal, Jan, M.A. *The Temperament Perspective: Working with Children's Behavioral Styles.* New York: Paul H. Brookes, 2005.

Kurcinka, Mary Sheedy. *Raising Your Spirited Child.* New York: HarperCollins, 1992.

Levine, Melvin, M.D., William Carey, M.D., and Allen Crocker, M.D. *Developmental-Behavioral Pediatrics,* 3rd edition. New York: W. B. Saunders Co., 1999.

Neville, Helen and Mona Halaby. *No Fault Parenting.* New York: Facts on File, 1984.

Phelan, Thomas W. *1-2-3-Magic: Effective Discipline for Children 2–12,* 3rd edition. Glen Ellyn, Ill.: Child Management, 1995

Rowe, K. S. and K. J. Rowe. "Synthetic Food Coloring and Behavior: A Dose Response Effect in a Double-Blind, Placebo-Controlled, Repeated-Measures Study." *Journal of Pediatrics* 125, no. 5, pt 1 (Nov. 1994): 691–98.

Spock, Benjamin, M.D. "Mommy Don't Go." *Parenting,* June/July 1996, 86–90.

Statman, Paula. *On the Safe Side: Teach Your Child to Be Safe, Strong, and Street-Smart.* New York: Harper Perennial, 1995.

Thomas, Alexander, M.D. and Stella Chess, M.D. *Temperament and Development.* New York: Brunner/Mazel, 1977.

Wright, Lawrence. *Twins.* New York: Wiley and Sons, Inc., 1997.

Development—General

American Academy of Pediatrics, Shelov, Steven P., M.D. *Caring for Your Baby and Young Child: Birth to Age 5.* New York: Bantam Books, 1998.

Ames, Louise Bates, Ph.D. *Questions Parents Ask.* New York: Clarkson N Potter, Inc., 1988.

Ames, Louise Bates, Ph.D., and Frances L. Ilg, M.D. *Your Five-Year-Old: Sunny and Serene.* New York: Dell, 1979.

Ames, Louise Bates, Ph.D., and Frances L. Ilg, M.D. *Your Four-Year-Old: Wild and Wonderful.* New York: Dell, 1979.

Ames, Louise Bates, Ph.D., and Frances L. Ilg, M.D. *Your Three-Year-Old: Friend or Enemy.* New York: Dell, 1985.

Ames, Louise Bates, Ph.D., and Frances L. Ilg, M.D. *Your Two-Year-Old: Terrible or Tender.* New York: Dell, 1976.

Ames, Louise Bates, Ph.D., Frances L. Ilg, M.D. and Carol Chase Haber. *Your One-Year Old: Fun-Loving and Fussy.* New York: Dell, 1982.

Berk, Laura E. *Infants, Children, and Adolescents.* 5th edition. Boston: Pearson/Allyn and Bacon, 2004.

Brazelton, T. Berry, M.D. and Stanley I. Greenspan, M.D. *The Irreducible Needs of Children.* Cambridge, Mass.: Perseus, 2000.

Gesell, Arnold, M.D., Frances L. Ilg, M.D., and Louise Bates Ames, Ph.D. *The Child from Five to Ten.* New York: Harper and Row, 1977.

Sroufe, L. Alan, Robert G. Cooper, Gaine DeHart, and Mary Marshall. *Child Development: Its Nature and Course.* New York: McGraw-Hill, 1996

Development—Physical and Health

Alta Bates Medical Center. *When to Refer Children for Occupational Therapy Evaluation.* Berkeley, Calif.: Alta Bates Medical Center, Outpatient Rehabilitation Dept., 1995.

American Academy of Pediatric Dentistry. *Policy on Oral Habits.* www.aapd.org (Nov. 2006.)

Behrman, Richard, M.D., Robert Kliegman, M.D., and Hal B. Jensen, M.D. *Nelson Textbook of Pediatrics,* 16th edition. Philadelphia: W. B. Sanders, 2000.

Center for Disease Control: www.cdc.gov (Nov. 2006).

Child Stats at www.childstats.gov/americaschildren/

index.asp (Nov. 2006).

Feingold Association: www.feingold.org.

Gillenwater, Jay Y., M.D. et al. *Adult and Pediatric Urology.* St. Louis: Mosby, 1996.

Kranowitz, Carol S., M.A. *The Out-of-Sync Child.* New York: Skylight Press/Putnam, 1998.

Leat, Susan J., Rosalyn H. Shute, and Carol A. Westall. *Assessing Children's Vision.* Boston: Butterworth Heinemann, 1999.

National Clearinghouse on Child Abuse and Neglect at www.childwelfare.gov (Nov. 2006).

National Easter Seal Society. *Are You Listening to What Your Child May Not Be Saying?* New York: Macmillan, Inc., 1985.

National Institutes of Child Health at www.nichd.nih.gov (Nov. 2006).

National Institutes of Health at www.nih.gov (Nov. 2006).

Rudolph, Abraham M., MD. et al. *Rudolph's Pediatrics,* 20th edition. Stamford, Conn.: Appleton & Lange, 1996.

VORT Corp. *HELP (Hawaii Early Learning Profile).* Palo Alto, Calif.: VORT Corp., 1994.

VORT Corp. *HELP for Preschoolers Checklist: Ages 3–6.* Palo Alto, Calif.: VORT Corp., 1994.

U.S. Department of Health and Human Services: Administration for Children and Families. *Child Maltreatment 2003.* www.acf.hhs.gov/programs/cb/pubs/cm03/cm2003 (Nov. 2006).

U.S. Department of Justice, Office of Juvenile Justice and Delinquency Prevention. *Homicides of Children and Youth.* www.ncjrs.org/pdffiles1/ojjdp/187239. (Nov. 2006).

World Health Organization. *Reducing Mortality from Major Childhood Killer Diseases.* www.who.int/en/ (Nov. 2006).

Diversity, Spirituality, and Bilingual Learning

Chopra, Deepak. *The Seven Spiritual Laws for Parents: Guiding Our Children to Success and Fulfillment.* New York: Harmony Books, 1997.

Derman-Sparks, Louise. *Anti-Bias Curriculum: Tools for Empowering Young Children.* Washington, D.C.: NAEYC (National Association for the Education of Young Children), 1989.

Genesee, Fred, ed. *Educating Second Language Children.* New York: Cambridge University Press, 1994.

Fowler, James W. *Stages of Faith.* San Francisco: Harper and Row, 1981.

Gonzalez-Mena, Janet. *Multicultural Issues in Child Care.* Mountain View, Calif.: Mayfield, 1993.

Harding, Edith, and Philip Riley. *The Bilingual Family.* New York: Cambridge University Press, 1986.

Hart, Tobin, Ph.D. *The Secret Spiritual World of Children.* Makawao, Maui, Ha.: Inner Ocean Publishing, 2003.

Lyon, Jean. *Becoming Bilingual: Language Acquisition in a Bilingual Community.* Philadelphia: Multilingual Matters, 1996.

Murray, Thomas, R. *Human Development Theories: Windows on Culture.* Thousand Oaks, Calif.: Sage, 1999.

Ortiz, Alba. *Second Language Acquisition.* Austin: University of Texas, College of Education, Department of Special Education, 1994.

Samway, Katharine Davies and Denise McKeon. *Myths and Realities: Best Practices for Language Minority Students.* Portsmouth, N.H.: Heinemann, 1999.

Umbel, Vivian, and Barbara Pearson. "Measuring Bilingual Children's Receptive Vocabularies." *Child Development* 63, no. 4. (Aug. 1992): 1012–20.

Wright, Marguerite A. *I'm Chocolate, You're Vanilla: Raising Healthy Black and Biracial Children in a Race-Conscious World.* San Francisco: Jossey-Bass, 1998.

Emotions

Bybee, Jane. *Guilt and Children.* Boston: Academic Press, 1998.

Collier, Gary. *Emotional Expression.* Hillsdale, N.J.: Lawrence Erlbaum Associates, 1985.

Corr, Charles, A. "Developmental Perspectives on Grief and Mourning." Chapter 12 of *Living with Grief: Who We Are and How We Grieve.* Edited by Doka, Kenneth J. and Joyce D. Davidson. Philadelphia: Brunner/Mazel, 1998.

Denham, Susanne. *Emotional Development in Young Children.* New York: Guilford Press, 1998.

Ehrensaft, Barbara. *Spoiling Childhood.* New York: Guilford Press, 1997.

Flanagan, Cara. *Early Socialisation: Sociability and Attachment.* New York: Routledge, 1999.

Frankel, Herman M., M.D. *Dealing with Loss: A Guidebook for Helping Your Children During and After Divorce.* www.divorcework.com. Click on "Tools for You."

Gottman, John. *Why Marriages Succeed or Fail.* New York:

Simon and Schuster, 1994.

Greenspan, Stanley, M.D. and Nancy Thorndike Greenspan. *First Feelings*. New York: Penguin Books, 1985.

Hesse, Erik and Mary Maine. "Second-Generation Effects of Unresolved Trauma in Nonmaltreating Parents: Dissociated, Frightened and Threatening Parental Behavior." *Psychoanalytic Inquiry* 19 no. 4 (1999): 481–540.

Izard, Carroll. *The Psychology of Emotions*. New York: Plenum Press, 1991.

Russell, James A., and Faye A. Paris. "Children's Complex Emotions." *International Journal of Behavioral Development* 12 no. 2 (June 1994): 349–65.

Russell, James A. and Faye A. Paris. "Do Children Acquire Concepts of Complex Emotions Abruptly?" *International Journal of Behavioral Development* 17, no. 2 (June1994): 349–65.

Seligman, Martin, Ph.D. *Learned Optimism*. New York: Pocket Books, 1992.

Shapiro, Lawrence E., Ph.D. *How to Raise a Child with a High EQ*. New York: Harper Collins, 1997.

Wingert, Pat and Martha Brant. "Reading Your Baby's Mind." *Newsweek*. August 15, 2005, pp. 33–39.

World Association for Infant Mental Health at www.waimh.org (Nov. 2006).

Youngs, Bettie B., Ph.D., Ed.D. *How to Develop Self-Esteem in Your Child*. New York: Fawcett Columbine, 1991.

Gender and Sex

Barron-Cohen, Simon. *The Essential Difference: The Truth about the Male and Female Brain*. New York: Basic Books, 2003.

Bernstein, Anne. "How Children Learn About Sex and Birth." *Psychology Today*. Jan. 1976, pp. 31–66.

Bernstein, Anne. "What You Tell Your Child about Sex (Without Saying a Word)." *Parents*, Oct. 1979, pp. 40–43.

Brannon, Linda. *Gender: Psychological Perspectives*. Boston: Allyn and Bacon, 1999.

Caldwell, Bettye. "How and When to Talk to Your Child About Sex Abuse." *Working Mother,* Jan. 1995, pp. 26–28.

Christen, Yves. *Sex Differences: Modern Biology and the Unisex Fallacy*. New Brunswick: Transaction Publishers, 1990 (IQ tests, page 69).

Gurian, Michael. *The Wonder of Boys*. New York: Tarcher/

Putnam, 1996.

Maccoby, Eleanor E, ed. *Development of Sex Differences*. Stanford, Calif.: Stanford University Press, 1966.

Maccoby, Eleanor and Carol Jacklin. *The Psychology of Sex Differences*. Stanford, Calif.: Stanford University Press, 1974.

Roughgarden, Joan. *Diversity, Gender, and Sexuality in Nature and People*. Berkeley: University of California Press, 2004.

Study Group of New York. *Children and Sex: The Parents Speak*. New York: Facts on File, 1983.

Learning

Acredolo, Linda, Ph.D., and Susan Goodwyn, Ph.D. *Baby Signs: How to Talk with Your Baby Before Your Baby Can Talk*. Chicago: Contemporary Books, 1996.

Battin, R. Ray, Ph.D. *Speech and Language Delay*. Springfield: Charles C Thomas Publishers, 1964.

Begley, Sharon. "How to Build a Baby's Brain." *Newsweek,* Spring/Summer 1997, pp. 28–32.

Begley, Sharon. "Your Child's Brain." *Newsweek,* Feb. 19, 1996, pp. 55–62.

Brooks, Mary and Deedra Hartung. *Speech and Language Handouts*. Austin, Texas: Pro-ed Inc., 1995.

DiLeo, Joseph, M.D. *Interpreting Children's Drawings*. New York: Brunner/Mazel, 1983.

Edwards, Betty, *Drawing on the Right Side of the Brain*. New York: Jeremy P. Tarcher, 2002.

Garcia, Joseph, *Sign with Your Baby: How to Communicate with Infants Before They Can Speak*. Bellingham, Wash.: Stratton Kehl, 1999.

Gardner, Howard. *Artful Scribbles: The Significance of Children's Drawings*. New York: Basic Books, 1980.

Gold, Svea J. *If Kids Just Came with Instruction Sheets!* Eugene, Ore.: Fern Ridge Press, 1997.

Gopnik, Alison, Ph.D., Andrew N. Meltzoff, Ph.D., and Patricia K. Kuhl, Ph.D. *The Scientist in the Crib*. New York: William Morrow & Co. 1999.

Gurian, Michael. *Boys and Girls Learn Differently: A Guide for Teachers and Parents*. San Francisco: Jossey-Bass, 2001.

Hart, Tobin, Ph.D. *The Secret Spiritual World of Children*. Makawao, Maui, Ha.: Inner Ocean Publishing, 2003.

Katz, Lillian G. "What Should Preschoolers Be Taught?" *Parents*, Sept. 1987, p. 207.

National Association of School Psychologists. *Position*

Statement on Student Grade Retention and Social Promotion. www.nasponline.org/information/pospaper_graderetent (Nov. 2006).

National Association for the Education of Young Children. www.naeyc.org (Nov. 2006).

Riera, Michael. *Right from Wrong: Instilling a Sense of Integrity in Your Children.* Cambridge, Mass.: Perseus, 2002.

Ochshorn, Susan. "How Smart Is Your Baby?" *Parenting,* Feb. 1995, pp. 69–75.

Shaywitz, Sally, M.D. *Overcoming Dyslexia: A New and Complete Science-Based Program for Reading Problems at Any Level.* New York: Alfred A. Knopf, 2003.

Wright, Karen. "Babies, Bonds and Brains." *Discover,* Oct. 1997, pp. 75–78.

Zill, Nicholas and Jerry West. *Entering Kindergarten—A Portrait of American Children When They Begin School.* Washington D.C.: National Center for Educational Statistics, NCES publication #2001–035, 2000.

Sleep and SIDS

American Academy of Pediatrics Task Force on Sudden Infant Death Syndrome. "The Changing Concept of Sudden Infant Death Syndrome: Diagnostic Coding Shifts, Controversies Regarding the Sleeping Environment, and New Variables to Consider in Reducing Risk." *Pediatrics* 116, no. 5 (Nov. 2005): 1245–55.

Blair, P. S., P. Sidebotham et al. "Major Epidemiological Changes in Sudden Infant Death Syndrome: A 20-Year Population-Based Study in the UK." *Lancet* 367, no. 9507 (Jan. 28, 2006): 277–78.

Blair, P. S., P. J. Fleming et al. "Babies Sleeping with Parents: Case-Control Study of Factors Influencing the Risk of the Sudden Infant Death Syndrome." *British Medical Journal* 319, no. 7223 (Dec. 4, 1999): 1457–61.

Carpenter, R. G., L. M. Irgens et al. "Sudden Unexplained Infant Death in 20 Regions in Europe: Case-Control Study." *Lancet* 363, no. 9404 (Jan. 17, 2004): 185–91.

Cohen, George J., M.D. *American Academy of Pediatrics Guide to Your Child's Sleep.* New York: Villard, 1999.

Dahl, Ronald E., M.D. "The Development and Disorders of Sleep." *Advances in Pediatrics* 45 (1998): Chap. 3.

Dement, William, M.D., Ph.D. *The Promise of Sleep.* New York: Dell, 1999.

Drago, D. A., A. L. Dannenberg. "Infant Mechanical Suffocation Deaths in the United States," 1980–1997. *Pediatrics* 103, no. 5 (May 1999): e59.

Ghaem, M., K. L. Armstrong and O. Trocki. "The Sleep Patterns of Infants and Young Children with Gastro-Oesophageal Reflux." *Journal of Paediatric Child Health.* (Queensland, Australia) 34 (1998): 160–63.

Guilleminault, Christian, M.D. *Sleep and Its Disorders in Children.* New York: Raven Press, 1987.

Hauck, F. R., S. M. Herman et al. "Sleep Environment and the Risk of Sudden Infant Death Syndrome in an Urban Population: the Chicago Infant Mortality Study." *Pediatrics* 111, no. 5, pt. 2 (May 2003): 1207–14.

International Lactation Consultant's Association. *Response to Policy Statement by AAP Task Force on SIDS.* www.ilca.org/news/SIDSstatementresponse.php (Nov. 2006).

Kemp, J. S., B. Unger et al. "Unsafe Sleep Practices and an Analysis of Bedsharing Among Infants Dying Suddenly and Unexpectedly: Results of a Four-Year, Population-Based, Death-Scene Investigation Study of Sudden Infant Death Syndrome and Related Deaths." *Pediatrics* 106, no. 3 (Sept. 2000): e41.

Kurcinka, Mary Sheedy. *Sleepless in America: Is Your Child Misbehaving or Missing Sleep?* New York: Harper Collins, 2006.

McGarvey, C., M. McDonnell et al. "Factors Relating to the Infant's Last Sleep Environment in Sudden Infant Death Syndrome in the Republic of Ireland." *Archives of Diseases of Childhood* 88, no. 12 (Dec. 2003): 1058–64.

Tappin, D., R. Ecob and H. Brooke. "Bedsharing, Room-sharing, and Sudden Infant Death Syndrome in Scotland: Case-Control Study." *Journal of Pediatrics* 147, no. 1 (July 2005): 32–37.

Sears, William, M.D. *The Baby Sleep Book: The Complete Guide to a Good Night's Rest for the Whole Family.* New York: Little, Brown and Co., 2005.

Scheers, N. J. et al. "Where Should Infants Sleep? A Comparison of Risk for Suffocation of Infants Sleeping in Cribs, Adult Beds, and Other Sleeping Locations." *Pediatrics* 112, no. 4 (Oct. 2003): 883–89.

Weissbluth, Marc, M.D. *Healthy Sleep Habits, Happy Child.* New York: Fawcett Books, 1999.

Index

LEARNING AND THINKING

Family Notes

Family Notes